HISTORY OF COMMONWEALTH LITERATURE

P. K. Sinha
Jagdish K. Ghosh

Commonwealth

History of Commonwealth Literature

Edition : 2021

ISBN 978-81-311-0327-2

Published by :
COMMONWEALTH PUBLISHERS PVT. LTD.
4831/24, Prahlad Street,
Ansari Road, Darya Ganj,
New Delhi - 110002
Ph. : 23275511, 23257835
e-mail : commonwealthbooks@gmail.com

Laser Typesetting by :
Rishu Computers
Delhi

Printed at :
Roshan Offset Printers
Delhi

Preface

The Commonwealth of Nations, normally referred to as the Commonwealth and previously as the British Commonwealth, is an intergovernmental organisation of fifty-four independent member states, all but two of which were formerly part of the British Empire.

The shared history of British presence has produced a substantial body of writing in many languages, known as Commonwealth literature. There is an Association for Commonwealth Literature and Language Studies, with nine chapters worldwide and an international conference is held every three years.

The present book *History of Commonwealth Literature* offers the general reader help of every kind in understanding of Commonwealth Literature. The main focus of this book remains the lives and works of the principal Commonwealth authors.

This book is intended for advanced level students of literature, who are taking exams or modules in this field. It may also be suitable for teachers, researchers and the general reader who is interested in the history of literature. The breadth and accuracy of this volume will surely make it the standard reference book of its kind for years to come.

Authors

Contents

1

Introduction to Commonwealth Literature

The Commonwealth of Nations, often referred to as the Commonwealth and previously as the British Commonwealth, is an intergovernmental organisation of fifty-four independent member states, all but two of which were formerly part of the British Empire. The member states co-operate within a framework of common values and goals as outlined in the Singapore Declaration. These include the promotion of democracy, human rights, good governance, the rule of law, individual liberty, egalitarianism, free trade, multilateralism and world peace.

The Commonwealth is not a political union, but an intergovernmental organisation through which countries with diverse social, political and economic backgrounds are regarded as equal in status. Its activities are carried out through the permanent Commonwealth Secretariat, headed by the Secretary-General; biennial Meetings between Commonwealth Heads of Government; and the Commonwealth Foundation, which facilitates activities of non-governmental organisations in the so-called "Commonwealth Family". The symbol of this free association is the Head of the Commonwealth, which is a ceremonial position currently held by Queen Elizabeth II.

Elizabeth II is also the monarch, separately, of sixteen members of the Commonwealth, informally known as the Commonwealth realms. As each realm is an independent kingdom, the Queen, as monarch, holds a distinct title for each, though, by a Meeting of Commonwealth Prime Ministers in 1952, all include the style *Head of the Commonwealth* at the end; for example: *Elizabeth the Second, by the Grace of God, Queen of Australia and of Her other Realms and Territories, Head of the Commonwealth*. Beyond the realms, the majority of the members of the Commonwealth have separate heads of state: thirty-three members are republics, and five members have distinct monarchs: the Sultan of Brunei; the King of Lesotho; the Yang di-Pertuan Agong (or King) of Malaysia; the King of Swaziland; and the King of Tonga.

The Commonwealth's objectives were first outlined in the 1971 Singapore Declaration, which committed the Commonwealth to the institution of world peace; promotion of representative democracy and individual liberty; the pursuit of equality and opposition to racism; the fight against poverty, ignorance, and disease; and free trade. To these were added opposition to discrimination on the basis of gender by the Lusaka Declaration of 1979 and environmental sustainability by the Langkawi Declaration of 1989. These objectives were reinforced by the Harare Declaration in 1991.

The Commonwealth's current highest-priority aims are on the promotion of democracy and development, as outlined in the 2003 Aso Rock

Declaration, which built on those in Singapore and Harare and clarified their terms of reference, stating: "We are committed to democracy, good governance, human rights, gender equality, and a more equitable sharing of the benefits of globalisation."

The Commonwealth has long been distinctive as an international forum where highly developed economies (such as the United Kingdom, Australia, Canada, Singapore, and New Zealand) and many of the world's poorer countries seek to reach agreement by consensus. This aim has sometimes been difficult to achieve, as when disagreements over Rhodesia in the late 1960s and 1970s and over apartheid in South Africa in the 1980s led to a cooling of relations between the United Kingdom and African members.

Culture and Literature

Mostly due to their history of British rule, many Commonwealth nations possess certain identifiable traditions and customs that are elements of a shared Commonwealth culture. Examples include common sports such as cricket and rugby, driving on the left, the Westminster system of parliamentary democracy, common law, widespread use of the English language, designation of English as an official language, military and naval ranks, and the use of British rather than American spelling conventions. None of these is universal amongst, nor exclusive to, the Commonwealth, but are more commonly found within its members than elsewhere

The shared history of British presence has also produced a substantial body of writing in many languages, known as Commonwealth Literature. There is an Association for Commonwealth Literature and

Language Studies, with nine chapters worldwide and an international conference is held every three years.In 1987, the Commonwealth Foundation established the Commonwealth Writers Prize "to encourage and reward the upsurge of new Commonwealth fiction and ensure that works of merit reach a wider audience outside their country of origin". Caryl Phillips won the Commonwealth Writers Prize 2004 for *A Distant Shore.* Mark Haddon beat out runner-up Michael Anthony Young to win the Commonwealth Writers' Prize 2004 Best First Book prize worth £3,000 for *The Curious Incident of the Dog in the Night-time.*

Although not affiliated with the Commonwealth in an official manner, the prestigious Man Booker Prize is awarded annually to an author from a Commonwealth country or the Republic of Ireland. This honour is one of the highest in literature.

The Commonwealth is an association of fifty-three independent states working together for their citizens in the interests of development, democracy and peace. The Harare Declaration of 1991 asserts that the special strength of the Commonwealth is to be found in the diversity of its membership and a shared inheritance of language and the rule of law. Freedom of speech including the right to hold opinions without interference is thought to be essential for the maintenance of strong and efficient governments throughout the Commonwealth, subject to respecting the reputations of others and laws for the protection of national security, public health or morals.

These values have been woven into the fabric of the common law over many centuries and form part of the Westminster system from which governmental habits in the Commonwealth are principally derived.

Their continuance depends upon an underlying respect for the rule of law, and that in turn depends not only upon the words used in a statute but also upon an awareness of the way things work in practice. "Give me the liberty to know, to utter, and to argue freely according to conscience, above all liberties," declared John Milton in a time of upheaval.

The rules of evidence in most Commonwealth countries assume that the intention with which a criminal act was done can be proved as a matter of fact. A man's intention can be inferred from what he said or did at the time the act was done. Moreover, if an accused person should seek to cover up his actions by telling lies after the deed, these lies can be used against him.

The author of a leading text on evidence once contended that the struggle of a victim for his life may leave upon the perpetrator the indelible traces of blood, or wounds or rent clothing, which point back to the deed as done by him. But a deed may also leave traces upon the doer through a psychological process. Thus, in certain circumstances a lie can constitute an admission against interest by an accused person if the court is satisfied that the only explanation for the lie is that he knew the truth would implicate him in the offence.

This rule is fraught with the possibility of error. An accused person may lie for many reasons: to shore up a true defence, to protect someone else, to conceal some other disgraceful conduct which is unrelated to the offence charged, or simply out of panic or confusion. The jury must therefore be warned against a natural tendency to assume that if an accused is lying it must be because he is guilty. If the jury thinks that there is, or might be, some innocent explanation for the lies, then it should take no notice of them.

The Application of these rules, which are difficult to grasp in the abstract, can be graphically illustrated by a trial scene in Alan Paton's well-known novel *Cry, the Beloved Country,* a seminal work foreshadowing the injustices of the apartheid regime in South Africa.

A father looking for a missing son in the slums of Johannesburg learns that his son is to stand trial as one of three housebreakers involved in the death by shooting of an enlightened social reformer named Jarvis. The defendants admit that they were on the premises with a loaded firearm, and assaulted the deceased's servant with an iron bar, but deny liability for murder on the grounds that the fatal shot was fired in a moment of panic, not with an intent to kill.

In the course of his summing up, the judge notes that during the police investigation the woman Baby Mkize misled the police about her role in the affair. With an eye to the rules that we have been discussing, the judge says this:

> The woman Baby Mkize is a most unsatisfactory witness and while the prosecution, and the Counsel for the defence of the first accused, demonstrated this most clearly, neither was able to produce that conclusive proof that the murder had been discussed. The woman at first lied to the Police, telling them that she had not seen the first accused for a year. She was a confused, contradictory, and frightened witness, but was this fear and its resulting confusion caused by mere presence in a Court, or by knowledge of other crimes to which she had been a party, or by the guilty knowledge that the murder was in fact discussed? That does not seem to us to have been clearly established.

In the end, as a consequence of the cautionary approach required by the rules concerning lies, two of the accused are given the benefit of the doubt and are acquitted. Certain admissions made by the first accused (the missing son) mean that the prosecution case against him is stronger, with the result that he is convicted, and eventually hanged. Paton's novel is haunted throughout by a poignant irony: the deceased has been a friend and supporter of the black fringe dwellers with whom his killer has been associating.

This story can be regarded as a graphic illustration of the workings of the legal system. It shows how the right to a fair trial can be affected by the subtleties of various evidentiary rules and by the sense of fairness of those involved in the investigative and judicial processes. On the other hand, inherent in the story is a darker prospect. If rules of evidence in the common-law world allow for conclusions to be drawn about the vagaries of a person's mind, it might not take much in an era of rapidly changing attitudes to weight these rules in favour of conviction.

Truth telling is an issue that doesn't arise only at trial. Prevarication or guilty conduct may be of use during the pre-trial or investigative phase, for there are no restrictions on the leads or clues that the police may act on in deciding what to look for and where to search. A suspect who has been caught out in some incidental falsehood, perhaps as to how much he drank on the night in question, or whom he was with, can always have this used against him in an interview. Whenever the suspect asserts that he is being truthful about the principal issue, it will be open to the interrogator to remind the suspect that he lied a moment ago. The undermining of a suspect's confidence in this way may ultimately lead to a full confession.

Cry, the Beloved Country was written in the 1940s. We now know that, as the practices of the apartheid regime worsened, the prospects of being dealt with fairly, especially at the investigation phase of many political and quasi-political crimes, steadily diminished, although the outward form of the trial process remained. This is evident in the plays of Athol Fugard and in the novels of Nadine Gordimer and Andre Brink.

Well-told stories not only illustrate the workings of the legal system, they can add a graphic sense of reality to the abstractions known as "human rights". It doesn't take much imagination to realise that the possession of a right will be meaningless if the description of it in a legal tome isn't matched by an individual's capacity to enforce the right, or by the realities of daily life. By creating works of fiction based on what is happening around them, by telling inspired lies if you like, writers of fiction have a way of revealing truths that might otherwise stay hidden. It is a lesson rooted in ancient Greek theatre: "Give a man a mask and he'll tell the truth."

George Orwell was alive to these concerns in the aftermath of the Second World War. It was then that he wrote his famous novel Nineteen Eighty-Four, a dystopian satire in which corruption of language—called Newspeak—becomes a means of controlling opinions and preserving the authority of the rulers. "Who controls the past, controls the future," runs the Party slogan. "Who controls the present, controls the past." Any rebellious or unorthodox opinion is characterised as a "thought crime".

A Party functionary in the book reminds the principal character, Winston Smith, that the whole aim of Newspeak is to narrow the range of thought. "In the end," he says, "we shall make thought crime literally impossible, because there will be no words in which to express it." This prompts Winston Smith to write in his forbidden diary: "Thought crime does not entail death: thought crime is death."

With the collapse of the Soviet regime, Orwell's satire has lost much of its point, but this is seldom said. Most readers seem to appreciate that, like the eerie parables of his precursor, Franz Kafka, Orwell's tale endures. It continues to evoke a shiver of apprehension. Big Brother's features resemble those of Stalin but they might also be said to recall a famous recruiting poster of the First World War, depicting a heavily moustached military man (Lord Kitchener) pointing a finger at the populace, with the caption: Your Country Needs You". This, in a small way, illustrates some of the themes to be found in Nineteen Eighty-Four—the power of surveillance, the corruption of language, the manipulation of public opinion, the subversion of social realities. As in modern political campaigning, no slogan is too obvious if it accommodates the public's secret wish to believe in it.

We can see much of this at work in J.M. Coetzee's novel Waiting for the Barbarians, which was written prior to the dismantling of the apartheid regime in South Africa. An ageing magistrate, serving out his time at a peaceful frontier outpost on the edge of an unnamed empire, is visited by Colonel Joll of the Third Bureau. The rumour in the capital is that the barbarian tribes of the north and west may at last be uniting. The empire has to take precautionary measures, for there will almost certainly be a war.

The magistrate has not seen any signs of unrest. Indeed, the so-called barbarians are scarcely visible apart from a few traders selling trinkets outside the walls of the fort and fishermen who bring their catch to the daily market. Nonetheless, to appease his visitor, the magistrate takes Colonel Joll to an elderly prisoner who is being held for cattle stealing. "This gentleman is visiting us from the capital," the magistrate explains. "He visits all the forts along the frontier. His work is to find out the truth."

When the magistrate learns that Colonel Joll and his men have beaten the old prisoner to a pulp, the magistrate protests. This leads to the magistrate himself being arrested and beaten to a pulp. In the meantime, the empire's expeditionary forces have ventured beyond the frontier to confront the barbarians, but to no avail. The barbarians can't be found, although they are certainly thought to be responsible when the empire's expeditionary forces limp home, half-crazed by heat and thirst.

The magistrate is reinstated eventually as a servant of the empire, but he feels "like a man who lost his way long ago but presses on along a road that may lead nowhere". By the end of the book the reader is left in no doubt that the barbarians are to be found not beyond the frontier, but in the capital.

These bring to *The Native Commissioner* by Shaun Johnson, which was entered for the Commonwealth Writers Prize 2007 and won the regional award for Africa in the Best Book category. This book touches upon Orwellian themes, but in a realistic manner. The reader is gradually drawn into the corrupting world of the apartheid regime that steadily expanded after *Cry, the Beloved Country* was written.

The Native Commissioner at the heart of Shaun Johnson's story is a kind and conscientious man. George Jameson joins the South African Department of Native Affairs during the era when his linguistic skills and familiarity with indigenous customs provided him with opportunities to fulfil his dream of balanced race relations. Then, Smuts is defeated in the first national election after the war and the National Party is swept into office.

The mood in the bureaucracy changes. Jameson is now an officer employed by the Department of Bantu Administration and Development. He has never been a political person but he soon perceives that even his comparatively mild views are no longer welcome. His skill at mastering tribal languages in far places is not appreciated. The Bantu is seen as an "unperson". Jameson and his family are shunted from one outpost to another, but he is now too old to find other employment.

Jameson's attempts to ameliorate the injustices of the system lead him eventually to a state of crippling depression, then to suicide. The book breaks new ground in showing how apartheid injured even those working for it by the gradual erosion of their humanity.

At one stage during the 1950s, while working under the new regime, Jameson presides over a trial in which a group of Xhosa leaders have been charged with what appears to be an unprovoked attack upon a neighbouring group. Having mastered Xhosa as well as the Zulu language, Jameson senses that somewhere beneath the welter of brutal and apparently senseless acts there is an explanation which the formal rules of court procedure have failed to uncover. This turns out to be the presence of certain fighting sticks held by th rival group, which is construed as an act of aggressior

The trial ends with a speech by the principa defendant which, from that day on, Jameson wi characterise in the privacy of his mind as Ntabaka' question:

> My Lord, I understand that we will be found guilty of these beatings we have been talking about all these days now and that we will be punished. This I understand. But I wish to ask this. What has it to do with you, Sir?

Alone in his office at nightfall, after the penalties hav been imposed, after the case is over, Jameson watche the sun going down over the hills of the Transke These are his reflections:

> He concluded that this day, this accidental trial over which he had been called to preside, was truly the first time since he embarked on his career that the uncertainty which before had nagged sporadically, now really gnawed at him like a constant and ravaging illness, if still not fully clear in its meaning. He sorted out and sifted through his own thought processes. Since 1948, he agreed with himself, he had worried primarily that his own advancement was being seriously Curtailed by the political change in the country. But now he could not avoid questioning the career itself, the point of his working life, inside and outside of himself; he questioned the meaning and validity and morality of everything he was doing and everything he was standing for, everything about himself. He felt come over him, not dilettantishly now, a sense of hopelessness and purposelessness that weighed a ton, and he said out loud in his good English accent: It's all wrong.

In Jameson's reflections one can hear the spectr voices of George Orwell's Winston Smith and J.N Coetzee's ageing magistrate, although it is clear fro the nature of Shaun Johnson's book that Jamesor career is based on real events. It is fascinating to see the way in which entirely speculative works can bring into sharper focus tendencies emerging in the world of actuality. Indeed, as the philosopher George Santayana observed: truth is only believed when someone has invented it well. The Native Commissioner's final admonition to his sons is to remember the Zulu greeting he taught them: *Nyabonana. We See Each Other.*

The works we have been discussing are concerned in part with the formation and gradual shaping of opinions; they are works about what happens when someone holds the wrong opinion. They cast light upon a matter of importance to the Commonwealth, namely, the preservation of certain crucial rights—the freedom to hold differing opinions, the freedom to speak freely. Freedom of speech will be illusory if we all hold, or are expected to hold, the same opinion. Too often we are prepared to overlook this fact. In social situations conformity has always been with us, brought about too often by long-standing social habits, or by inertia. In the case of political correctness, an outlook that was supposed to nurture the expression of dissenting opinions is now, paradoxically, inclined to stifle that expression. This is why the works of our greatest writers remain essential to our Social well-being. They respond to change, but they make us ponder. In holding up a mirror to life their task is to inform, to challenge, and to enlighten.

Commonwealth Writers' Prize

The Commonwealth Writers' Prize, organised and funded by the Commonwealth Foundation, is a leading award for fiction that was first awarded in 1987. The Commonwealth Foundation is an intergovernmental organisation working in the 53 countries of the Commonwealth of Nations. The aim of the Prize is to encourage new Commonwealth fiction, and to ensure that works of merit reach a wider audience outside their country of origin.

The Commonwealth Writers' Prize is sponsored and administered by the Commonwealth Foundation with the support of the Macquarie Foundation in the Europe and South Asia and South East Asia and South Pacific regions. The Commonwealth Foundation is an intergovernmental body working to help civil society organisations promote democracy, development and cultural understanding in Commonwealth countries.

The Commonwealth Writers' Prize is established as a noted annual event in both the media and literary calendar. Since 2006, the regional sections of the Prize have been open for sponsorship and the Canada/ Caribbean and Africa regions are still seeking partners. It is established as a noted annual event in both the media and literary calendar. Last year, the CWP achieved a high level of exposure in both regional and international media. Over the past years media coverage has increased year-on-year and it is expected to continue to do so.

The Commonwealth Writers' Prize is chaired by Justice Nicholas Hasluck, distinguished Australian author and leading judicial officer. Justice Hasluck has published ten works of fiction, including the award-winning novels *The Bellarmine Jug* and *The Country Without Music.*

The Commonwealth Writers' Prize covers the Commonwealth regions of Africa, Europe and South Asia, The Caribbean and Canada, and South East Asia and the South Pacific. Entries are first assessed by four regional panels of judges and the selection of the overall winner is made by a distinguished pan-Commonwealth panel. In each of the four regions of the Commonwealth two prizes of £1,000 are awarded: one for the Best Book and one for the Best First Book. The resulting eight regional winners' books are then judged by the pan-Commonwealth panel. Authors win £10,000 for the overall Best Book and £5,000 for the Best First Book. Writers and judges come together in a final literary programme in a different Commonwealth country each year.

Winners

Best Book Winners 1987-2009

1) 1987 - Olive Senior, *Summer Lightning*
2) 1988 - Festus Iyayi, *Heroes*
3) 1989 - Janet Frame, *The Carpathians*
4) 1990 - Mordecai Richler, *Solomon Gursky Was Here*
5) 1991 - David Malouf, *The Great World*
6) 1992 - Rohinton Mistry, *Such a Long Journey*
7) 1993 - Alex Miller, *The Ancestor Game*
8) 1994 - Vikram Seth, *A Suitable Boy*
9) 1995 - Louis de Bernières, *Captain Corelli's Mandolin*
10) 1996 - Rohinton Mistry, *A Fine Balance*
11) 1997 - Earl Lovelace, *Salt*
12) 1998 - Peter Carey, *Jack Maggs*
13) 1999 - Murray Bail, *Eucalyptus*
14) 2000 - John Maxwell Coetzee, *Disgrace*
15) 2001 - Peter Carey, *True History of the Kelly Gang*
16) 2002 - Richard Flanagan, *Gould's Book of Fish*
17) 2003 - Austin Clarke, *The Polished Hoe*

18) 2004 - Caryl Phillips, *A Distant Shore*
19) 2005 - Andrea Levy, *Small Island*
20) 2006 - Kate Grenville, *The Secret River*
21) 2007 - Lloyd Jones, *Mister Pip*
22) 2008 - Lawrence Hill, *The Book of Negroes*
23) 2009 - Christos Tsiolkas, *The Slap*

Best First Book Winners 1987-2009

1) 1989 - Bonnie Burnard, *Women of Influence*
2) 1990 - John Cranna, *Visitors*
3) 1991 - Pauline Melville, *Shape-Shifter*
4) 1992 - Robert Antoni, *Divina Trace*
5) 1993 - Gita Hariharan, *The Thousand Faces of Night*
6) 1994 - Keith Oatley, *The Case of Emily V*
7) 1995 - Adib Khan, *Seasonal Adjustments*
8) 1996 - Vikram Chandra, *Red Earth, Pouring Rain*
9) 1997 - Ann-Marie MacDonald, *Fall on Your Knees*
10) 1998 - Tim Wynveen, *Angel Falls*
11) 1999 - Kerri Sakamoto, *The Electrical Field*
12) 2000 - Jeffrey Moore, *Prisoner in a Red-Rose Chain*
13) 2001 - Zadie Smith, *White Teeth*
14) 2002 - Manu Herbstein, *Ama, A Story of the Atlantic Slave Trade*
15) 2003 - Sarah Hall, *Haweswater*
16) 2004 - Mark Haddon, *The Curious Incident of the Dog in the Night-time*
17) 2005 - Chimamanda Ngozi Adichie, *Purple Hibiscus*
18) 2006 - Mark McWatt, *Suspended Sentences: Fictions of Atonement*
19) 2007 - D. Y. Béchard, *Vandal Love*
20) 2008 - Tahmima Anam, *A Golden Age*
21) 2009 - Mohammed Hanif, *A Case of Exploding Mangoes*

2

History of British Literature

As use of language is the exercise of understanding, the literature of a community is the record of the nature of that community's understanding at the time. So the rise then decline of the English speaking public's understanding, which is the rise then decline of English speaking civilization, is reflected by the history of English literature.

Chaucer is recognised as the *father* of the English language, which became a national tongue in the latter part of the 14th century, marking the beginning of English civilization. The gradual rise of the community's ability to think clearly is demonstrated by the improvement from the awkward verse of Chaucer, to the brilliant prose of such writers as Edmund Burke, Edward Gibbon, Locke and Hume published in the eighteenth century.

The Concise Oxford English Dictionary (1938) defines *Augustan* as: '*connected with reign of* [Ancient Roman Emperor] *Augustus Caesar, best period of Latin literature*'; which reveals that the *Golden Age* of Ancient Roman civilization was the age of Augustus. But the Oxford English Dictionary also states that *Augustan* may be applied to 'any national literature', and the

Augustan period of English literature was 1660-1780, which means this period was the *Golden Age* of English civilization.

The decline of English civilization is confirmed by the subsequent deterioration of its literature to the present day. W.H. Hudson stated in *English Literature Of The XIXTH Century*:

> "That a great chapter in the annals of our literature came to a close about the beginning of the seventh decade of the nineteen century is universally admitted by historians and critics."

The use of English in contemporary works (circa 2001) stands condemned by the textbooks of the twentieth century that set down the correct use of English needed for clear understanding. These works include *Plain Words* (1948) and *The Complete Plain Words* (1954) by Sir Ernest Gower, and *Modern English Usage* (1926) and *The King's English* (1908) by Fowler.

The growing vagueness creeping into modern expression was also condemned by George Orwell in *Politics And The English Language* (1946). The *very existence* of these works show that people in the twentieth century were concerned that the popular use of language was becoming less precise and harder to understand. And this group included England's department of the Treasury, who commissioned Sir Ernest Gower to write books meant to repair the poor use of English by their own staff. Fowler revealed in '*Modern English Usage*' that the use of words with no sensible meaning was becoming popular, especially with the young!

The decay of our language is so widespread and continual that Lord Dunsany claimed in 1943 that he could tell within ten years when any book of the twentieth century was written by the progress of the decay. The level of the decay in the year 2003 was described in detail by Don Watson in his book *'Death Sentence: The Decay Of Public Language'*.

Old English

English, as we know it, descends from the language spoken by the north Germanic tribes who settled in England from the 5th century A.D. onwards. They had no writing (except runes, used as charms) until they learned the Latin alphabet from Roman missionaries. The earliest written works in Old English (as their language is now known to scholars) were probably composed orally at first, and may have been passed on from speaker to speaker before being written. We know the names of some of the later writers but most writing is anonymous. Old English literature is mostly chronicle and poetry - lyric, descriptive but chiefly narrative or epic. By the time literacy becomes widespread, Old English is effectively a foreign and dead language. And its forms do not significantly affect subsequent developments in English literature. (With the scholarly exception of the 19th century poet, Gerard Manley Hopkins, who finds in Old English verse the model for his metrical system of "sprung rhythm".)

Middle English and Chaucer

From 1066 onwards, the language is known to scholars as Middle English. Ideas and themes from French and Celtic literature appear in English writing at about this time, but the first great name in English literature is that of Geoffrey Chaucer (?1343-1400). Chaucer introduces the iambic pentameter line, the rhyming couplet and other rhymes used in Italian poetry (a language in which rhyming is arguably much easier than in English, thanks to the frequency of terminal vowels). Some of Chaucer's work is prose and some is lyric poetry, but his greatest work is mostly narrative poetry, which we find in *Troilus and Criseyde* and *The Canterbury Tales*. Other notable mediaeval works are the anonymous *Pearl* and *Gawain and the Green Knight* (probably by the same author) and William Langlands' *Piers Plowman*.

Tudor Lyric Poetry

Modern lyric poetry in English begins in the early 16th century with the work of Sir Thomas Wyatt (1503-1542) and Henry Howard, Earl of Surrey (1517-1547). Wyatt, who is greatly influenced by the Italian, Francesco Petrarca (Petrarch) introduces the sonnet and a range of short lyrics to English, while Surrey (as he is known) develops unrhymed pentameters (or blank verse) thus inventing the verse form which will be of great use to contemporary dramatists. A flowering of lyric poetry in the reign of Elizabeth comes with such writers as Sir Philip Sidney (1554-1586), Edmund Spenser (1552-1599), Sir Walter Ralegh (1552-1618), Christopher Marlowe (1564-1593) and William Shakespeare (1564-1616). The major works of the time are Spenser's *Faerie Queene*, Sidney's *Astrophil and Stella* and Shakespeare's sonnets.

Renaissance Drama

The first great English dramatist is Marlowe. Before the 16th century English drama meant the amateur performances of Bible stories by craft guilds on public holidays. Marlowe's plays (*Tamburlaine; Dr. Faustus;*

Edward II and *The Jew of Malta*) use the five act structure and the medium of blank verse, which Shakespeare finds so productive. Shakespeare develops and virtually exhausts this form, his Jacobean successors producing work which is rarely performed today, though some pieces have literary merit, notably *The Duchess of Malfi* and *The White Devil* by John Webster (1580-1625) and *The Revenger's Tragedy* by Cyril Tourneur (1575-1626). The excessive and gratuitous violence of Jacobean plays leads to the clamour for closing down the theatres, which is enacted by parliament after the Civil war.

Metaphysical Poetry

The greatest of Elizabethan lyric poets is John Donne (1572-1631), whose short love poems are characterized by wit and irony, as he seeks to wrest meaning from experience. The preoccupation with the big questions of love, death and religious faith marks out Donne and his successors who are often called metaphysical poets. (This name, coined by Dr. Samuel Johnson in an essay of 1779, was revived and popularized by T.S. Eliot, in an essay of 1921. It can be unhelpful to modern students who are unfamiliar with this adjective, and who are led to think that these poets belonged to some kind of school or group - which is not the case.) After his wife's death, Donne underwent a serious religious conversion, and wrote much fine devotional verse. The best known of the other metaphysicals are George Herbert (1593-1633), Andrew Marvell (1621-1678) and Henry Vaughan (1621-1695).

Epic Poetry

Long narrative poems on heroic subjects mark the best

work of classical Greek (Homer's *Iliad* and *Odyssey*) and Roman (Virgil's *Æneid*) poetry. John Milton (1608-1674) who was Cromwell's secretary, set out to write a great biblical epic, unsure whether to write in Latin or English, but settling for the latter in *Paradise Lost*. John Dryden (1631-1700) also wrote epic poetry, on classical and biblical subjects.

Though Dryden's work is little read today it leads to a comic parody of the epic form, or mock-heroic. The best poetry of the mid 18th century is the comic writing of Alexander Pope (1688-1744). Pope is the best-regarded comic writer and satirist of English poetry.

Among his many masterpieces, one of the more accessible is *The Rape of the Lock* (seekers of sensation should note that "rape" here has its archaic sense of "removal by force"; the "lock" is a curl of the heroine's hair). Serious poetry of the period is well represented by the neo-classical Thomas Gray (1716-1771) whose *Elegy Written in a Country Churchyard* virtually perfects the elegant style favoured at the time.

Restoration Comedy

On the death of Oliver Cromwell (in 1658) plays were no longer prohibited. A new kind of comic drama, dealing with issues of sexual politics among the wealthy and the bourgeois, arose. This is Restoration Comedy, and the style developed well beyond the restoration period into the mid 18th century almost. The total number of plays performed is vast, and many lack real merit, but the best drama uses the restoration conventions for a serious examination of contemporary morality. A play which exemplifies this well is *The Country Wife* by William Wycherley (1640-1716).

Prose Fiction and the Novel

Jonathan Swift (1667-1745), wrote satires in verse and prose. He is best-known for the extended prose work *Gulliver's Travels*, in which a fantastic account of a series of travels is the vehicle for satirizing familiar English institutions, such as religion, politics and law. Another writer who uses prose fiction, this time much more naturalistic, to explore other questions of politics or economics is Daniel Defoe (1661-1731), author of *Robinson Crusoe* and *Moll Flanders*.

The first English novel is generally accepted to be *Pamela* (1740), by Samuel Richardson (1689-1761): this novel takes the form of a series of letters; Pamela, a virtuous housemaid resists the advances of her rich employer, who eventually marries her. Richardson's work was almost at once satirized by Henry Fielding (1707-1754) in *Joseph Andrews* (Joseph is depicted as the brother of Richardson's Pamela Andrews) and *Tom Jones*.

After Fielding, the novel is dominated by the two great figures of Sir Walter Scott (1771-1832) and Jane Austen (1775-1817), who typify, respectively, the new regional, historical romanticism and the established, urbane classical views.

Novels depicting extreme behaviour, madness or cruelty, often in historically remote or exotic settings are called Gothic. They are ridiculed by Austen in *Northanger Abbey* but include one undisputed masterpiece, *Frankenstein*, by Mary Shelley (1797-1851).

Romanticism

A movement in philosophy but especially in literature, romanticism is the revolt of the senses or passions against the intellect and of the individual against the consensus. Its first stirrings may be seen in the work of William Blake (1757-1827), and in continental writers such as the Swiss philosopher Jean-Jacques Rousseau and the German playwrights Johann Christoph Friedrich Schiller and Johann Wolfgang von Goethe.

The publication, in 1798, by the poets William Wordsworth (1770-1850) and Samuel Taylor Coleridge (1772-1834) of a volume entitled *Lyrical Ballads* is a significant event in English literary history, though the poems were poorly received and few books sold. The elegant latinisms of Gray are dropped in favour of a kind of English closer to that spoken by real people (supposedly).

Actually, the attempts to render the speech of ordinary people are not wholly convincing. Robert Burns (1759 1796) writes lyric verse in the dialect of lowland Scots (a variety of English). After Shakespeare, Burns is perhaps the most often quoted of writers in English: we sing his *Auld Lang Syne* every New Year's Eve.

The work of the later romantics John Keats (1795-1821) and his friend Percy Bysshe Shelley (1792-1822; husband of Mary Shelley) is marked by an attempt to make language beautiful, and by an interest in remote history and exotic places. George Gordon, Lord Byron (1788-1824) uses romantic themes, sometimes comically, to explain contemporary events. Romanticism begins as a revolt against established views, but eventually becomes the established outlook. Wordsworth becomes a kind of national monument, while the Victorians make what was at first revolutionary seem familiar, domestic and sentimental.

Victorian Poetry

The major poets of the Victorian era are Alfred, Lord Tennyson (1809-1892) and Robert Browning (1812-1889). Both are prolific and varied, and their work defies easy classification. Tennyson makes extensive use of classical myth and Arthurian legend, and has been praised for the beautiful and musical qualities of his writing.

Browning's chief interest is in people; he uses blank verse in writing dramatic monologues in which the speaker achieves a kind of self-portraiture: his subjects are both historical individuals (*Fra Lippo Lippi, Andrea del Sarto*) and representative types or caricatures (*Mr. Sludge the Medium*).

Other Victorian poets of note include Browning's wife, Elizabeth Barrett Browning (1806-1861) and Christina Rossetti (1830-1894). Gerard Manley Hopkins (1844-1889) is notable for his use of what he calls "sprung rhythm"; as in Old English verse syllables are not counted, but there is a pattern of stresses. Hopkins' work was not well-known until very long after his death.

Victorian Novel

In the 19th century, adult literacy increases markedly: attempts to provide education by the state, and self-help schemes are partly the cause and partly the result of the popularity of the novel. Publication in instalments means that works are affordable for people of modest means. The change in the reading public is reflected in a change in the subjects of novels: the high bourgeois world of Austen gives way to an interest in characters of humble origins. The great novelists write works which in some ways transcend their own period, but which in detail very much explore the preoccupations of their time.

Dickens and the Brontës

Certainly the greatest English novelist of the 19th century, and possibly of all time, is Charles Dickens (1812-1870). The complexity of his best work, the variety of tone, the use of irony and caricature create surface problems for the modern reader, who may not readily persist in reading. But *Great Expectations, Bleak House, Our Mutual Friend* and *Little Dorrit* are works with which every student should be acquainted.

Charlotte Brontë (1816-1855) and her sisters Emily (1818-1848) and Anne (1820-1849) are understandably linked together, but their work differs greatly. Charlotte is notable for several good novels, among which her masterpiece is *Jane Eyre,* in which we see the heroine, after much adversity, achieve happiness on her own terms. Emily Brontë's *Wüthering Heights* is a strange work, which enjoys almost cult status. Its concerns are more romantic, less contemporary than those of *Jane Eyre* - but its themes of obsessive love and self-destructive passion have proved popular with the 20th century reader.

Later Victorian Novelists

After the middle of the century, the novel, as a form, becomes firmly-established: sensational or melodramatic "popular" writing is represented by Mrs. Henry Wood's *East Lynne* (1861), but the best novelists achieved serious critical acclaim while reaching a wide public, notable authors being Anthony Trollope (1815-82), Wilkie Collins (1824-89), William Makepeace

Thackeray (1811-63), George Eliot (Mary Ann Evans; 1819-80) and Thomas Hardy (1840-1928). Among the best novels are Collins's *The Moonstone,* Thackeray's *Vanity Fair,* Eliot's *The Mill on the Floss, Adam Bede* and *Middlemarch,* and Hardy's *The Mayor of Casterbridge, The Return of the Native, Tess of the d'Urbervilles* and *Jude the Obscure.*

Modern Literature

Early 20th Century Poets

W.B. (William Butler) Yeats (1865-1939) is one of two figures who dominate modern poetry, the other being T.S. (Thomas Stearns) Eliot (1888-1965). Yeats was Irish; Eliot was born in the USA but settled in England, and took UK citizenship in 1927. Yeats uses conventional lyric forms, but explores the connection between modern themes and classical and romantic ideas. Eliot uses elements of conventional forms, within an unconventionally structured whole in his greatest works. Where Yeats is prolific as a poet, Eliot's reputation largely rests on two long and complex works: *The Waste Land* (1922) and *Four Quartets* (1943).

The work of these two has overshadowed the work of the best late Victorian, Edwardian and Georgian poets, some of whom came to prominence during the First World War. Among these are Thomas Hardy, Rudyard Kipling (1865-1936), A.E. Housman (1859-1936), Edward Thomas (1878-1917), Rupert Brooke (1887-1915), Siegfried Sassoon (1886-1967), Wilfred Owen (1893-1918) and Isaac Rosenberg (1890-1918). The most celebrated modern American poet, is Robert Frost (1874-1963), who befriended Edward Thomas before the war of 1914-1918.

Early Modern Writers

The late Victorian and early modern periods are spanned by two novelists of foreign birth: the American Henry James (1843-1916) and the Pole Joseph Conrad (Josef Korzeniowski; 1857-1924). James relates character to issues of culture and ethics, but his style can be opaque; Conrad's narratives may resemble adventure stories in incident and setting, but his real concern is with issues of character and morality. The best of their work would include James's *The Portrait of a Lady* and Conrad's *Heart of Darkness, Nostromo* and *The Secret Agent.*

Other notable writers of the early part of the century include George Bernard Shaw (1856-1950), H.G. Wells (1866-1946), and E.M. Forster (1879-1970). Shaw was an essay-writer, language scholar and critic, but is best-remembered as a playwright. Of his many plays, the best-known is *Pygmalion* (even better known today in its form as the musical *My Fair Lady*). Wells is celebrated as a popularizer of science, but his best novels explore serious social and cultural themes, *The History of Mr. Polly* being perhaps his masterpiece. Forster's novels include *Howard's End, A Room with a View* and *A Passage to India.*

Joyce and Woolf

Where these writers show continuity with the Victorian tradition of the novel, more radically modern writing is found in the novels of James Joyce (1882-1941), of Virginia Woolf (1882-1941), and of D.H. Lawrence (1885-1930). Where Joyce and Woolf challenge traditional narrative methods of viewpoint and structure, Lawrence is concerned to explore human relationships more profoundly than his predecessors, attempting to marry the insights of the new psychology with his own acute observation. Working-class characters are presented as serious and dignified; their manners and speech are not objects of ridicule. Other notable novelists include George Orwell (1903-50), Evelyn Waugh (1903-1966), Graham Greene (1904-1991) and the 1983 Nobel prize-winner, William Golding (1911-1993).

Poetry in the Later 20th Century

Between the two wars, a revival of romanticism in poetry is associated with the work of W.H. (Wystan Hugh) Auden (1907-73), Louis MacNeice (1907-63) and Cecil Day-Lewis (1904-72). Auden seems to be a major figure on the poetic landscape, but is almost too contemporary to see in perspective. The Welsh poet, Dylan Thomas (1914-53) is notable for strange effects of language, alternating from extreme simplicity to massive overstatement.

Of poets who have achieved celebrity in the second half of the century, evaluation is even more difficult, but writers of note include the American Robert Lowell (1917-77), Philip Larkin (1922-1985), R.S. Thomas (1913-2000), Thom Gunn (1929-2004), Ted Hughes (1930-1998) and the 1995 Nobel laureate Seamus Heaney (b. 1939).

Notable Writers Outside Mainstream Movements

Any list of "important" names is bound to be uneven and selective. Identifying broad movements leads to the exclusion of those who do not easily fit into schematic outlines of history. Writers not referred to above, but highly regarded by some readers might include Laurence Sterne (1713-68), author of *Tristram*

Shandy, R.L. Stevenson (1850-94) writer of *Kidnapped* and *The Strange Case of Dr. Jekyll and Mr. Hyde,* Oscar Wilde (1854-1900), author of *The Importance of Being Earnest,* and novelists such as Arnold Bennett (1867-1931), John Galsworthy (1867-1933) and the Americans F. Scott Fitzgerald (1896-1940), Ernest Hemingway (1898-1961), John Steinbeck (1902-68) and J.D. Salinger (b. 1919). Two works notable not just for their literary merit but for their articulation of the spirit of the age are Fitzgerald's *The Great Gatsby* and Salinger's *The Catcher in the Rye.* The American dramatist Arthur Miller (b. 1915) has received similar acclaim for his play *Death of a Salesman* (1949). Miller is more popular in the UK than his native country, and is familiar to many teachers and students because his work is so often set for study in examinations.

Literature and Culture

Literature has a history, and this connects with cultural history more widely. Prose narratives were written in the 16th century, but the novel as we know it could not arise, in the absence of a literate public. The popular and very contemporary medium for narrative in the 16th century is the theatre. The earliest novels reflect a bourgeois view of the world because this is the world of the authors and their readers (working people are depicted, but patronizingly, not from inside knowledge). The growth of literacy in the Victorian era leads to enormous diversification in the subjects and settings of the novel.

Recent and Future Trends

In recent times the novel has developed different genres such as the thriller, the whodunnit, the potboiler, the western and works of science-fiction, horror and the sex-and-shopping novel. Some of these may be brief fashions (the western seems to be dying) while others such as the detective story or science-fiction have survived for well over a century. As the dominant form of narrative in contemporary western popular culture, the novel may have given way to the feature film and television drama. But it has proved surprisingly resilient. As society alters, so the novel may reflect or define this change; many works may be written, but few of them will fulfil this defining rôle; those which seem to do so now, may not speak to later generations in the same way.

The "test of time" may be a cliché, but is a genuine measure of how a work of imagination can transcend cultural boundaries; we should, perhaps, now speak of the "test of time and place", as the best works cross boundaries of both kinds. We may not "like" or "enjoy" works such as *Wüthering Heights, Heart of Darkness* or *The Waste Land,* but they are the perfect expression of particular ways of looking at the world; the author has articulated a view which connects with the reader's search for meaning. It is, of course, perfectly possible for a work of imagination to make sense of the world or of experience (or love, or God, or death) while also entertaining or delighting the reader or audience with the detail and eloquence of the work, as in *A Midsummer Night's Dream, The Rime of the Ancient Mariner* or *Great Expectations.*

3

Historical Development of Australian Literature

Australian literature began soon after the settlement of the country by Europeans. Common themes include indigenous and settler identity, alienation, exile and relationship to place—but it is a varied and contested area.

Early Works

Early popular works tended to be of the 'ripping yarn' variety, telling tales of derring-do against the new frontier of the Australian outback. Writers such as Rolf Boldrewood, Marcus Clarke and Joseph Furphy embodied these stirring ideals in their tales and, particularly the latter, tried to accurately record the vernacular language of the common Australian. These novelists also gave valuable insights into the penal colonies which helped form the country and also the early rural settlements.

Australia's first novel, *Quintus Servinton: A Tale founded upon Incidents of Real Occurrence* was written and published in Tasmania in 1831. It was written by the convicted English forger Henry Savery and published anonymously though the authorship became a public secret. It is regarded as a thinly disguised autobiography designed to demonstrate how his fictional equivalent was different from the general convict population.

In 1838 *The Guardian: a tale* by Anna Maria Bunn was published in Sydney. It was the first Australian novel printed and published in mainland Australia and the first Australian novel written by a woman. It is a Gothic romance.

Poetry

Poetry played an important part in the founding of Australian literature. Henry Lawson, son of a Norwegian sailor born in 1867, was widely recognised as Australia's poet of the people and, in 1922, became the first Australian writer to be honoured with a state funeral. Two poets who are amongst the great Australian poets are Christopher Brennan and Adam Lindsay Gordon; Gordon was once referred to as the "national poet of Australia" and is the only Australian with a monument in Poets' Corner of Westminster Abbey in England.

Both Gordon's and Brennan's (but particularly Brennan's) works conformed to traditional styles of poetry, with many classical allusions, and therefore fell within the domain of high culture. However, at the same time Australia was blessed with a competing, vibrant tradition of folk songs and ballads. Henry Lawson and Banjo Paterson were two of the chief exponents of these popular ballads, and 'Banjo' himself was responsible for creating what is probably the most famous Australian verse, *Waltzing Matilda*. Romanticised views of the outback and the rugged characters that inhabited it played an important part in shaping the Australian nation's psyche, just as the cowboys of the American Old West and the gauchos of the Argentine pampa became part of the self-image of those nations.

Prominent Australian poets of the twentieth century include A. D. Hope, Judith Wright, Gwen Harwood, Kenneth Slessor, Les Murray and more recently John Forbes and John Tranter. More recent and emerging Australian poets include Peter Minter and Judith Beveridge.

Contemporary Australian poetry is mostly published by small, independent book publishers. However, other kinds of publication, including new media and online journals, spoken word and live events, and public poetry projects are gaining an increasingly vibrant and popular presence. Red Room Company is a major exponent of innovative projects.

From the 1830s, distinctive early Australian poetic voices began to emerge. Charles Harpur was regarded as the country's leading poet. Harpur wrote of the solitude and grandeur of a landscape that dwarfs its people. Henry Kendall, encouraged by Harpur, was the first Australian poet to draw his inspiration from the life, landscape and traditions of Australian, and its influence on human beings. George Gordon McCrae incorporated Aboriginal themes into his poetry. The English-born Adam Lindsay Gordon, with his *Bush Ballads and Galloping Rhymes* (1870), 'revitalised the traditional ballad form by infusing it with bush themes'.

The names of early Australian poets and authors are well known today. Indeed they conjure images of a time of exploration, adventure and excitement, as well as a poignant reminder of the hardships of living in the newly formed colonies. Adam Lindsay Gordon, Dorothea MacKellar, Harry 'Breaker' Morant, Barcroft Boake, Henry Kendall and Henry Handel Richardson, chronicled the early settlement days in poetry and prose.

Modern Poets

Modern Australian poets were influenced both by the 'literary nationalism' of the late 1890s which espoused Australian values as well as the contemporary modernist writings which challenged writers to use their imagination and be innovative in describing what was 'real'. AD Hope and Judith Wright were seen as the giants of post war poetry circles in Australia. Hope wrote about love, faith and spirituality. Wright was regarded as 'marvelously lucid... rich and clear' as well as being the first white Australian poet to publicly name and explore the experiences of its Indigenous people.

In the 1950s and 1960s, Melbourne verse expressed a solemn, ironic, concern for social and moral issues and, in the work of Vincent Buckley and Chris Wallace Crabb, an academic literariness. Whereas in Sydney, where Kenneth Slessor, R D Fitzgerald and Douglas Steward were influential, a more relaxed, popular, and various style of poetry flourished. Kenneth Slessor was probably the most talented poet to have written in Australia at this time.

Other influential poets outside of the east coast capitals were the 'Sandgropers and Islanders' - Dorothy Hewett (1923 - 2002) and Jack Davis (1917 - 2000) from the sand country of Western Australian and Oodgeroo (Kath Walker) (of the tribe Noonuccal) (1920

- 1995), born Kathleen Jean Mary Ruska, on Minjerribah, of the Stradbroke Islands. John Tranter describes the focus of the 1980s and 1990s in Sydney as being a mood 'of passive recollection' which tells of an 'adult life tormented by decay, women gained and lost and dead animals'. Dorothy Hewett's *Greenhouse* (1980) has love and betrayal, death, travel, politics and passion as its subjects.

Dorothy Porter is credited with Australian poetry making a comeback in the late 1990s by re-visiting one of the oldest forms of literature - the verse novel. David Malouf's first poetry collection in 26 years, *Typewriter Music,* was released at the Sydney Writers Festival in June 2007, selling out of its print run of 3,000 in three days.

Other leading contemporary poets include:Les Murray, John Tranter, Fay Zwicky and Billy Marshall-Stoneking and Indigenous authors Bobby Sykes and Samuel Wagan Watson.

Novels

Like other literary forms, early and many later novels were often concerned with the 'quintessential' Australian qualities: convicts, the bush, bushrangers, folklore, tales of pioneering, family sagas, floods, droughts, bushfires, battlers, Aboriginal people, Irishmen and lost children.

Early Australian novelists included Marcus Clarke, (Stella Maria Sarah) Miles Franklin, Clarence (Clarrie or Den) Michael James Stanislaus (CJ) Dennis, Edward Dyson and Doris Pilkington. The slow, or non-existent, rate of publication did not deter them from continuing to write their poems, books and plays.

A new breed of writers was born in the 20th century. They redefined what could be expected from writing even if they used the same backdrop of the bush as early writers had done. Published in 1901, *My Brilliant Career* by Miles Franklin is often said to be the first authentic Australian novel.

The most eminent fiction writer after 1945 was Patrick White, who won the Nobel Prize for literature in 1973. In a dozen novels from *Happy Valley* (1939) to *Memoirs of Many in One* (1986), White examined, often satirically, the conflict between inner consciousness and social existence.

In the Miles Franklin tradition, other novelists, particularly the women, relied upon both social realism and also a surreal or imaginary life linked to the everyday lives of their characters.

Christina Stead (1902 - 1983) highly praised novel *The Man Who Loved Children* appeared in 1940. Ruth Park (b. 1922)'s most famous books are the trilogy of *Missus, The Harp in the South* and *Poor Man's Orange,* along with *Swords and Crowns and Rings* which won the Miles Franklin Literary Award in 1977. *The Newspaper of Claremont Street: a Novel* by Elizabeth Jolley (1923 - 2007) relates the story of an old cleaning woman known as The Newspaper, who dreams of escape from the parasitic demands of both her past and her present.

These were followed by David Malouf's *Remembering Babylon* (1996) which was considered by the International IMPAC Dublin Literary Award judges to be the best novel written by anyone, anywhere, in any language, in the last three years. Richard Flanagan's (b. 1961, Tasmania) three novels adopted a similar form with great lucidity. Peter

Carey's novel *True History of the Kelly Gang,* which evokes the tradition of literary nationalism and the imaginary life of Ned Kelly, was short-listed for the 2001 Miles Franklin Award and won the 2001 Commonwealth Writers Prize, and the 2001 Man Booker Prize.

Children's Literature

Australia has a strong tradition of children's books. The earliest books published for children were mostly instructive tales - stories to teach children how to behave. By the late 19th century, Australian writers began to focus on stories showing real life experiences and everyday adventures, such as settling in Australia and family life. Ethel Turner is a well-known writer of that time - her highly successful book, *Seven Little Australians,* was published in 1894.

Some children's books of the early 20th century are now Australian classics, such as Norman Lindsay's *The Magic Pudding* and May Gibbs' *Snugglepot and Cuddlepie.* Ruth Park also wrote the famous children's series *The Muddle-Headed Wombat.* In the last few decades there has also been a steady growth in the writing of children's literature by authors like May Gibbs, Nan Chauncy, Mem Fox and John Marsden. People such as Pamela Allen, Kerry Argent, Jeannie Baker, Graeme Base, Louise Elliott, Bob Graham and Junko Morimoto have displayed creative abilities as both storytellers and artists.

Today, there is a large diversity of children's books for all ages, including picture books, and books for young and older readers. Awards for children's books, such as the The Children's Book Council (CBC) Awards, celebrate the high quality of children's literature.

Plays and Theatre Scripts

Australian playwrights were largely ignored for a hundred years or so. Betty Roland had to wait 70 years to see her play performed, as the theatre owners were much more interested in bringing new overseas plays to Australia than taking a risk with local material. *The Lighthouse Keeper's Wife* by Mary Wilkinson was performed briefly in 1922, but the work of Tasmanian Catherine Shepherd has not been performed since its debut in 1942. However, the ABC began radio broadcasts of live drama in 1932, which focused attention on plays.

Since the late 18th century, there has been a number of prominent scripts written for theatre. Notable plays were Alfred Dampier's *His Natural Life* in 1886, Steele Rudd's *On Our Selection* in 1912, *Summer of the Seventeenth Doll* in 1955 and Louis Nowra's *Capricornia* in 1988.

Writing and Identity

A complicated, multi-faceted relationship to Australia is displayed in much Australian writing, often through writing about landscape. Barbara Baynton's short stories from the late 1800s/early 1900s convey people living in the bush, a landscape that is alive but also threatening and alienating. Kenneth Cook's *Wake in Fright* (1961) portrayed the outback as a nightmare with a blazing sun, from which there is no escape. Colin Thiele's novels reflected the life and times of rural and regional Australians in the 20th century, showing aspects of Australian life unknown to many city dwellers.

What it means to be Australian is another issue that Australian literature explores. Miles Franklin struggled to find a place for herself as a female writer in Australia, fictionalising this experience in *My Brilliant Career* (1901). Marie Bjelke Petersen's popular romance novels, published between 1917 and 1937, offered a fresh upbeat interpretation of the Australian bush. The central character in Patrick White's *The Twyborn Affair* tries to conform to expectations of pre-WWII Australian masculinity but cannot, and instead, post-war, tries out another identity - and gender - overseas. Peter Carey has toyed with the idea of a national Australian identity as a series of 'beautiful lies', and this is a recurrent theme in his novels. Andrew McGahan's *Praise* (1992) and Christos Tsiolkas's *Loaded* (1995) introduced a 'gritty realism' take on questions of Australian identity in the 1990s, though an important precursor to such work was Helen Garner's *Monkey Grip* (1977).

Australian literature has had several scandals surrounding the identity of writers. The 1944 Ern Malley affair led to an obscenity trial and is often blamed for the lack of modernist poetry in Australia. To mark the 60th anniversary of the Ern Malley affair another Australian writer, Leon Carmen, set out to make a point about the prejudice of Australian publishers against white Australians. Unable to find publication as a white Australian he was an instant success using the false Aboriginal identity of Wanda Koolmatrie with *My Own Sweet Time*. In the 1980s Streten Bozik also managed to become published by assuming the Aboriginal identity of B Wongar.In the 1990s, Helen Darville used the pen-name "Helen Demidenko" and won major literary prizes for her *Hand that Signed the Paper* before being discovered, sparking a controversy over the content of her novel, a fictionalised and highly tendentious account of the

Nazi occupation of the Ukraine. Mudrooroo - previously known as Colin Johnson - was acclaimed as an Aboriginal writer until his Aboriginality came under question (his mother was Irish/English and his father was Irish/African-American, however he has strong connections with Aboriginal tribes); he now avoids adopting a specific ethnic identity and his works deconstruct such notions.

Other writers have felt that, whatever Australia was, it needed to be escaped. Clive James, Robert Hughes, Barry Humphries and Germaine Greer are all Australian writers who left Australia in the 1960s for England and America. Greer, author of The Female Eunuch, has spent much of her career in England and has been a fierce critic of her native land, and she does not return there often.

Other Developments

Australian literature can be thought of as coming of age in 1973 when Patrick White became the first (and so far only) Australian to be awarded the Nobel Prize for Literature. (2003 laureate John M. Coetzee lives in Adelaide, South Australia, but was born in South Africa and is not widely regarded as Australian.) Other notable writers to have emerged since the 1970s include Peter Carey, Kate Grenville, David Malouf, Janette Turner Hospital, Marion Halligan, Christopher Koch, Alex Miller, Shirley Hazzard, Richard Flanagan and Tim Winton.

James Clavell in The Asian Saga discusses an important feature of Australian literature: its portrayal of far eastern culture, from the admittedly even further east, but nevertheless western cultural viewpoint, as Nevil Shute did. Clavell was also a successful screenwriter and along with such writers as Thomas Keneally, who won the Booker Prize for *Schindler's Ark* (the book *Schindler's List* is based on), has expanded the topics of Australian literature far beyond that one country. Other novelists to use international themes are Gerald Murnane and Brenda Walker.

Letters

Australian language, letters and literature in Australia has been influenced by Aboriginal storytelling, convict tales and the desire by colonists to relate their experiences in a new country.

Some of those early works have remained part of the Australian ethos. Marcus Clarke's *For the term of his natural life*, for example, is still being published today, more than 100 years after it was written.

Similarly, the bush ballads of Henry Lawson and Andrew 'Banjo' Paterson have become so ingrained in Australian history, that most Australians are word-perfect when singing *Waltzing Matilda.* C J Dennis's *The Sentimental Bloke* remains another favourite with its use of slang language.

Some famous writings include the *Jerilderie Letter*, which was dictated by Ned Kelly to Joe Byrne in February 1879. It is the only document providing a direct link to the Kelly Gang and the events with which they were associated. The letter articulates Kelly's pleas of innocence and desire for justice for both his family and the poor Irish selectors of Victoria's north-east.

The *Coranderrk Letter* was written in 1882 by William Barak, an Aborigine living on Coranderrk Station. Barak wrote the letter protesting about the management and treatment of Aborigines. He and other Aboriginal Elders continued to petition, including a letter to Queen Victoria.

Another famous petition was by the Yolngu people. In 1963, the Yolngu sent the *Yirrkala Bark Petitions* to the House of Representatives in protest against the Commonwealth's granting of mining rights to Nabalco over land excised from Arnhem Land reserve. The result was a parliamentary inquiry which recommended that compensation was owed to the Yolngu.

In another vein, the letters of Judith Wright, published as *With Love and Fury* (2006) explore the complex relationships that fed the poet's creative life. The correspondence with Jack McKinney (later her husband) between 1945-46, coincides with the most fertile periods of her poetic career. Judith's correspondence with Queensland poet, Jack Blight 'constitute a running commentary on the Australian literary scene as well as what she was reading and thinking about poetry and writing in general' (Meredith McKinney, 2007).

Gwen Harwood's letters published as *A Steady Storm of Correspondence: Selected Letters of Gwen Harwood 1943-1995* (2001) are described as:

Spirited and witty, warm, reflective, at times enraged, often overcome by laughter, the letters are so varied that this large volume can be read as one might read a novel or an autobiography. It would be a pity just to dip in at random: this is the story of the making of a poet.

Literary Magazines

Australia's literary magazine industry developed

rapidly in the late nineteenth century through popular titles such as *The Bulletin*. Australian poetry and writing, in general, in the period from 1890 to 1919 was dominated by a feeling of optimism about Australia's federation, democratic potential and pride in Australia's distinctive society and national character. The weekly magazine *The Bulletin*, founded in Sydney in 1880, reflected this spirit and encouraged the development of a national literature by inviting its readers to contribute fiction and verse of Australian interest.

The bush ballad was the poetic form favoured by *The Bulletin*. The characteristic subjects developed from the early ballads about convict life, gold mining, bushranging, and campfire themes. Banjo Paterson and Henry Lawson, the duelling banjos of late 19th century Australian writing, came to the fore - explaining and exploring the Australian landscape in verse, ballads and stories.

Meanjin began its publishing life in Brisbane in 1940. The magazine attracted a high calibre of Australian and international writers which, during the 1950s and 1960s, included Xavier Herbert, Katherine Susannah Pritchard, Anais Nin and Jean-Paul Sartre. A range of prints and designs from influential artists such as Margaret Preston and Noel Counihan also appeared in these early editions.

In the 1970s and 1980s, *Meanjin* continued to support both established and emerging writers. Writing by women and migrants to Australia were acknowledged as two important community issues for Australia. Contributors during this period included Bruce Dawe, Chris Wallace-Crabbe, Tom Shapcott, Marion Halligan, Les Murray, Patrick White, Tim Winton and Frank Moorhouse.

Quadrant was founded as an initiative of the Australian Committee for Cultural Freedom in 1956 to protect liberty and creativity in the face of the perceived threat of communism. Many of Australia's most prominent poets have appeared in the magazine, however fiction has also been regularly published.

Southerly magazine quickly grew from a four-page bulletin in 1932. Under Kenneth Slessor's editorial stint in the late 1950s, the sub-title *a review of Australian literature* was added and the publication continued to develop as an outlet for academic discussion of local literary issues. It now produces regular editions of up to 200 pages.

Newspapers

Australia's first newspaper, the *Sydney Gazette and New South Wales Advertiser* first printed in 1803, was followed by a succession of government and privately-produced newspapers.

By the late 1800s, cheaper wood pulp, improvements in printing technology, railways and streamlined news services all enabled a more efficient and influential newspaper industry. The passing of legislation making education compulsory for children over the age of six years, such as the Education Act 1872 (Vic) and the Public Instruction Act of 1880 (NSW), led to increases in literacy as more of the population learnt to read and write.

The Sydney *Sun* was the first daily paper to carry a news story on its front page in 1910 and Melbourne's *Sun News-Pictorial* was the first daily pictorial tabloid (newspaper with pictures) in 1922. Four prominent daily newspapers emerged during this period - the *The*

Age, the *Argus*, *The Sydney Morning Herald* and *The Daily Telegraph*.

Clashes with government were not unusual, and newspapers increasingly expressed anti-authoritarian opinions. *The Age* was launched in 1854, during the turmoil of Victoria's gold rush era and prided itself on voicing a radical viewpoint, including support for the miners at Ballarat, the eight-hour working day and reform of land laws.

Australian historian Clive Turnbull proposed that the era of modern journalism began in the 1920s as companies took over control of newspapers and the popularity of a news story became increasingly important. (Source: Turnbull, Clive, 'Journalism' in C H Grattan (ed.) 1947, *Australia*, University of California Press, Berkeley.)

In any form, stories about the 'Australian experience' are still much sought after, despite declining publication lists. Dorothy Porter's verse novels and David Malouf's recent poetry collection outsell their print runs. An increasing number of hopeful novelists attempt their hands at the elusive 'bunyip of Australian Literature... The Great Australian novel' (A D Hope). The joy is that, in the attempt to capture the congruities and contradictions, there are some wonderful works of literature created.

Aboriginal Writing

The voices of indigenous Australians have begun to be noticed and include the playwright Jack Davis, Kevin Gilbert, and poet and activist Oodgeroo Noonuccal. Sally Morgan's *My Place* was considered a breakthrough memoir in terms of bringing indigenous stories to wider notice. The allegedly indigenous writer

Mudrooroo was later shown not to be indigenous, but of Irish, English, and African-American descent. Writers coming to prominence in the 21st century include Alexis Wright and Tara June Winch.

4

Origin and Growth of Canadian Literature

As a young, pioneering country, Canada put more of its energies into economic development than into the arts. As material circumstances improved, however, two literatures developed, reflecting Canada's dual cultural heritage. At first they evinced a common interest in the wilderness and in regional locales and tended to imitate European styles. In the 20th century a growing sense of national identity was reflected in literatures of maturity and distinction.

Canada's literature, whether written in English or French, often reflects the Canadian perspective on nature, frontier life, and Canada's position in the world, all three of which tie in to the garrison mentality. Canada's ethnic and cultural diversity are reflected in its literature, with many of its most prominent writers focusing on ethnic life.

Criticism of Canadian literature has focused on nationalistic and regional themes. Critics against such thematic criticism in Canadian literature, such as Frank Davey, have argued that a focus on theme diminishes the appreciation of complexity of the literature produced in the country, and creates the impression that Canadian literature is sociologically-oriented.

While Canadian literature, like the literature of every nation state, is influenced by its socio-political contexts, Canadian writers have produced a variety of genres. Influences on Canadian writers are broad, both geographically and historically.

Canada's dominant cultures were originally British and French, as well as aboriginal. After Prime Minister Trudeau's "Announcement of Implementation of Policy of Multiculturalism within Bilingual Framework," in 1971, Canada gradually became home to a more diverse population of readers and writers. The country's literature has been strongly influenced by international immigration, particularly in recent decades.

Categories of Canadian literature

Because of its size and breadth, Canadian literature is often divided into sub-categories.

1) The most common is to categorize it by region or province.
2) Another way is to categorize it by author. For instance, the literature of Canadian women, Acadians, Aboriginal peoples in Canada, and Irish Canadians have been anthologized as bodies of work.
3) A third is to divide it by literary period, such as "Canadian postmoderns" or "Canadian Poets Between the Wars."

Traits of Canadian Literature

Traits common to works of Canadian literature include:

1) *Failure as a theme:* Failure and futility feature heavily as themes in many notable works; for instance, *Not Wanted on the Voyage* by Timothy Findley or *Kamouraska* by Anne Hebert.

2) *Humour:* Serious subject matter is often laced with humour.

3) *Mild anti-Americanism:* There is marked sentiment of anti-American often in the form of gentle satire. While it is sometimes perceived as malicious, it often presents a friendly rivalry between the two nations

4) *Multiculturalism:* Since World War Two, multiculturalism has been an important theme. Writers using this theme include Mordecai Richler (known for novels such as *The Apprenticeship of Duddy Kravitz*), Margaret Laurence (known for novels such as *The Stone Angel*), Rohinton Mistry, Michael Ondaatje — The English Patient— *and prolific Chinese Canadian writer Wayson Choy.*

5) *Nature (and a "human vs. nature" tension)*: Reference to nature is common in Canada's literature. Nature is sometimes portrayed like an enemy, and sometimes like a divine force.

6) *Satire and irony*: Satire is probably one of the main elements of Canadian literature.

7) *Self-deprecation*: Another common theme in Canadian literature.

8) Self-evaluation by the reader

9) *Search for Self-Identity*: Some Canadian novels revolve around the theme of the search for one's identity and the need to justify one's existence. A good example is Robertson Davies's *Fifth Business,* in which the main character Dunstan Ramsay

searches for a new identity by leaving his old town of Deptford.

10) *Southern Ontario Gothic*: A sub-genre which critiques the stereotypical Protestant mentality of Southern Ontario; many of Canada's most internationally famous authors write in this style.

11) *The underdog hero*: The most common hero of Canadian literature, an ordinary person who must overcome challenges from a large corporation, a bank, a rich tycoon, a government, a natural disaster, and so on.

12) Urban vs. rural: A variant of the underdog theme which involves a conflict between urban culture and rural culture, usually portraying the rural characters as morally superior. Often, as in Stephen Leacock's *Sunshine Sketches of a Little Town* or Alistair MacLeod's *No Great Mischief*, the simplicity of rural living is lost in the city.

Canadian-English Literature

Because English-speaking Canadians were more numerous and diversified than French-speaking Canadians, Canadian literature written in English has been until recently more abundant and varied than that written in French.

Colonial Period

Among early Canadian works in English were the accounts of 18th- and early 19th-century explorers such as Samuel Hearne (1745–92), Sir Alexander Mackenzie, Simon Fraser (1776–1862), and David Thompson. The first novel produced in Canada, indeed in North America, was *The History of Emily Montague* (1769), an account of contemporary Québec, realistically written by Frances Moore Brooke (1724–89), wife of an English army chaplain.

In the early 19th century, Oliver Goldsmith (1794–1861) wrote *The Rising Village* (1825), a book-length poem extolling a pioneer community, in reply to *The Deserted Village* (1770) by the British writer Oliver Goldsmith, his great-uncle. Charles Sangster (1822–93), in *St. Lawrence and the Saguenay* (1856), was one of the first poets to describe the natural beauties of the land.

Wacousta (1832) by John Richardson (1796–1852), about Pontiac's Rebellion (1763) was the first novel based on Canadian history. In the humorous essays of *The Clockmaster* (1836), Thomas Chandler Haliburton (1796–1865) presented the vulgar but enterprising Yankee peddler San Slick as a satire on the comparatively lazy Nova Scotians. The rigors of pioneer life were described in two autobiographical books, *Backwoods of Canada* (1836) by Catherine Parr Traill (1802–99) and *Roughing It in the Bush* (1852) by her sister Susanna Moodie (1803–85).

Confederation to World War I

The Confederation of 1867 encouraged a sense of national identity, which stimulated literary activity. Inspired by the English romantics' and early Victorians' love of nature. Canadians looked for themes in their own natural landscape.

Poetry

The first significant Canadian poets were those of the Confederation school, led by Sir Charles G. D. Roberts (1860–1943). His romantic *Orion and Other Poems* (1880) stimulated other writers, and in his *Songs of the*

Common Day (1893) he vividly described his native New Brunswick countryside. Bliss Carman, Roberts's cousin, gained fame through love songs and nature poems, tinged with romantic melancholy and nostalgia. Among his best-known collections are *Low Tide on Grand Pré* (1893) and *The Pipes of Pan* (5 vol., 1902–5).

Other important Confederation poets were Archibald Lampman (1861–99) and Duncan Campbell Scott. Lampman described rural Ontario in *Among the Miller* (1888). Scott took the most dramatic view of the Ontario landscape in *New World Lyrics and Ballads* (1905) and *Beauty and Life* (1921). As head of the Department of Indian Affairs, he wrote poems sympathetic to Indian culture. His volumes of short stories, *In the Village of Viger* (1896) and *The Witching of Elspie* (1923), reveal a deep interest in psychology as well. Wilfred Campbell (1858?–1918) described contrasts in Canadian climate and landscape.

The most popular Canadian poet of the early 20th century was English-born Robert W. Service. His *Songs of a Sourdough* (1907), including "The Shooting of Dan McGrew," was the product of his years in the Yukon. Although his work has been highly praised, Service himself never pretended to be anything but a rhymester.

Prose

The two principal novelists of the late 19th century, William Kirby (1817–1906) and Sir Gilbert Parker, wrote historical romances concerning the trials and pleasures of life in a vast new land. Kirby's *Golden Dog* (1877) and Parker's *The Seats of the Mighty* (1897), both set in Québec, began a trend toward colorful novels of a glorified past.Around the turn of the century, a literary taste developed for regional novels that gave a rather idyllic description of rural life of the time. Ralph Connor (pseudonym of C. W. Gordon, 1860–1937), once a missionary in the Rockies, wrote *Black Rock* (1898) and *The Man from Glengarry* (1901) about the west. Lucy Maud Montgomery (1874–1942) set her classic children's story, *Anne of Green Gables* (1908), on her native Prince Edward Island; perennially popular, it has been staged and filmed several times.

The English-born humorist Stephen Leacock, a professor of economics at McGill University, wrote sharp, witty social criticism in such works as *Sunshine Sketches of a Little Town* (1912), set in Ontario, and *Arcadian Adventures with the Idle Rich* (1914).

1920s to World War II

During the 1920s realist writers were critical of Canadian values and institutions, a tendency strengthened by Canadians' experience of the Great Depression and World War I.

Poetry

One of the finest poets of this period was the Newfoundland-born English professor Edwin John Pratt (1882–1964). His poetry reflects his fascination with the sea, his sense of the impersonal violence of nature, and his fundamentally tragic world view. In *The Titanic* (1935) and *Brébeuf and His Brethren* (1940), he amply proved that the ancient epic form is vital in the 20th century.

Poets living in Montréal made the 1930s and 1940s one of the most exciting periods in the history of Canadian poetry in English. They published in little literary magazines, cheaper than books in a depressed economy, which encouraged rivalry and urged them to be aware of their roots and guard against excessive British or American influence. The leaders were Francis Reginald Scott (1899–1985) and A. J. M. Smith (1902–80), who were also concerned with social issues and with literary criticism. Later they compiled *The Blasted Pine: An Anthology of Satire, Invective, and Disrespectful Verse: Chiefly by Canadians* (1957), which perhaps belies the cliché that Canadians are incapable of self-criticism. Another of these early Montréal poets was Abraham Moses Klein (1909–72). Steeped in Jewish tradition, he wrote lyrically and with deep understanding of Jews and other minorities.

Prose

One of the first writers of sociological novels was the European-born Frederick Philip Grove (1871–1948). Years as a farmhand and schoolmaster on the Manitoba prairies inspired his book of sketches, *Over Prairie Trails* (1922), and the two powerful novels *Settlers of the Marsh* (1925) and *Fruits of the Earth* (1933), in which he described pioneer life with strength, vigor, and an astute eye. He is often weak and tedious in style and characterization, however.

Combining the traditions of the late 19th-century historical romances and early 20th-century regional idylls was Mazo de la Roche, the most widely read Canadian novelist of her day. Beginning with *Jalna* (1927), she created a 16-volume chronicle of the Whiteoak family and of Jalna, their Ontario estate.

Morley Callaghan sympathetically explored individuals in conflict with society in *They Shall Inherit the Earth* (1935) and *The Loved and the Lost* (1951). Hugh

MacLennan studied various strains of the Canadian heritage in *Barometer Rising* (1941), *Two Solitudes* (1945), and *The Watch That Ends the Night* (1959). Early in their careers both Callaghan and MacLennan were commended for their realism, psychological honesty, and contributions to defining Canadian character. Since then, however, their reputations have declined. Other social realist novels are *As for Me and My House* (1941), an affecting picture of the depression years on the prairies, by Sinclair Ross (1908–96), and *Who Has Seen the Wind?* (1947), a boy's experience of a Saskatchewan village, by W. O. Mitchell.

Late 20th Century

Since World War II, Canadian literature has gained in volume and creativity, reflecting and encouraging a heightened national consciousness. Produced in a time of rebellion and of breaks with tradition, it has become more experimental in approach and universal in theme. Many critics considered Canadian poetry of the 1970s the best being written in the English-speaking world.

Poetry

Perhaps the most significant voices in poetry were those of Earle Birney (1904–95) and Dorothy Livesay (1909–96), both of whom had written of social problems in the 1930s. Birney's *David* (1942), set in the Canadian Rockies of his youth, continues to captivate readers by its powerful language and intriguing story of a man's search for truth through encountering nature. Birney's lyrical style and controlled humanism have never faltered in such later works as *Ice, Cod, Bell, or Stone* (1962) and *Near False Creek Mouth* (1964). His

Collected Poems appeared in 1975. Livesay has been humanistically concerned with the individual's efforts to overcome the forces of destruction within and without. Her work, such as *The Unquiet Bed* (1967), *Collected Poems* (1972), and *The Phases of Love* (1982), seemed to become more youthful and accomplished as she grew older, revealing a sensitive, understanding mind.

Raymond Souster (1921–), Louis Dudek (1918–), and Irving Layton (1912–2006) criticized materialist Canadian society. Using colorful, earthy language, the Romanian-born Layton attacked smugly complacent middle-class morality in *The Laughing Rooster* (1964) and *Periods of* the Moon (1967). A selection of his verse was published in 1977. Also important were Patricia K. Page (1916–), interested in psychology, the neoromantic Anne Wilkinson (1910–61), and Miriam Waddington (1917–), who emphasized the beneficence of nature.

Margaret Avison (1918–), in *Winter Sun* (1960) and *The Dumbfounding* (1966), lyrically expressed her Christian faith. Leonard Cohen (1934–) wrote emotionally of his own love and art and of 20th-century evil. Margaret Atwood explored the anxieties accompanying poetic self-realization. Other noteworthy figures were Al Purdy (1918– ; *The Stone Bird,* 1981), Phyllis Webb (1927–), Alden Nowlan (1933–83), and experimental aural and oral poets Bill Bissett (1939–) and B. P. Nichol.

Prose

Major novelists of the 1950s included Ernest Buckler (1908–84), whose *Mountain and the Valley* (1952) concerns frustrated artists in Nova Scotia, and Ethel

Wilson (1890–1980), who wrote of women's self-fulfillment in *The Equations of Love* (1952) and *Swamp Angel* (1954), both set in British Columbia. Aspects of the Jewish experience are treated by Abraham Moses Klein in his novel *The Second Scroll* (1951), a modern search for Israel, and by Mordecai Richler in his satiric, antimaterialist *Apprenticeship of Duddy Kravitz* (1959).

According to many critics, the best novelists of the 1960s and 1970s were Robertson Davies and Margaret Laurence (1926–87). Davies moved from satirical novels and plays to Jungian psychological examination of oddly assorted characters in his *Deptford Trilogy: Fifth Business* (1970), *The Manticore* (1972), and *World of Wonders* (1975). His popularity continued with *The Rebel Angels* (1982), *What's Bred in the Bone* (1985), and *The Cunning Man* (1995). Laurence's writing is distinguished by penetrating characterizations and fine technique. In *The Stone Angel* (1964), *A Jest of God* (1966), and *The Diviners* (1974), she traces a heroine's progress toward self-realization.

Other contemporary novelists produced more experimental works, such as *The Double Hook* (1959) by Sheila Watson (1909–), *The Studhorse Man* (1969) by Robert Kroetsch (1927–), and *Bear* (1976) by Marian Engel (1933–85). Several poets turned to fiction, including Leonard Cohen, who wrote *The Favorite Game* (1963) and *Beautiful Losers* (1966), and Margaret Atwood. Her feminist outlook shapes her several novels, including *Surfacing* (1972), *Life Before Man* (1979), *Bodily Harm* (1981), and *The Handmaid's Tale* (1986); *The Blind Assassin* (2000), the saga of an Ontario family in the 1930s, won her the Booker Prize for that year. Among writers of short stories are Alice Munro, Norman Levine (1924–), and Jane Rule (1931–). Mavis Gallant (1922–), although a longtime resident of

France, appraises her native country clearly in *Home Truths: Selected Canadian Stories* (1981). Michael Ondaatje combines autobiographical elements with the history of his native Sri Lanka where he lived until the age of 19. His novel *The English Patient* (1992) received the Booker Prize (1992) and was made into a successful film in 1995. In 2002 Yann Martel (1963–) became the third Canadian to win the Booker Prize, for his novel *Life of Pi* (2001), which explores issues of faith and religion.

Farley Mowat (1921–) has written several very popular nonfiction books on Native Americans (*People of the Deer,* 1952), on the survival of endangered species (*Never Cry Wolf,* 1963, and *A Whale for the Killing,* 1972), and on problems of the Canadian North (*The Great Betrayal: Arctic Canada Now,* 1976). Mordecai Richler's nonfictional *Home Sweet Home: My Canadian Album* (1984) mingles autobiography and journalistic essays.

Drama has been slower to develop in a country of widely spaced small communities. In the mid-20th century, increased interest in drama was reflected in the establishment of theaters such as the repertory theater in Stratford, Ont.; the Shaw Festival in Niagara, Ont.; and the Vancouver Playhouse in British Columbia.

Two of the most noteworthy literary critics were George Woodcock (1912–95) and Northrop Frye. Woodcock, a believer in social revolution, wrote poetry, history, drama, and travel books in addition to criticism. Frye's *Anatomy of Criticism* (1957) is a highly influential study of English literary themes; he also wrote *The Bush Garden: Essays on the Canadian Imagination* (1971) and *The Great Code: The Bible and*

Literature (1981), among other works.. University of Toronto professor Marshall McLuhan received wide attention for his theory proclaiming that printed literature is being superseded by electronic means of mass communication. Somewhat ironically, his own book *The Medium Is the Massage: An Inventory of Effects* (1967) enjoyed a great vogue.

Canadian literature in French

Until the mid-20th century Canadian literature in French focused primarily on religion, Canadian history, and patriotism. Since then it has become more involved in the concerns of contemporary Western society.

Colonial Period

The earliest Canadian works in French were written by 16th- and 17th-century explorers and missionaries. Particularly informative are the accounts of the 1534–35 voyage of Jacques Cartier and Samuel de Champlain's *Voyages de la Nouvelle France occidentale, dicte Canada* (Voyages in Western New France, called Canada, 2 vol., 1632) and *Les relations des Jésuites* (Jesuit Reports, 1632–73), annual reports of Jesuit missionaries about their lives among the Indians. Letters by the Ursuline nun Marie de l'Incarnation (1599–1672) are filled with details of life in New France.

19th Century

Resentment of the English conquest, intensified by the Union Act of 1840 and Confederation in 1867, strengthened a deep sense of French-Canadian patriotism. It affected the first novelists, P. I. F. Aubert de Gaspé (1814–41), who filled his *Influence d'un livre*

(Influence of a Book, 1837) with Québec folklore, and P. J. O. Chauveau (1820–90), who described the decline of French Canada after the conquest in *Charles Guérin* (1852). This patriotism found its classic expression in the *Histoire du Canada* (1845–48), written by François Xavier Garneau (1809–66) to disprove Governor-General Lord Durham's statement that French Canada had neither a history nor a literature.

Taking Garneau as their prophet, poets, novelists, historians, and journalists met at the Québec city bookshop of Octave Crémazie. At its height in the 1860s, this Québec group set the style for oratorical patriotic works, modeled on French romantic poetry, that dominated French-Canadian literature for the rest of the century. Crémazie, considered the father of French-Canadian poetry, influenced the younger poet Louis Honoré Fréchette, who based his *Légende d'un peuple* (1887) on French-Canadian history. Pamphile Lemay (1837–1918), author of *Les gouttelettes* (1904), and William Chapman (1850–1917) in *Les rayons du nord* (The Northern Lights, 1910) vividly recreated rural Québec life in poetic form.

Also prominent in the Québec group was Abbé Henri Raymond Casgrain, who wrote *Légendes canadiennes* (1861), literary criticism, and histories such as *Montcalm et Lévis* (1891; *Wolfe and Montcalm*, 1964). Joseph Charles Taché (1820–94) told tales of lumbermen and trappers in *Forestiers et voyageurs* (1884), and Antoine Gérin-Lajoie (1824–82) tried to discourage French-Canadian emigration in the propaganda novel *Jean Rivard: le defricheur* (Jean Rivard: the Settler, 1862). Other novelists wrote historical romances set in New France; they include Napoléon Bourassa (1827–1916) and Philippe Joseph

Aubert de Gaspé (1786–1871), whose *Les anciens canadiens* (1863) became a classic.

Early 20th Century

French-Canadian life continued to be a major theme in early 20th-century literature through the *terroir* ("country"), or regionalist, school, which stressed the bonds between the habitant, or farmer, and the ancestral land. One of the best *terroir* poets was Nérée Beauchemin (1850–1931), whose *Floraisons matutinales* (Morning Efflorescence, 1897) and *Patrie intime* (Intimate Birthplace, 1928) express his devotion to Québec. Among *terroir* novelists were Ernest Choquette (1862–1941), Harry Bernard (1898–1979), and especially French-born Louis Hémon, who lived with a habitant family in order to write *Maria Chapdelaine* (posthumously serialized, 1914; pub. 1916). Abbé Lionel Adolphe Groulx (1878–1967) vehemently expressed his patriotism in *Vers L'émancipation* (Towards Emancipation, 1921) and *Histoire du Canada Français. . .* (2 vol., 1962).

The Montréal school of poets, which flourished in Montréal between 1895 and 1930, was influenced by French Parnassians and symbolists; its members emphasized aesthetics and technique. Particularly original and sensuous was the work of Émile Nelligan (1879–1941) before he lost his reason at the age of 20. Paul Morin (1889–1963) drew on his Mediterranean travels for the vivid, technically complex *Paon d'émail* (Enamel Peacock, 1911) and *Poèmes de cendre et d'or* (Poems of Ashes and Gold, 1922). Also noteworthy are the nostalgic lyrics of the lapsed Jesuit Louis Dantin (pseudonym of Eugène Seers, 1865–1945) and the reflective works of Albert Lozeau (1878–1924) and Jean Charbonneau (1875–1960).

As a result of urbanization, the Great Depression, and World War II, the proud cultural isolation of French Canada began to break down, and writers became more introspective, realistic, and innovative. The poets Hector de Saint-Denys-Garneau (1912–43), François Hertel (pseudonym of Rodolphe Dubé, 1905–85), and Alain Grandbois (1900–75) experimented with free verse and symbolism to express philosophical abstractions and awareness of death. The novelist Albert Laberge (1871–1960) had already subjected Québec tradition to harsh realism in *La scouine* (1918; *Bitter Bread,* 1977). That culture was further criticized and exposed by Claude Henri Grignon (1894–1976) in *Un homme et son péché* (A Man and His Sin, 1933), Jean Charles Harvey (1891–1967) in *Les demi-civilisés* (1934; *Sackcloth for Barner,* 1938), and Ringuet (pseudonym of Philippe Panneton, 1895–1960) in *Trente arpents* (1938; *Thirty Acres,* 1940).

Late 20th Century

After World War II and especially in the nationalist 1960s, new writers appeared, writing in many different modes with great technical skill.

A poet of major stature was Anne Hébert, whose surrealist, symbolist works such as *Les songes en équilibre* (Dreams in Equilibrium, 1942) and *Le tombeau des rois* (The Tomb of Kings, 1953) concerned mental anguish, solitude, and death; she also was noted for her powrful and evocative novels, set mostly in her native Québec. Pierre Trottier (1925–) in *Le combat contre Tristan* (The Battle Against Tristan; 1951) presented a tragic drama of love and death that evoked the troubled disunity of Canada. Also criticizing or lamenting the modern world were Paul Marie Lapointe (1929–), Gatien Lapointe (1931–83), and Fernand Ouellette (1930–). Among other notable poets was Jacques Poulin (1937–), author of the experimental "novel-poem" *Coeur de la baleine bleue* (Heart of the Blue Whale, 1970).

Many novelists turned to social satire. In *Bonheur d'occasion* (1945; *The Tin Flute,* 1947) and *Alexandre Chenevert* (1954; *The Cashier,* 1955), Gabrielle Roy (1909–83) described the disturbing effect of industrialization and the city on human dignity, suggesting that such pressures may be withstood by cultivating compassion and love. *La détresse et l'enchantement* (Distress and Enchantment), the first volume of her autobiography, was published posthumously in 1984. Roger Lemelin (1919–) wrote of urban working-class life in *Les Plouffe* (1948; *The Plouffe Family,* 1948). This seemingly benign satire, popular in both French- and English-speaking Canada, was made into a film in 1982. Germaine Guèvremont (1900–68), on the other hand, realistically depicted rural life. The prolific writer Yves Thériault (1916–83), as well as Gerard Bessette (1920–), and Jean Simard (1916–), criticized the puritanical attitudes and other negative aspects of French-Canadian culture.

Other novelists were concerned with human inner nature. André Giroux (1916–) and Robert Élie (1915–73) expressed some confidence in the human spirit. Particularly sensitive is *Poussière sur la ville* (1953; *Dust over the City,* 1955), a study of despair, by André Langevin (1927–). The French Jewish immigrant Monique Bosco (1927–) wrote of postwar rootlessness in *Un amour maladroit* (An Awkward Love, 1961), and the symbolist Hubert Aquin (1929–77) concluded the impossibility of freedom in *Prochain episode* (The Next Installment, 1965). One of the most devastating psychological novels is *Une saison dans la vie d'Emmanuel* (1965; *A Season in the Life of Emmanuel,*

1966) by Marie Claire Blais. Also notable is *L'avalée des avalés* (1966; *The Swallower Swallowed,* 1968) by Rejean Ducharme (1942–). Reflecting French-Canadian nationalism, Michel Tremblay (1942–) used the Montréal vernacular in dramas, which, in translation, were also enjoyed by English audiences. His first play was *Les belles-soeurs* (1968; trans. *The Sisters-in-law,* 1973); he was also known for his mostly biographical novels, written in the late 1970s and '80s.

Beginning about the 1980s, writers whose ethnic origins were other than French, such as the Italian-born Canadian playwright Marco Micone (1945–) and the Chinese-born Canadian novelist Ying Chen (1961–), introduced new themes and styles of expression to French-Canadian literature.

Contemporary Canadian Literature

Following World War II, writers such as Mavis Gallant, Mordecai Richler, Norman Levine, Margaret Laurence and Irving Layton brought added to the Modernist influence to Canadian literature previously introduced by F.R. Scott, A.J.M. Smith and others associated with the *McGill Fortnightly*. This influence, at first, was not broadly appreciated. Norman Levine's *Canada Made Me,* a travelogue that presented a sour interpretation of the country in 1958, for example, was widely rejected.

After 1967, the country's centennial year, the national government increased funding to publishers and numerous small presses began operating throughout the country.

In the late 1970s, science fiction fan and scholar of Canadian literature Susan Wood helped pioneer the study of feminist science fiction, and (along with immigrant editor Judith Merril) brought new respectability to the study of Canadian science fiction, paving the way for the rise of such phenomena as the French-Canadian science fiction magazine *Solaris.*

By the 1990s, Canadian literature was viewed as some of the world's best.

Canadian authors have accumulated international awards:

1) In 1992, Michael Ondaatje became the first Canadian to win the Booker Prize for *The English Patient.*
2) Margaret Atwood won the Booker in 2000 for *The Blind Assassin* and Yann Martel won it in 2002 for *Life of Pi.*
3) Alistair MacLeod won the 2001 IMPAC Award for *No Great Mischief* and Rawi Hage won it in 2008 for *De Niro's Game.*
4) Carol Shields's *The Stone Diaries* won the 1995 Pulitzer Prize for Fiction, and in 1998 her novel *Larry's Party* won the Orange Prize.

Notable Figures

Because Canada only officially became a country on July 1, 1867, it has been argued that literature written before this time was colonial. For example, Susanna Moodie and Catherine Parr Traill, English sisters who adopted the country as their own, moved to Canada in 1832. They recorded their experiences as pioneers in Parr Traill's *The Backwoods of Canada* (1836) and *Canadian Crusoes* (1852), and Moodie's *Roughing It in the Bush* (1852) and *Life in the Clearings* (1853). However, both women wrote until their deaths, placing them in the country for more than 50 years and certainly well past Confederation. Moreover, their books often dealt with survival and the rugged Canadian environment; these themes re-appear in other Canadian works, including Margaret Atwood's *Survival*. Moodie and Parr Traill's sister, Agnes Strickland, remained in England and wrote elegant royal biographies, creating a stark contrast between Canadian and English literatures.

However, one of the earliest "Canadian" writers virtually always included in Canadian literary anthologies is Thomas Chandler Haliburton (1796–1865), who died just two years before Canada's official birth. He is remembered for his comic character, Sam Slick, who appeared in *The Clockmaker* and other humorous works throughout Haliburton's life.

Arguably, the best-known living Canadian writer internationally (especially after the recent passing of Robertson Davies and Mordecai Richler) is Margaret Atwood, a prolific novelist, poet, and literary critic.

This group, along with Alice Munro, who has been called the best living writer of short stories in English, were the first to elevate Canadian Literature to the world stage. During the post-war decades only a handful of books of any literary merit were published each year in Canada, and Canadian literature was viewed as an appendage to British and American writing.

Much of what was produced dealt with extremely typical Canadiana such as the outdoors and animals, or events in Canadian history. A reaction against this tradition, poet Leonard Cohen's novel *Beautiful Losers* (1966), was labelled by one reviewer "the most revolting book ever written in Canada".

Canadian poet Leonard Cohen is perhaps best known as a folk singer and songwriter, with an international following.

Canadian Author Farley Mowat, best known for his work "Never Cry Wolf", also author of "Lost in the Barrens" (1956), Governor General's Award-winning children's book.

5

India Literature—Status and Trends

The Indian literary tradition is primarily one of verse and is also essentially oral. The earliest works were composed to be sung or recited and were so transmitted for many generations before being written down. As a result, the earliest records of a text may be later by several centuries than the conjectured date of its composition. Furthermore, perhaps because so much Indian literature is either religious or a reworking of familiar stories from the Sanskrit epics, the *Ramayana* and the *Mahabharata,* and the mythological writings known as *Puranas,* the authors often remain anonymous. Biographical details of the lives of most of the earlier Indian writers exist only in much later stories and legends.

In medieval Indian literature the earliest works in many of the languages were sectarian, designed to advance or to celebrate some unorthodox regional belief. Examples are the *Caryapadas* in Bengali, Tantric verses of the 12th century, and the *Lilacaritra* (circa 1280), in Marathi. In Kannada (Kanarese) from the 10th century, and later in Gujarati from the 13th century, the first truly indigenous works are Jain romances; ostensibly the lives of Jain saints, these are actually popular tales based on Sanskrit and Pali themes. Other example was in Rajasthani of the bardic tales of chivalry and heroic resistance to the first Muslim invasions - such as the 12th-century epic poem *Prithiraja-raso* by Chand Bardai of Lahore.

Most important of all for later Indian literature were the first traces in the vernacular languages of the northern Indian cults of Krishna and of Rama. Included are the 12th-century poems by Jaydev, called the *Gitagovinda* (The Cowherd's Song); and about 1400, a group of religious love poems written in Maithili (eastern Hindi of Bihar) by the poet Vidyapati were a seminal influence on the cult of Radha-Krishna in Bengal.

Bhakti Tradition

The full flowering of the Radha-Krishna cult, under the Hindu mystics Chaitanya in Bengal and Vallabhacharya at Mathura, involved *bhakti* (a personal devotion to a god). Although earlier traces of this attitude are found in the work of the Tamil Alvars (mystics who wrote ecstatic hymns to Vishnu between the 7th and 10th centuries), a later surge of *bhakti* flooded every channel of Indian intellectual and religious life beginning in the late 15th century. *Bhakti* was also addressed to Rama (an avatar of Vishnu), most notably in the Avadhi (eastern Hindi) works of Tulsi Das; his *Ramcharitmanas* (Lake of the Acts of Rama, 1574-77; trans. 1952) has become the authoritative. The early gurus or founders of the Sikh religion, especially Nanak and Arjun, composed *bhakti* hymns to their concepts of deity. These are the first written documents in Punjabi (Panjabi) and form part of the *Adi Granth* (First, or Original, Book), the sacred scripture of the Sikhs, which was first compiled by

Arjun in 1604. In the 16th century, the Rajaasthani princess and poet Mira Bai addressed her *bhakti* lyric verse to Krishna, as did the Gujarati poet Narsimh Mehta.

In the 16th century, Jagannath Das wrote an Oriya version of the *Bhagavata* and Tuncattu Eruttacchan, the so-called father of Malayalam literature, wrote recensions of traditional literature. Added, in the 18th century, was a deliberate imitation of Sanskritic forms and vocabulary by *pandits*. In 18th-century evolved Assamese and Marathi prose chronicles, ballads, and folk drama involving much dance and song.

The only Indian writings that incontestably predate the influence of classical Sanskrit are those in the Tamil language. Anthologies of secular lyrics on the themes of love and war, together with the grammatical-stylistic work *Tolkappiyam* (Old Composition), are thought to be very ancient. Later, between the 6th and 9th centuries, Tamil sectarian devotional poems were composed, often claimed as the first examples of the Indian *bhakti* tradition. At some indeterminate date between the 2nd and 5th centuries, two long Tamil verse romances (sometimes called epics) were written: *Cilappatikaram* (The Jeweled Anklet) by Ilanko Atikal, which has been translated into English (1939 and 1965); and its sequel *Manimekalai* (The Girdle of Gems), a Buddhist work by Cattanar.

Linguistic and Cultural Influences

Much traditional Indian literature is derived in theme and form not only from Sanskrit literature but from the Buddhist and Jain texts written in the Pali language and the other Prakrits (medieval dialects of

Sanskrit). This applies to literature in the Dravidian languages of the south as well as to literature in the Indo-Iranian languages of the north. Invasions of Persians and Turks, beginning in the 14th century, resulted in the influence of Persian and Islamic culture in Urdu, although important Islamic strands can be found in other literatures as well, especially those written in Bengali, Gujarati, and Kashmiri. After 1817, entirely new literary values were established that remain dominant today.

The Urdu poets almost always wrote in Persian forms, using the ghazal for love poetry in addition to an Islamic form of *bhakti,* the *masnavi* for narrative verse, and the *marsiya* for elegies. Urdu then gained use as a literary language in Delhi and Lucknow. The ghazals of Mir and Ghalib mark the highest achievement of Urdu lyric verse. The Urdu poets were mostly sophisticated, urban artists, but some adopted the idiom of folk poetry, as is typical of the verses in Punjabi, Pushtu, Sindhi or other regional languages.

Modern Period

Poets such as Ghalib, lived and worked during the British era, when a literary revolution occurred in all the Indian languages as a result of contact with Western thought, when the printing press was introduced (by Christian missionaries), and when the influence of Western educational institutions was strong. During the mid-19th century in the great ports of Mumbai, Calcutta, and Chennai, a prose literary tradition arose—encompassing the novel, short story, essay, and literary drama (this last incorporating both classical Sanskrit and Western models)—that gradually engulfed the customary Indian verse genres. Urdu poets remained faithful to the old forms while Bengalis were imitating such English poets as Percy Bysshe Shelley or T.S. Eliot.

Ram Mohan Roy's (1774-1833) campaign for introduction of scientific education in India and Swami Vivekananda's work are considered to be great examples of the English literature in India.

During the last 150 years many writers have contributed to the development of modern Indian literature, writing in any of the 18 major languages (as well as in English). Bengali has led the way and today has one of the most extensive literatures of any Indian language. One of its greatest representatives is Sir Rabindranath Tagore, the first Indian to win the Nobel Prize for literature (1913). Much of his prose and verse is available in his own English translations.

Work by two other great 20th-century Indian leaders and writers is also widely known: the verse of the Islamic leader and philosopher Sir Muhammad Iqbal, originally written in Urdu and Persian; and the autobiography of Mohandas K. Gandhi, *My Experiments with Truth,* originally written in Gujarati between 1927 and 1929, is now considered a classic.

Several other writers are relatively well known to the West. They include Jawaharlal Nehru (1889-1964) for his Glimpses of World History, Discovery of India and An Autobiography (1936); Mulk Raj Anand, among whose many works the early affectionate *Untouchable* (1935) and *Coolie* (1936) are novels of social protest; and R. K. Narayan, writer of novels and tales of village life in southern India. The first of Narayan's many works, *Swami and Friends,* appeared in 1935; among his more recent titles are *The English Teacher* (1980), *The Vendor of Sweets* (1983), and *Under the*

Banyan Tree (1985). Among the younger authors writing of modern India with nostalgia for the past is Anita Desai—as in *Clear Light of Day* (1980). Her *In Custody* (1984) is the story of a teacher's fatal enchantment with poetry. Ved Mehta, although long resident in the U.S., recalls his Indian roots in a series of memoirs of his family and of his education at schools for the blind in India and America; among these works are *Vedi* (1982) and *Sound Shadows of the New World* (1986).

The other well-known novelist/ writers are Dom Moraes (A Beginning), Nlissim E Zekiel (The Unfurnished Man), P Lal, A.K.Ramanujan (whose translations of Tamil classics are internationally known), Kamala Das, Arun Kolatkar and R. Parthasarathy; Toru Dutt; Sarojini Naidu; Aurobindo; Raja Rao, GV Desani, M Ananthanarayanan, Bhadani Bhattacharya, Monohar Malgonkar, Arun Joshi, Kamala Markandaya, Khushwant Singh, Nayantara Sahgal, O.V. Vijayan; Salman Rushdie; K.R. Sreenivasa Iyengar, C.D. Narasimhaiah and M.K. Naik.

Among the latest are Vikram Seth (A Suitable Boy), Allan Sealy (The Trotter-Nama), Sashi Tharoor (Show Business, The Great Indian Novel, Amitav Ghosh (Circle of Reason, Shadow Lines), Upamanyu Chatterjee (English August) and Vikram Chandra (Red Earth and Pouring Rain).

Regional Literature

Literary activities burst forth with the playwright Bharata's (200 BC) Natya Shastra, the Bible of dramatic criticism. The earliest plays were soon overshadowed by Kalidasa's Shakuntala, a heroic play, a model for ages. While Shudraka's *Mrichchhakatika,* was a play of the social class. Bhavabhuti (circa 700AD) was another well-known figure, his best being *Malatimadhava* and *Uttaramacharita* (based on Ramayana).

The great Sanskrit poems are five – Kalidasa's Raghuvamsa and Kumarasambhava, Kiratarjuniya of Bharavi (550AD), Sishupalavadha of Magha (7th century AD) and Naishadhiyacharita of Sriharsha (12th century AD). All of them draw from the Mahabharata. Shorter poems of great depth were composed on a single theme like love, morality, detachment and sometimes of grave matters. The earliest and best collections of such verses called Muktakas are those of Bhartrihari and Amaruka.

Much of the early prose work in Sanskrit has not survived. Of the remaining, some of the best are Vasavadatta of Subandhu, Kadambari and Harshacharita of Bana (7th century AD) and Dasakumaracharita of Dandin (7th century AD). The Panchatantra and Hitopadesha are collections of wit and wisdom in the Indian style, teaching polity and proper conduct through animal fables and aphorisms.

With a glorious life of over 3000 years, Sanskrit continues to be a living language even today, bobbing up during Hindu ceremonies when mantras (ritual verses) are chanted. And though restricted, it's still a medium of literary expression, but 'great works' have long stopped being written.

Assamese Literature

The Charyapadas are often cited as the earliest example of Assamese literature. The Charyapadas are Buddhist songs composed in 8th-12th century. These writings bear similarities to Oriya and Bengali languages as well. The phonological and morphological traits of these songs bear very strong resemblance to Assamese some of which are extant.

After the Charyapadas, the period may again be split into Pre-Vaishnavite and Vaishnative sub-periods. The earliest known Assamese writer is Hema Saraswati, who wrote a small poem "Prahlada Charita". In the time of the King Indranarayana (1350-1365) of Kamatapur the two poets Harihara Vipra and Kaviratna Saraswati composed Asvamedha Parva and Jayadratha Vadha respectively. Another poet named Rudra Kandali translated Drona Parva into Assamese. But the most well-known poet of the Pre-Vaishnavite sub period is Madhav Kandali, who rendered Valmiki's Ramayana into Assamese verse (Kotha Ramayana, 11th century) under the patronage of Mahamanikya, a Kachari king of Jayantapura.

The most famous modern Assamese writers are Indira Goswami, Nirupama Bargohain, Birendra Kumar Bhattacharya, Homen Borgohain, Bhabendra Nath Saikia, Amulya Barua, Nabakanta Barua, Atul Chandra Hazarika, Nalini Bala Devi, Nirmal Prabha Bordoloi, Mahim Bora, Arupa Patangia Kalita, Bhabananda Deka, Purobi Bormudoi, Arun Sharma, Anuradha Sharma Pujari, Atulananda Deva Goswami, etc.

Bengali Literature

The first evidence of Bengali literature is known as Charyapada or Charyageeti, which were Buddhist hymns from the 8th century. Charyapada is in the oldest known written form of Bengali. The famous Bengali linguist Harprashad Shastri discovered the palm leaf Charyapada manuscript in the Nepal Royal Court Library in 1907. The most internationally famous

Bengali writer is Nobel laureate Rabindranath Tagore, who received the Nobel Prize for Literature in 1913 for his work "Gitanjali". He wrote the national anthem of India and Bangladesh namely, "Jana Gana Mana" and "Amar Sonar Bangla", respectively. He was the first Asian who won the Nobel Prize. Rabindranath has written enormous amount of Poems, Songs, Essays, Novels, Plays and Short-stories. His songs remain popular and are still widely sung in Bengal.

Another poet, one generation younger is equally popular, valuable, and influential in his country, though virtually unknown in foreign countries: Kazi Nazrul Islam. Other famous Indian Bengali writers were Sharat Chandra Chattopadhyay, Bankim Chandra Chattopadhyay, and Michael Madhusudan Dutt. Bengali is the second most commonly spoken language in India (after Hindi). As a result of the Bengal Renaissance in the 19th and 20th centuries, many of India's most famous, and relatively recent, literature, poetry, and songs are in Bengali.

In the history of Bengali literature there has been only one path-breaking literary movement by a group of poets and artists who called themselves Hungryalists.

Hindi Literature

Hindi literature started as religious and philosophical poetry in medieval periods in dialects like Avadhi and Brij. The most famous figures from this period are Kabir and Tulsidas. In modern times, the *Khadi* dialect became more prominent and Sanskrit.

Chandrakanta, written by Devaki Nandan Khatri, is considered to be the first work of prose in Hindi. Munshi Premchand was the most famous Hindi novelist. The *chhayavadi* poets include Suryakant Tripathi 'Nirala', Jaishankar Prasad, Sumitranandan Pant, and Mahadevi Varma. Other renowned poets include Ramdhari Singh 'Dinkar', Maithili Sharan Gupt, Agyeya, Harivansh Rai Bachchan, and Dharmveer Bharti.

Kannada Literature

The oldest existing record of Kannada poetry in *tripadi* metre is the Kappe Arabhatta record of 700 CE. *Kavirajamarga* by King Nripatunga Amoghavarsha I (850 CE) is the earliest existing literary work in Kannada. It is a writing on literary criticism and poetics meant to standardize various written Kannada dialects used in literature in previous centuries. The book makes reference to Kannada works by early writers such as King Durvinita of the sixth century and Ravikirti, the author of the Aihole record of 636 CE. An early extant prose work, the *Vaddaradhane* by Shivakotiacharya of 900 CE provides an elaborate description of the life of Bhadrabahu of Shravanabelagola. Since the earliest available Kannada work is one on grammar and a guide of sorts to unify existing variants of Kannada grammar and literary styles, it can be safely assumed that literature in Kannada must have started several centuries earlier.

The works of the midieval period are based on Jain and Hindu principles. The Vachana Sahitya tradition of the twelfth century is purely native and unique in world literature. It is the sum of contributions by all sections of society. Vachanas were pithy comments on that period's social, religious and economic conditions. More importantly, they held a mirror to the seed of social revolution, which caused a radical re-examination of the ideas of caste, creed and religion. Some of the important writers of Vachana literature include Basavanna, Allama Prabhu and Akka Mahadevi. Kumara Vyasa, who wrote the *Karnata Bharata Katamanjari*, has arguably been the most famous and most influential Kannada writer of the fifteenth century.

The Bhakti movement gave rise to Dasa Sahitya around the fifteenth century which significantly contributed to the evolution of Carnatic music in its present form. This period witnessed great Haridasas like Purandara Dasa who has been aptly called the *Pioneer of Carnatic music*, Kanaka Dasa, Vyasathirtha and Vijaya Dasa. Modern Kannada in the twentieth century has been influenced by many movements, notably *Navodaya, Navya, Navyottara, Dalita* and *Bandaya*. Contemporary Kannada literature has been highly successful in reaching people of all classes in society. Works of Kannada literature have received seven Jnanpith awards, which is the highest number awarded for the literature in any Indian language. It has also received forty-seven Sahitya Academy awards.

Malayalam Literature

Even up to 500 years since the start of the Malayalam calendar which commenced in 825 AD, Malayalam literature remained in preliminary stage. During this time, Malayalam literature consisted mainly of various genres of songs. *Ramacharitham* written by *Cheeramakavi* is a collection of poems written at the end of preliminary stage in Malayalam literaure's evolution, and is the oldest Malayalam book available. Thunchaththu Ramanujan Ezhuthachan (17th century) is considered as the Father of the Malayalam language, because of his influence on the acceptance of the Malayalam alphabet and his extremely popular poetic works like Adhyathmaramayanam. Several noted works were written during the 19th century, but it was in the 20th century the Malayalam literary movement came to prominence. Malayalam literature flourished under various genres and today it is a fully developed part of Indian literature.

Manipuri Literature

Manipuri literature is the literature written in the Manipuri Language, including literature composed in Manipuri Language by writers from Manipur, Assam, Tripura, Myanmar and Bangladesh.The history of Manipuri literature trace back to thousands of years with flourish of its civilization. The survival of Manipuri literature after passing through the massive devastation, the terror event of history, by burning of Meetei Scriptures, which is known as Puya Meithaba, was a miracle. The resilience that Meeteis could acquire in the event of devastation proved her ability to survive in history. Most of the early literary works found in Manipuri Literature were in Poetry and Prose. Some of the books were written with combination of both the Prose and Poetry.

Marathi Literature

Marathi literature began with saint-poets like Dnyaneshwar, Tukaram, Ramdas, and Eknath. Modern Marathi literature was marked by a theme of social reform. Well-known figures from this phase include Mahatma Jyotiba Phule, Lokhitwadi, and others. Prominent modern literary figures include Vishnu Sakharam Khandekar, P.L. Deshpande, Vijay

Tendulkar, Indira Sant and Vishnu Vaman Shirvadakar (*Kavi Kusumagraj*).

Oriya Literature

Oriya has a rich literary heritage dating back to the thirteenth century. Sarala Dasa who lived in the fourteenth century is known as the Vyasa of Orissa. He translated the Mahabharata into Oriya. In fact the language was initially standardised through a process of translation of classical Sanskrit texts like the Mahabharata, the Ramayana and the Srimad Bhagabatam. Jagannatha Das translated the Srimad Bhagabatam into Oriya and his translation standardized the written form of the language. Oriya has had a strong tradition of poetry, especially that of devotional poetry. Some other eminent ancient Oriya Poets include Kabi Samrat Upendra Bhanja and Kabi Surya Bala Dev Ratha.

In nineteenth Century, Fakir Mohan Senapati (1843-1918), Gouri Shankar Ray, Gopal Chandra Praharaj, Pandit Nilmani Vidyaratna, Kabibar Radhanath Ray were prominent figure in prose and poetry writinga of Oriya Literature. In twentieth century Godabarish Mohapatra, Kalindi Charana Panigrahi, Kanhu Charan Mohanty (1906-1994), Gopinath Mohanty, Sachchidananda Routray, Surendra Mohanty, Manoj Das, Kishori Charan Das, Sitakanta Mohapatra, Ramakanta Rath, Binapani Mohanty, Jagadish Mohanty, Sarojini Sahoo, Rajendra Kishore Panda, Padmaj Pal, Ramchandra Behera, Pratibha Satpathy are few names who made the Oriya Literature and Oriya language worthy.

Punjabi Literature

The history of Punjabi literature starts with advent of

Aryan in Punjab. Punjab provided them the perfect environment in which to compose the ancient texts. The Rig-Veda is first example in which references are made to the rivers, flora and fauna of Punjab.

Tamil Literature

Tamil literature has a rich and long literary tradition spanning more than 2000 years. Tolkaappiyam has been credited as the oldest work in Tamil available today. The history of Tamil literature follows the history of Tamil Nadu, closely following the social and political trends of various periods. The secular nature of the early Sangam poetry gave way to works of religious and didactic nature during the Middle Ages. Tirukkural is a fine example of such work on human behaviour and political morals. A wave of religious revival helped generate a great volume of literary output by Saivite and Vaishnavite authors. Jain and Buddhist authors during the medieval period and Muslim and European authors later also contributed to the growth of Tamil literature.

A revival of Tamil literature took place from the late nineteenth century when works of religious and philosophical nature were written in a style that made it easier for the common people to enjoy. Nationalist poets began to utilise the power of poetry in influencing the masses. Short stories and novels began to appear. The popularity of Tamil Cinema has also provided opportunities for modern Tamil poets to emerge.

Telugu Literature

Telugu, the second largest language (after Hindi) spoken in India, is rich in literary traditions. The earliest written literature dates back to the seventh century. The epic literary tradition started with Nannayya who is acclaimed as Telugu's *Aadikavi* meaning the first poet. He belongs to the tenth or eleventh century.

Vemana who lived in the fourteenth century (a prince called Pedakomati. Vemaa Reddy) wrote in the language of the common man. He wrote poems in a simple style. He questioned the prevailing pseudo values and conventions and religious practices in his poems. His philosophy made him a unique poet of the masses.

Viswanadha Satyanarayana (*Veyipadagalu*), a doyen of conventional yet creative literature, was the first to receive the Jnanpith Award for Telugu followed by C. Narayana Reddy.

Srirangam Srinivasarao or Sri Sri was a popular modern poet and lyricist. Srisri took the "Telugu literary band wagon that travelled in roads of kings and queens in to that of muddy roads of common man".

Literary Movements: Old Era: Telugu literature has been enriched by many literary movements like Veera Shaiva movement which gave birth sto dwipada kavitvam (ccuplets). Bhakti movement which gave us immortal compilations by Annamayya, Kshetrayya and Tyagaraja and kancharla Gopanna (Ramadasu). The renaissance movement heralded by Vemana stand for the old Telugu literary movements.

New era: Romantic Movemnet (led by Krishna-sashtri, Rayaprolu, Vedula), Progressive Writers Movement, Digambara Kavitvam (Nagnamuni, Cherabanda Raju, Jwalamukhi, Nikhileswar, Bhairavayya and Mahaswapna Revolutionary Writers'

Movement, Streevada Kavitvam and Dalita Kavitvam all flourished in Telugu Literature and in fact, Telugu Literature has been the standard bearer of Indian Literature in these respects.

Fiction and Prose literature: Kadukuri Veeresalingam, is said to be the father of Modern Telugu fiction. Kodavatiganti Kutumba Rao laid foundation for the realistic modern Telugu Novel and Short Story, Rachakonda and Kalipatnam carried the flag in to excellency.

Annamaya, Gurajada Appa Rao, Kandukuri, Devulapalli, Jashuva, Unnava Laxminarayana (*Malapalli*), Bucchi Babu, Tripuraneni Gopichand and many more had a profound impact on Telugu literature.

Urdu Literature

Among other traditions, Urdu poetry is a fine example of linguistic and cultural synthesis. Arab and Persian vocabulary based on the Hindi language resulted in a vast and extremely beloved class of ghazal literature, usually written by Muslims in contexts ranging from romance and society to philosophy and devotion to Allah. Urdu soon became the court language of the Mughals and in its higher forms was once called the "Kohinoor" of Indian languages.

Indian Literature in Foreign Languages

Indian Persian Literature

During the early Muslim period, Persian became the lingua franca of the subcontinent, used by most of the educated and the government. Although Persian literature from Persia itself was popular, several

Indians became major Persian poets, the most notable being Amir Khusro and in more modern times Allama Iqbal. Much of the older Sanskrit literature was also translated into Persian. For a time, it remained the court language of the Mughals, soon to be replaced by Urdu. Persian still held its status, despite the spread of Urdu, well into the early years of the British rule in India. Most British officials had to learn Persian on coming to India and concluded their conversations in Persian. In 1837, however, the British, in an effort to expand their influence, made a government ruling to discontinue the use of Persian and commence the use of English instead. Thus started the decline of Persian as the subcontinent's lingua franca, a position to be taken up by the new language of the British Raj, English. Many modern Indian languages still show signs of heavy Persian influence, most notably Urdu and Hindi.

Indian English Literature

India has a sizable number of populations that have English as either primary or secondary language of communication. This is precisely because India had been a colony of the then British Empire for close to 200 years. Its association with British and hence English is even older. Emperor Jahangir granted William Hawkins permission to trade in India in the year 1608 and that was when English put its first step.

In the due course of history, British concluded their conquest of India and spread English language along with the empire. English replaced Persian as the court language in early 19th century and understanding English became a matter of survival for the urban class rather that a matter of pride. As a new block of population started to emerge from the grassroots, English spread its wings.

Most of the early exponents of English Literature in India were British though. The likes of George Orwell, Rudyard Kipling and Jim Corbett gave the initial push that was later carried on by several British authors. Rabindra Nath Tagore and Sarojini Naidu who contributed a lot to the English literature initially represented the natives but it was only in mid seventies that a new breed of boarding-school educated, elite brand of English authors started to appear on the radar. These writers gave a much-needed oxygen to English literature with their crisp, tongue-in-cheek and realistic fictions that were read all over the world.

The present condition of Indian English literature is heartening. New crops of English language writers are replacing the old breed and are representing India through their unique writings. Some of them have even won prestigious Booker Award. This has led to a sudden surge in the number of books published in English every year. New breed of English writers are trying to break glass ceiling. They are venturing in to newer genres by refusing to follow dotted lines. With English language becoming part of curriculum, the number of people knowing English language is increasing rapidly in every consecutive census. This is opening newer windows for the Indian English writers to experiment. In present context, with its all pros and cons, the future of English Literature in India looks nothing but bright.

History of Indian English Literature

History of English language and literature in India

starts with the advent of East India Company in India. It all started in the summers of 1608 when Emperor Jahangir, in the courts of Moguls, welcomed Captain William Hawkins, Commander of British Naval Expedition Hector. It was India's first tryst with an Englishman and English. Jahangir later allowed Britain to open a permanent port and factory on the special request of King James IV that was conveyed by his ambassador Sir Thomas Roe. English were here to stay.

As East India Company spread its wing in southern peninsula, English language started to get newer pockets of influence. But it was still time for the first English book to capitalize. Late 17th century saw the coming of printing press in India but the publication were largely confined to either printing Bible or government decrees. Then came newspapers. It was in 1779 that the first English Newspaper named Hickey's Bengal Gazette was published in India. The breakthrough in Indian English literature came in 1793 A.D. when a person by the name of Sake Dean Mahomet published a book in London titled Travels of Dean Mahomet. This was essentially Mahomet's travel narrative that can be put somewhere between a Non-Fiction and a Travelogue.

In its early stages, the Indian writings in English were heavily influenced by the Western art form of the novel. It was typical for the early Indian English language writers to use English unadulterated by Indian words to convey experiences that were primarily Indian. The core reason behind this step was the fact that most of the readers were either British or British educated Indians. In the coming century, the writings were largely confined to writing history chronicles and government gazettes.

In the early 20th century, when the British conquest of India was achieved, a new breed of writers started to emerge on the block. These writers were essentially British who were born or brought up or both in India. Their writing consisted of Indian themes and sentiments but the way of storytelling was primarily western. They had no reservation in using native words, though, to signify the context. This group consisted likes of Rudyard Kipling, Jim Corbett and George Orwell among others. Books such as Kim, The Jungle Book, 1984, Animal Farm and The man-eaters of Kumaon etc were liked and read all over the English-speaking world. In fact, some of the writings of that era are still considered to be the masterpieces of English Literature. In those periods, natives were represented by the likes of Rabindra Nath Tagore and Sarojini Naidu. In fact, Geetanjali helped Tagore win Nobel Prize for Literature in the year 1913.

There was a lull for more than 3 decades when India was passing through the era of aspiration and reconstruction. Some sporadic works such as 'A Passage to India' by E M Foster, 'The Wonder that was India' by E L. Basham and ' Autobiography of an unknown Indian' by Nirad C Chaudhuri though set the stage on fire but were unsuccessful in catalyzing and explosion.

It was in late seventies that a new breed of Convent, boarding school educated and elite class of novelists and writers started to come on block. The likes of Salman Rushdie, Vikram Seth, Amitabh Ghosh and Dominique Lepierre set the literature world on fire. Rushdie' s ' Midnight Children' won Booker in 1981 and send the message loud and clear that Indians are here to stay. Arundhati Roy and Kiran Desai repeated the feat when they won Man Booker in the year 1997 and 2006 respectively. In the mean time, a new crop of authors such as Pankaj Misra, Chetan Bhagat, Jhumpa Lahiri, William Dalrymple, Hari Kunzuru have arrived on the international scene and their writings are being appreciated round the globe.

India became independent from Britain in 1947, and the English language was supposed to be phased out by 1965. However, today English and Hindi are the official languages. Indian English is characterized by treating mass nouns as count nouns, frequent use of the "isn't it?" tag, use of more compounds, and a different use of prepositions. With its distinct flavor, Indian English writings are there to stay. With he surge of English speaking population, the future looks anything but bleak.

History of English language and literature in India starts with the advent of East India Company in India. It all started in the summers of 1608 when Emperor Jahangir, in the courts of Moguls, welcomed Captain William Hawkins, Commander of British Naval Expedition Hector. It was India's first tryst with an Englishman and English. Jahangir later allowed Britain to open a permanent port and factory on the special request of King James IV that was conveyed by his ambassador Sir Thomas Roe. English were here to stay.

As East India Company spread its wing in southern peninsula, English language started to get newer pockets of influence. But it was still time for the first English book to capitalize. Late 17th century saw the coming of printing press in India but the publication were largely confined to either printing Bible or government decrees. Then came newspapers. It was in 1779 that the first English Newspaper named

Hickey's Bengal Gazette was published in India. The breakthrough in Indian English literature came in 1793 A.D. when a person by the name of Sake Dean Mahomet published a book in London titled Travels of Dean Mahomet. This was essentially Mahomet's travel narrative that can be put somewhere between a Non-Fiction and a Travelogue.

In its early stages, the Indian writings in English were heavily influenced by the Western art form of the novel. It was typical for the early Indian English language writers to use English unadulterated by Indian words to convey experiences that were primarily Indian. The core reason behind this step was the fact that most of the readers were either British or British educated Indians. In the coming century, the writings were largely confined to writing history chronicles and government gazettes.

In the early 20th century, when the British conquest of India was achieved, a new breed of writers started to emerge on the block. These writers were essentially British who were born or brought up or both in India. Their writing consisted of Indian themes and sentiments but the way of storytelling was primarily western. They had no reservation in using native words, though, to signify the context. This group consisted likes of Rudyard Kipling, Jim Corbett and George Orwell among others. Books such as Kim, The Jungle Book, 1984, Animal Farm and The man-eaters of Kumaon etc were liked and read all over the English-speaking world. In fact, some of the writings of that era are still considered to be the masterpieces of English Literature. In those periods, natives were represented by the likes of Rabindra Nath Tagore and Sarojini Naidu. In fact, Geetanjali helped Tagore win Nobel Prize for Literature in the year 1913.

There was a lull for more than 3 decades when India was passing through the era of aspiration and reconstruction. Some sporadic works such as 'A Passage to India' by E M Foster, 'The Wonder that was India' by E L. Basham and ' Autobiography of an unknown Indian' by Nirad C Chaudhuri though set the stage on fire but were unsuccessful in catalyzing and explosion.

It was in late seventies that a new breed of Convent, boarding school educated and elite class of novelists and writers started to come on block. The likes of Salman Rushdie, Vikram Seth, Amitabh Ghosh and Dominique Lepierre set the literature world on fire. Rushdie' s ' Midnight Children' won Booker in 1981 and send the message loud and clear that Indians are here to stay. Arundhati Roy and Kiran Desai repeated the feat when they won Man Booker in the year 1997 and 2006 respectively. In the mean time, a new crop of authors such as Pankaj Misra, Chetan Bhagat, Jhumpa Lahiri, William Dalrymple, Hari Kunzuru have arrived on the international scene and their writings are being appreciated round the globe.

India became independent from Britain in 1947, and the English language was supposed to be phased out by 1965. However, today English and Hindi are the official languages. Indian English is characterized by treating mass nouns as count nouns, frequent use of the "isn't it?" tag, use of more compounds, and a different use of prepositions. With its distinct flavor, Indian English writings are there to stay. With he surge of English speaking population, the future looks anything but bleak.

There is no dearth of Indian authors who write in English language, as of today. But it was not same a century ago. English literature and writing was still in its nascent phase in India and most of the Indian writers were either used to be Indian born British or Britain educated Indians. The list includes exponents such as George Orwell, Rudyard Kipling, Jim Corbett, Tagore and Sarojini Naidu among others.

The post independence decades were largely dormant with only few names such as Nirad C Chaudhuri and R K Narayan inciting curiosity if any. It was as late as early eighties that the new breed of writers such as Salman Rushdie, Vikram Seth, Amitabh Ghosh and Anita Desai started popping upon the international literary map. The new breed of authors and writers who emerged in post reform era carried the initiative forward. These writers have created a niche for themselves among the readers across the globe and have given signal loud and clear that they are here to stay. The list includes the likes of Pankaj Misra, William Dalrymple, Chetan Bhagat, Anurag Mathur, Kiran Desai, Kamla Das, Hari Kunzuru, Jhumpa Lahiri and Arundhati Roy among others.

Though foreign in its origin, English has been adopted in India as a language of education and literary expression besides being an important medium of communication amongst the people of various regions. The beginning of Indian literature in English is traced to the end of the 18th century and the beginning of the 19th, by which time English education was more or less firmly established in the three major centers of British power in India - Calcutta, Madras and Bombay. Ram Mohan Roy (1774-1833), a social reformist from Bengal who fought for widow remarriage and voting rights for women, was the pioneer of Indian writing in English. Roy insisted that for India to be included among the world's nations, education in English was essential. He, therefore, campaigned for introduction of scientific education in India through the English medium.

Raja Ram Mohan Roy was followed in the early 19th century in Bengal by the poets Henry Derozio and Michael Madhusudan Dutt. Dutt started out writing epic verse in English, but returned to his native Bengali later in life. The poems of Toru Dutt (1855-1876), who died at a tender age of 21, and the novel Rajmohan's Wife by Bankimchandra Chatterjee have received academic acceptance as the earliest examples of Indian literature written in English. Toru Dutt not composed poetry in English, but more interestingly, translated French poetry as well. Her best works include Ancient Ballads and Legends of Hindustan. However, the most famous literary figure of this era was Rabindranath Tagore (1861-1941), who won the Nobel Prize for literature in 1913 for his book Gitanjali, which is a free rendering of his poems in Bengali.

Sarojini Naidu (1879-1949) was a great poetess whose romanticism charmed readers in India and Europe. *Her Golden Threshold* (1905) and *The Broken Wing* (1917) are works of great literary merit. Aurobindo Gosh (1872-1950) was a poet philosopher and sage, for whom poetry was akin to a form of mediation. His epic, *Savitri* and *Life Divine* (2 vols.) are outstanding works in English literature. It may be mentioned that most Indian writers in English from the early period hailed from Calcutta, the first stronghold of the British, than other places in the country.

The freedom struggle resulted in a revolutionary brand of writing that voiced sentiments against the

British Empire. Several political l'eaders from different parts of the country emerged as literary figures such as Bal Gangadhar Tilak, Lala Lajpath Rai, Kasturi Ranga Iyengar and T. Prakasham. The English language became a sharp and strong instrument in the hands of Gandhiji, who edited and wrote for papers like 'Young India' and '*Harijan*'. He also wrote his autobiography, '*My Experiments With Truth*', which is known for its literary flair. Jawaharlal Nehru (1889-1964) stands out as another prominent leader who excelled in writing prose. He is particularly remembered for his *Glimpses of World History, Discovery of India* and *An Autobiography* (1936).

Mulk Raj Anand, R K Narayan and Raja Rao were among the earliest Indian novelist writing in English, who began to write in the early thirties. Mulk Raj Anand (b.1905), best known for his short story '*The Lost Child*', has written numerous works of prose, poetry and drama. His novels *Coolie* (1933), *Untouchable* (1935) and *The Woman and the Cow* (1960) reveal his concern for the downtrodden and underprivileged in India. R.K. Narayan is another prolific figure in Indian English writing. Most of his work, starting from his first novel *Swami and Friends* (1935) is set in the fictional town of Malgudi, which captures the Indian ethos in its entirety while having a unique identity of its own. Malgudi is perhaps the single most endearing "character" R.K.Narayan has ever created. Bachelor of Arts (1937), *The Financial Expert* (1952) *The Guide* (1959) and *Waiting for the Mahatma* (1955) are his other popular novels. The last of the harbingers of Indian English literature is Raja Rao (b.1909), whose novel *Kanthapura* (1938), set in rural India, established him as a major figure on the Indian literary scene. Raja Rao's other three novels are *The Serpent and the Rope* (1960) and *The Cat and Shakespeare* (1965). Nirad Choudhuri (1897-1999) was another internationally renowned Indian writer whose autobiography An Unknown Indian (1951) catapulted him into a celebrated international author.

Later novelists like Kamala Markandaya (*Nectar in a Sieve, Some Inner Fury, A Silence of Desire, Two Virgins*), Manohar Malgaonkar (*Distant Drum, Combat of Shadows, The Princes, A Bend in the Ganges* and *The Devil's Wind*), Anita Desai (*Clear Light of Day, The Accompanist, Fire on the Mountain, Games at Twilight*), and Nayantara Sehgal captured the spirit of an independent India, struggling to break away from the British and traditional Indian cultures and establish a distinct identity.

In the 1980's and 90's, India emerged as a major literary nation. Salman Rushdie's Midnight's Children became a rage around the world, even winning the Booker Prize. The worldwide success of Vikram Seth's The Golden Gate made him the first writer of the Indian Diaspora to enter the sphere of international writers and leave an indelible mark on the global literary scene. Other novelists of repute of the contemporary times include Shobha De (*Selective Memory*), G.V. Desani, M Ananthanarayanan, Bhadani Bhattacharya, Arun Joshi, Khushwant Singh, O.V. Vijayan, Allan Sealy (*The Trotternama*), Sashi Tharoor (*Show Business, The Great Indian Novel*), Amitav Ghosh (*Circle of Reason, Shadow Lines*), Upamanyu Chatterjee (*English August, The Mammaries of the Welfare State*), Raj Kamal Jha (*The Blue Bedspread*), Amit Chaudhuri (*A New World*), Pankaj Mishra (*Butter Chicken in Ludhiana, The Romantics*) and Vikram Chandra (*Red Earth and Pouring Rain, Love and Longing in Bombay*). The latest

Indian writer who took the world with a storm was Arundhati Roy, whose The God of Small Things won the 1997 Booker Prize and became an international best-seller. Rohinton Mistry, Firdaus Kanga, Kiran Desai (*Strange Happenings in the Guava Orchard*), Sudhir Kakar (*The Ascetic of Desire*), Ardeshir Vakil (*Beach Boy*) and Jhumpa Lahiri (*Interpreter of Maladies*) are some other renowned writers of Indian origin.

Former Prime Minister P.V.Narasimha Rao's *The Insider*; Satish Gujral's *A Brush with Life;* R.K.Laxman's *The Tunnel of Time,* Prof. Bipin Chandra's *India After Independence*, Sunil Khilnani's *The Idea of India,* J.N.Dixit's *Fifty Years of India's Foreign Policy,* Yogesh Chadha's *Rediscovering Gandhi* and Pavan K.Varma's *The Great Indian Middle Class* are notable works of the recent times.

The mid-20th century saw the emergence of poets such as Nissim Ezekiel (The Unfurnished Man), P Lal, A K Ramanujan (*The Striders, Relations, Second Sight, Selected Poems*), Dom Moraes (*A Beginning*), Keki Daruwalla, Geive Patel, Eunice de Souza, Adil Jussawala, Kamala Das, Arun Kolatkar and R. Parthasarathy, who were heavily influenced by literary movements taking place in the West such as Symbolism, Surrealism, Existentialism, Absurdism and Confessional Poetry. These authors used Indian phrases alongside English words and tried to reflect a blend of the Indian and the Western cultures.

Prominent Writers

Amitav Ghosh

Amitav Ghosh, a pioneer of English literature in India, was born in Calcutta (Now Kolkata) in the year 1956. Amitav Ghosh has been raised and educated at the same time in as different locations as Bangladesh, Sri Lanka, Iran, Egypt, India and the United Kingdom. He completed his higher studies in England where he went on to receive his Ph.D. in social anthropology from Oxford University. After completing his Ph.D. he decided to pursue his career in writing.

Amitav Ghosh is acclaimed in the literary world for his works on fiction, travel writing and journalism. His long list of accomplishment includes books like *The Circle of Reason, The Shadow Lines, In an Antique Land and Dancing in Cambodia.* His previous work, The *Glass Palace,* was an international bestseller that sold more than a half-million copies in Britain. Recently published there, *The Hungry Tide* has been sold for translation in twelve foreign countries and is also a bestseller abroad. Among awards, Ghosh has won France's Prix Medici Etranger, India's prestigious Sahitya Akademi Award, the Arthur C. Clarke Award, and the Pushcart Prize.

The fictions of Amitav Ghosh are marked by extreme themes that go side by side with post-colonialism. Nevertheless it will be nothing short of insult, for an author of his repute, to say that his works are formulaic. It is practically impossible to label his works. It can be added here that his topics are much more unique and personal. The appeal of Amitav' s work lies in his ability to weave "Indo-nostalgic" elements into more serious, heavier themes. The Government of India conferred Amitav Ghosh with Padma Bhushan. He now divides his time between Harvard University, where he is a visiting professor, and his homes in India and Brooklyn, New York. He is planning to shift back to India.

George Orwell

Born Eric Arthur Blair to an Anglo-Indian parent in the year 1903, George Orwell had a deep connection with India. It was in a barn in some sleepy village of Motihari district of the then Bihar that George Orwell had first tryst with the human world. His father, a famous Indigo planter of Champaran, wanted him to sail for England to study. His mother took him to England where he completed his primary education at Eton. He couldn't afford further studies therefore he joined the Indian Imperial Police and served in Burma. This was a phase of his turn around.

He returned from Burma disillusioned from Imperialism and wrote some of his splendid works such as *Down and Out in Paris and London* (1933), Burmese Days (1934), *A Clergyman's Daughter* (1935), A *Hanging* (1931) and *Shooting an Elephant* (1936) among others. This was the time when George Orwell felt early moorings for Communism. He even went on to fight alongside his comrades in Spanish Civil War but it was during this war that he got disillusioned from the Stalinist brand of communism. The stage was set for some of his best works.

It started with *'Homage to Catalonia'* in the year 1938 and then came the very famous *'Animal Farm'*.

Animal Farm got published in the year 1945 and took the literary world by storm. In this work, George Orwell criticized the Stalinist brand of Communism and proved its vulnerability towards corruption and despotism. With quotes such as "...all men are equal but some are more equal than others..." Orwell had arrived. In the year 1949 Orwell wrote his magnum opus 1984. The novel feared the American dominion in coming centuries and its ultimate transition in to a totalitarian regime flourishing behind the veil of democracy. It is unbelievable that many of his predictions stand true as of today.

George Orwell spent last years of his life fighting against Zionism and the sinister designs of Britain and US in the formation of Israel. He championed the cause of Arabs and Palestinians and severely criticized the moves of west in strangulating human rights of Palestinians. He resigned from *'The Tribune'* that was controlled by Zionist lobby and championed the cause of Israel. All his life, George Orwell stood against traits like Fascism, Totalitarianism, Zionism, and most of his works reflected his ethos. This great literary figure finally closed his eyes in 1949 in London where he was later buried according to Anglican rites

Jim Corbett

Jim Corbett, a colonel in the British Indian Army, was best known for being a hunter, conservationist and naturalist. He held the honor of killing many man-eating tigers and leopards in India, especially the United Provinces (now the Indian states of Uttar Pradesh & Uttarakhand). Being a multi-faceted personality, he was also avid photographer and an author. In fact, after his retirement, Jim wrote a number of books on wildlife, describing his hunts and experiences, the most prominent ones being *'Maneaters of Kumaon'* and *'Jungle Lore'*. He is also credited for speaking on the need to save wildlife from extinction. For this very reason, the Corbett National Park in Kumaon has been named after him.

Jim Corbett was born as Edward James Corbett, on 25th July 1875, in Nainital, near the Kumaon foothills of the Himalayas, in the United Provinces (now in Uttarakhand). He was the eighth child of Christopher and Mary Jane Corbett, who had an Irish ancestry. They moved to Nainital in 1862, when Christopher was appointed as its postmaster.

Jim lost his father when he was very young and was brought up by his mother. Since a very tender age, he developed a love for the forests and their wildlife, especially those around his home in Kaladhungi.

In his free time, Jim used to make frequent trips to the nearby forests and gradually, he came to identify most of the animals and birds present there, by their calls. He developed excellent trekking as well as hunting skills. In the meantime, Jim attended Oak Openings School (later renamed Philander Smith College) and Sherwood College, Nainital. After completing his education, he joined Bengal and North Western Railway, initially working as a fuel inspector at Manakpur (Punjab). Later, he worked as a contractor at Mokameh Ghat (Bihar).

Initially, Jim Corbett indulged in regular hunting and fishing. However, with time, he started shooting the big game with camera, rather than rifles. As his love for wildlife photography grew, he vowed never to shoot tigers and leopards unless they turned man-eater or threatened cattle. In 1911, his hunt for man-eating tigers and leopards began and came to an end in 1938. During this time, he hunted at least a dozen man-eaters, who had killed more than 1500 people, men, women and children combined.

Jim used to hunt alone, taking great personal risk, since he knew that man-eaters are quite capable of stalking and killing the hunter as well. His sole companion was a small dog named Robin, about whom we see much information in his first book *'The Maneaters of Kumaon'*. Jim's most noted kills are the Champawat Tiger, the Leopard of Rudraprayag, the Tigers of Chowgarh and the Panar Leopard. He has shot 19 Tigers and 14 Leopards i.e. he has a total of 33 recorded and documented kills.

Apart from being a renowned hunter, Jim Corbett is also known for being a pioneer conservationist. He was constantly engaged in giving lectures at local schools and societies, to make people aware of the necessity to conserve natural beauty, including forests and their wildlife. He helped create the Association for the Preservation of Game in the United Provinces (now Uttar Pradesh), and the All-India Conference for the Preservation of Wild Life. Jim also helped create Hailey National Park, which was later renamed in his honor.

After the independence of India, in 1947, Jim Corbett went to Nyeri, Kenya, where he settled along with his sister Maggie. There, he continued to write and make people aware of the declining numbers of jungle cats and other wildlife. He spent the rest of his life in Kenya only. On 19th April 1955, a few days after writing his sixth book *'Tree Tops'*, Jim died of a heart attack. He was buried at St. Peter's Anglican Church in Nyeri. Two years later, the national park that he had founded in India was renamed, as 'Jim Corbett National Park', in his honor.

Rudyard Kipling

Joseph Rudyard Kipling was born in 1865 at Bombay to Lockwood Kipling. His father was then the principal prestigious Jeejabhoy School of Architecture at Bombay. As customary in those days, Kipling was sent to England to be educated at the United Services College. After completing his schooling, Kipling returned to India, as he didn't have required fund to get enlisted in Oxford. It was 1882 when Rudyard Kipling joined Civil and Military Gazette at Lahore as a journalist.

This was the phase of his making. His editor by the name of Dr. Wheelers encouraged him to write articles and poems that first appeared in the newspaper were later collected and published as Departmental Ditties (1886), Plain Tales from the Hills (1888), Soldiers Three (1890) and Wee Willie Winkie (1890).

When he was sure of his popularity in India, Kipling tried to pursue his career in writing in England. His plans hit a roadblock when his very first novel, based on his true-life encounters, by the name of ' The Light That Failed (1890)' failed miserably. He was shocked to death but kept calm.

His next ventures such as Barrack-Room Ballads (1892) and Jungle Book (1894) established Kipling's reputation however. Jungle Book went on to become one of the bestsellers in the history of English literature. However, some people find his work full of preconceived notions and typecasting. Due to his propagation of 'White Man's Burden' those hostile to imperialism accused Kipling of jingoism.

On the outbreak of the Boer War, Kipling traveled to South Africa. In South Africa, Rudyard Kipling worked with civil organizations that helped wounded soldiers. He even went on to produce a newspaper for the troops that propagated the infallibility of the British race. By the time he returned to England, Kipling was being described as the Laureate of the

Empire. In 1901 Kipling published the best-selling novel, Kim. Riding on the success of Kim, over the next few years Kipling concentrated on writing children's books such as *Just So Stories* (1902), Puck of Pook's Hill (1906) and *Rewards and Fairies* (1910). After the outbreak of First World War in 1914, the War Propaganda Bureau arranged for Kipling to tour of Britain's army camps. The visits resulted in the publication of *The New Army* (1914). He also visited the Western Front and wrote about his experiences in France at War (1915).

Soon after the outbreak of the First World War, Kipling' s only son, John attempted to enlist in the British Army. Kipling used his influence to get his seventeen-year-old son enlisted but he died in the Battle of Loos. He never really got over from the loss of his son and for many years suffered from depression. This was reflected in the somber mood of most of his later writing including his autobiography by the name '*Something of myself*' that was published in 1934. Rudyard Kipling died of a severe hemorrhage in London on 18th January 1936.

Ruskin Bond

Better perceived as the Indian 'William Wordsworth', Ruskin Bond was born in Kasauli in the then Punjab Province in the year 1934. Born to a first generation British migrant, Bond spent most of his childhood in amidst Himalayas. He was brought up at different places that included Jamnagar, Dehradun and Shimla. As customary in that period he went to England for his primary studies. Although Bond was studying in England, his mind rested in India. He had forged an intimate relationship with the Himalayas and longed for it.

Bond started displaying his literary talent in England. He wrote his first novel named *'Room On The Roof'* when he was all of 17 years. The book made him win prestigious 'John Llewellyn Rhys' Prize that is awarded to British Commonwealth Writers who are under the age of 30. The book was primarily based in and around Himalayas and was successful in capturing its beauty and ethos in a manner that was never tried before. Its sequel named 'Vagrants in the Valley' followed it. Riding on the success of these two novels, Ruskin took the journey back home.

Ruskin Bond has now been writing for more than 5 decades. He has stressed more on the local elements of Himalayas in his writings. His writing style is distinct in a way that it tries to make reader understand the landscape and ethos through carefully mastered words. His writings have won him both tremendous critical acclaim as well as a long list of fans through out the literary world. Replete with unassuming humor and quiet wisdom, his stories manifest a deep love for nature and people. His mesmerizing descriptions about the flora and fauna of Himalayas can not be missed in his 100 something short stories, essays, novels, and more than thirty books of children that he has written.

His works has inspired several generations of writers, authors and scriptwriters. His novel named 'The Flight of Pigeons' has been adapted into the acclaimed Merchant Ivory film Junoon. Another less known novel named *'The Room on the Roof'* has been adapted in to a BBC produced TV series. Nevertheless his greatest achievement comes from the fact that several of his short stories from his collections have been incorporated in the school curriculum all over India. It includes jewels such as The Night Train at

Deoli, Time Stops at Shamli and Our Trees Still Grow in Dehra. In spite of all these successes, Bond can be concluded today as a media-shy and reclusive literary genius. He spends his days with his adopted family at a place close to Dehradun. He received the Sahitya Akademi Award for English writing in India for 'Our Trees Still grows in Dehra' in 1992. He has also been conferred with Padma Shri, one of the most prestigious civil awards in India.

Sarojini Naidu

Sarojini Naidu was born Sarojini Chattopadhyay in Hyderabad on February 13, 1879. She was the eldest sibling of a comparatively large family that was educated in England. She passed her matriculation at the tender age of 12 from the then Madras University. Her early life was full of struggle. She fell on love with Dr. Govinduraju Naidu who was not a Brahmin as she was. This led to opposition from both side. She was thus sent to England for her studies much against her will. She remained in England till 1898, studying first at King's College, London and then at Girton. She returned to Hyderabad in September 1898 and married Dr. Naidu.

Though she went England much against her will but it was here that her poetic soul got liberated. It was here only that she met Arthur Simons, a poet and critic. The struck chord in the very first meeting and kept on corresponding even after her return to India. Simons persuaded her to publish some of her poems. She published her first collection of poems in 1905 under the title *"Golden Threshold"*.

The book sold like hot cakes both among natives as well as among the Indian Diasporas. Riding on the success, she published two other collections of poems namely "The Bird of Time" and "The Broken Wings". In 1918, " Feast of Youth" was published. Later, "The Magic Tree", "The Wizard Mask" and "A Treasury of Poems" were published. It is said that people of such caliber as Rabindra Nath Tagore and Jawaharlal Nehru were among the thousands of admirers of her work. Her works were characterized by their contents that were though English in wording, had an Indian soul.

Then in 1916, she met Mahatma Gandhi, and she totally directed her energy to the fight for freedom. The independence of India became the heart and soul of her work and most of her poems that were composed during that period reflected hope and aspirations of common Indians who were marred by slavery. She was responsible for awakening the women of India. She brought them out of the kitchen and was successful in reestablishing self-esteem, among the women in India. In 1925, she chaired the summit of Congress in Kanpur. And in 1930, when Gandhi Ji was arrested for a protest, she took the helms of his movement. In 1931, she participated in the Round Table Summit, along with Gandhi Ji. In 1942, she was arrested during the "Quit India" protest and stayed in jail for 21 months. After independence she became the Governor of Uttar Pradesh. She was the first woman governor. She passed away on March 2, 1949.

Jawaharlal Nehru

Jawaharlal Nehru was born on 14 November 1889 at Allahabad and educated in England, at Harrow and Cambridge. In 1912, Nehru returned home to play a central role in India's struggle for freedom from British colonial rule, and then, as prime minister of independent India for seventeen years, went on to shape the nation's future as a modern, secular and democratic state. He died in office, on 27 May 1964. Visionary and idealist, scholar and statesman of international stature, Nehru was also an outstanding writer. His three most renowned books—*An Autobiography, Glimpses of World History* and *The Discovery of India*—have acquired the status of classics, and are all published by Penguin

Mulk Raj Anand

Indian novelist, short-story writer, and art critic writing in English. Mulk Raj Anand was among the first writers to render Punjabi and Hindustani idioms into English. Called the Zola or Balzac of India, Anand drew a realistic and sympathetic portrait of the poor of his country. With Raja Rao and R.K. Narayan he has been regarded as one the "founding fathers" of the Indian English novel.

> "And he had soon become possessed with an overwhelming desire to live their life. He had been told they were sahibs, superior people. He had felt that to put on their clothes made one sahib too. So he tried to copy them as well as he could in the exigencies of his peculiarly Indian circumstances."
>
> (from Untouchable, 1935)

Mulk Raj Anand was born in Peshawar, as the son of Lal Chand, a coppersmith and soldier, and Ishwar Kaur. Anand rebelled early on against his father's subservience to the British authorities. His first texts were born as a reaction to the trauma of the suicide of an aunt, who had been excommunicated for dining with a Muslim woman. An unhappy love for a Muslim girl, who was married, inspired some of his poetry. Anand attended Khalsa College, Amritsar, and entered the University of Punjab in 1921, graduating with honors in 1924. Thereafter Anand did his additional studies at Cambridge and at London University, receiving his Ph.D. in 1929. He studied-and later lectured-at League of Nations School of Intellectual Cooperation in Geneva. Between 1932 and 1945 Anand lectured, on and off, at Workers Educational Association in London.

In the 1930s and 1940s, Anand divided his time between literary London and Gandhi's India. He joined the struggle for independence, but also fought with the Republicans in the Spanish Civil War. During World War II, he worked as a broadcaster and scriptwriter in the film division of the BBC in London. Among his friends was George Orwell.

After the war Anand returned permanently to India, making Bombay his hometown and center of activity. In 1946 he founded the fine-arts magazine Marg. He also became a director of Kutub Publishers. From 1948 to 1966 Anand taught at Indian universities. In the 1960s he was Tagore Professor of Literature and Fine Art at the University of Punjab and visiting professor at the Institute of Advanced Studies in Simla (1967-68). Between the years 1965 and 1970 Anand was fine art chairman at Lalit Kala Akademi (National Academy of Arts). In 1970 he was appointed president of Lokayata Trust, for creating a community and cultural center in the village of Hauz Khas, New Delhi.

Anand started to write at an early age. Although Punjabi and Hindustani were Anand's mother tongues, he wrote in English, because English language publisher did not reject his books due to their themes. His career as a writer Anand began in England by publishing short notes on books in T.S. Eliot's magazine Criterion. His acquaintances from this time included such authors as E.M. Forster, Herbert Read, Henry Miller, and George Orwell, who tired to get Anad a full-time post at the BBC. The most important influence upon Anand was Gandhi, who shaped his social conscience.

In the early 1930s Anand focused on books on art history. It was not until the appearance of the novels Untouchable (1935) and Coolie (1936), the story of a fifteen year-old child-labourer who dies of tuberculosis, that Anand gained a wide recognition. Untouchable narrates a day in the life of Bakha, an unclean outcaste, who suffers a number of humiliations in the course of his day. Bakha is eighteen, proud, "strong and able-bodied", a child of modern India, who has started to think himself as superior to his fellow-outcastes. The "touching" occurs in the morning, and subsequently shadows the rest of the day. Due to his low birth, Bakha's fate is to work as a latrine sweeper. The powerful critique of the Indian caste system suggested that British colonial domination of India has actually increased the suffering of outcastes, such as Bakha. After 19 rejection slips Anand's novel was published in England with a preface by E.M. Forster: "Untouchable could only have been written by an Indian. and by an Indian who observed from the outside. No European, however sympathetic, could have created the character of Bakha, because he would not have known enough about his troubles. And no Untouchable could have written the book, because he would have been involved in indignation and self-pity."

In Two Leaves and a Bud (1937) Anand continued his exploration of the Indian society. The story told about a poor Punjabi peasant. He is brutally exploited in a tea plantation and killed by a British official, who tries to rape his daughter. The socially conscious work shared much with the proletarian novels published in Britain and the United States during the 1930s.

Anand's famous trilogy, The Village (1939), Across the Black Waters (1940), and The Sword and the Sickle (1942), was a strong protest against social injustices. The story follows the life of Lai Sing from adolescent rebellion through his experiences in World War I, to his return home and revolutionary activities. In Anand's early novels his social and political analysis of oppression grows clearly from his involvement with the Left in England. Among Anand's later and most impressive works is The Private Life of an Indian Prince (1953). This time Anand focused more on human psyche and personal struggles than on class conflicts. The story had its origins in the betrayal of a hill-woman with whom the author was romantically involved while married to his first wife, the actress Kathleen van Gelder. Anand had met Gelder in London; they married in 1939.

After divorce in 1948, Anand married Shirin Vajibdar, a distinguished dancer. Anand's daughter from his first marriage became a writer, too. Since the 1950s, Anand intermittently worked on a projected seven-volume autobiography, entitled Seven Ages of Man. From the project appeared Seven Summers (1951), Morning Face (1968), Confessions of a Lover (1976), and The Bubble (1984). Anand also published books on subjects as diverse as Marx and Engels in India, Tagore, Nehru, Aesop's fables, the Kama Sutra, erotic sculpture, and Indian ivories. Mulk Raj Anand died in Pune on September 28, 2004. Along with the novelista and short story writer Munshi Premchand

(1880-1936), Anand was involved in forming dalit literature, used to refer to the "untouchable", casteless sects of India.

R. K. Narayan

R. K. Narayan was born in Madras in 1906 and educated there and at Maharajah's College in Mysore. He has lived in India ever since, apart from his travels. Most of his work, starting from his first novel Swami and friends (1935) is set in the fictional town of Malgudi which at the same time captures everything Indian while having a unique identity of its own. After having read only a few of his books it is difficult to shake off the feeling that you have vicariously lived in this town. Malgudi is perhaps the single most endearing "character" R. K. Narayan has ever created.

He has published numerous novels, five collections of short stories (A Horse and Two Goats, An Astrologer's Day, Lawley Road, Malgudi Days, and The Grandmother's Tale), two travel books (My Dateless Diary and The Emerald Route), four collections of essays (Next Sunday, Reluctant Guru, A Writer's Nightmare, and A Story-Teller's World), a memoir (My Days), and some translations of Indian epics and myths (The Ramayana, The Mahabharata, and Gods, Demons and Others).

In 1980, R. K. Narayan was awarded the A.C. Benson award by the Royal Society of Literature and was made an Honorary Member of the American Academy and Institute of Arts and Letters. In 1989 he was made a member of the Rajya Sabha (the non-elective House of Parliament in India). He received the Sahitya Akademi Award for The Guide (1958).

R. K. Narayan's full name is Rasipuram Krishnaswami Ayyar Naranayanaswami. In his early years he signed his name as R. K. Narayanaswami, but apparently at the time of the publication of Swami and Friends, he shortened it to R. K. Narayan on Graham Greene's suggestion.

Raja Rao

Indian writer of novels and short stories, whose works are deeply rooted in Brahmanism and Hinduism. Raja Rao's semi-autobiographical novel, The Serpent and the Rope (1960), is a story of a search for spiritual truth in Europe and India. It established him as one of the finest Indian stylists. "Writing is my dharma," he once said.

> I hear you saying that liberation is possible and that Socratic wisdom is identical with your guru's. No, Raja, I must start from what I am. I am those monsters which visit my dreams and reveal to me my hidden essence.
>
> (Czeslaw Milosz in 'To Raja Rao')

Raja Rao was born on November 8, 1908 in Hassan, in the state of Mysore in south India, into a well-known Brahman family. His native language was Kanarese, but his post-graduate education was in France, and all his publications in book form were in English. Like the Nigerian novelist Chinua Achebe, writing in English, Rao was concerned with language and consciousness. In the foreword to Kanthapura (1938) he admitted the difficulties in using "a language that is not one's own the spirit that is one's own," and conveying "the various shades and omissions of certain thought-movement that looks maltreated in an alien language."

Rao was educated at Muslim schools. After taking a degree from Madras University, he left India for

Europe, where he remained for a decade. He studied at the universities of Montpellier and the Sorbonne, doing research in Christian theology and history. In 1931 he married a French academic, Camille Mouly. Later he depicted the breakdown of their marriage in The Serpent and the Rope. His first stories Rao published in French and English. During 1931-32 he contributed four articles written in Kannada for Jaya Karnataka, an influential journal.

When his marriage disintegrated in 1939, Rao returned to India and began his first period of residence in an ashram. During WW II, he travelled widely in India in search of his spiritual heritage. In 1942 he was active in an underground movement against colonial rule. During these years he edited the literary magazine Tomorrow.

Rao's involvement in the nationalist movement is reflected in his first two books. The novel Kanthapura (1938) was an account of the impact of Gandhi's teaching on non-violent resistance against the British. The story is seen from the perspective of a small Mysore village in South India. Rao borrows the style and structure from Indian vernacular tales and folk-epic. The narrator is an old woman. She tells how the community obtains from daily life, with its millennia-old worship of the local deity, the strength to stand against the British Raj. In the character of the young Moorthy, who comes back from the city, Rao portrays an idealist and supporter of ahimsa and satyagraha, who wants to cross the traditional barriers of caste. The younger generation has city ways, they read city books, and they even call themselves Gandhi-men. Doré, as the old woman calls the "university graduate," has given up his "boots and hat and suit and had taken to dhoti and khadi, and it was said he had even given up his city habit of smoking." The work was highly praised by the English writer E.M. Forster, whose masterwork A Passage to India (1924) criticized British imperialism. However, Rao's India is not a certain geographical or historical entity, but more of a philosophical concept and a symbol of spiritual calling.

Rao returned to the theme of Gandhism in the short story collection The Cow of the Barricades (1947). In 1998 he published Gandhi's biography Great Indian Way: A Life of Mahatma Gandhi. After the war, Rao spent much of his time in France and travelling throughout the world. He visited America in 1950 and later spent some more time living in an ashram. In 1965 he married an actress, Katherine Jones. From 1965 to 1983 Rao lectured on Indian philosophy at the University of Texas, Austin. In 1988 he received the prestigious Neustadt International Prize for Literature. Several Neustadt Laureates have also received the Nobel Prize for literature, among them Gabriel García Márquez, Czeslaw Milosz, and Octavio Paz.

The Serpent and the Rope was written after a long silence during which Rao lived India, where he renewed a connection with his roots in the modern rendering of the Mahabharata legend of Satayavan and Savithri. The work also dramatized the relationships between Indian and Western culture. Ramaswamy, a young Brahmin studying in France, is married to a French college teacher, Madeleine, who sees her husband above all as a guru. As Ramaswamy struggles with commitments imposed on him by his Hindu family, his wife becomes a Buddhist in her spiritual quest and renounces worldly desires. She leaves her husband to find his own true self. The serpent in the title refers to the illusion and the rope to the reality.

Cat and Shakespeare (1965) was a metaphysical comedy that answered philosophical questions posed in the earlier novels. In the book the Hindu notion of karma is symbolized by a cat. The hero discovers in his attempts to receive divine grace, that there is no dichotomy between himself and God. Comrade Kirillov (1976) was written early in Rao's career and was first published in French. It satirized communism as an ideological misunderstanding of man's ultimate aims, and argued that all foreign creeds gradually become Indianized.

The Chessmaster and His Moves (1988) is peopled by characters from various cultures seeking their identities. Like Nabokov, Rao used the metaphor of the chess game to animate philosophical and psychological ideas. In the story Sivaram Sastri, an Indian mathematician in Paris, meets Proust, and recounts his love affairs and friendships. Rao has confessed: "I am no scholar. I am a creative writer. I love to play with ideas. It is like a chess game with horses, elephants, chamberlains and kings which might fight with one another. The game is not for winning. It is for rasa-delight." Raja Rao died of heart failure on July 8, 2006, at his home in Austin, Texas. He was 97.

A. K. Ramanujan

Attipat Krishnaswami Ramanujan or A. K. Ramanujan, as he is known, was born in Mysore, India in 1929. He was a transitional figure in the history of Indian English Literature, and also a trans-disciplinary scholar, working as a poet, translator, linguist, and folklorist. Although he wrote primarily in English, he was fluent in both Kannada and Tamil, the language of his family. Ramanujan received his BA and MA in English language and literature from the University of Mysore. He then spent some time teaching at several universities in South India before getting a graduate diploma in theoretical linguistics from Deccan University in Poona in 1958. He went to the U.S. in 1959. In 1962, he became an assistant professor at the University of Chicago, where he was affiliated throughout the rest of his career.

The following year, he went to Indiana University where he got a Ph.D. in linguistics in 1963. He taught at several U.S. universities, including Harvard, University of Wisconsin, University of Michigan, University of California at Berkeley, and Carlton College. At the University of Chicago, Ramanujan was instrumental in shaping the South Asian Studies program. He worked in the departments of South Asian Languages and Civilizations, Linguistics, and with the Committee on Social Thought. In 1976, the government of India awarded him the honorific title "Padma Sri," and in 1983, he was given the MacArthur Prize Fellowship. Ramanujan breathed his last in Chicago on July 13, 1993.

Kamala Das

Kamala Das was born on March 31, 1934 in Malabar in Kerala, India. She is the daughter of V.M. Nair, a former managing editor of the widely-circulated Malayalam daily Mathrubhumi, and Nalappatt Balamani Amma, a renowned Malayali poetess. In 1984, she was short-listed for the Nobel Prize for Literature along with Marguerite Yourcenar, Doris Lessing, and Nadine Gordimer. Kamala Das is probably the first Hindu woman to openly and honestly talk about sexual desires of Indian woman, which made her an iconoclast of her generation.

Kamala Das, is a well-known female Indian writer writing in English as well as Malayalam, her native language. She is considered one of the outstanding Indian poets writing in English, although her popularity in Kerala is based chiefly on her short stories and autobiography. Much of her writing in Malayalam came under the pen name Madhavikkutty

Anita Desai

Anita Desai was born in Mussoorie, a hill station north of Delhi, as the daughter of a D.N. Mazumdar, a Bengali businessman, and the former Toni Nime, of German origin. She grew up speaking German at home and Bengali, Urdu, Hindi and English at school and in the city streets. She has said that she grew up surrounded by Western literature and music, not realizing until she was older that this was an anomaly in her world where she also learned the Eastern culture and customs. She married a businessman at twenty-one and raised several children before becoming known for her writing. Her first book, Cry,the Peacock was published in England in 1963, and her better known novels include In Custody (1984) and Baumgartner's Bombay (1988). She once wrote: "I see India through my mother's eyes, as an outsider, but my feelings for India are my father's, of someone born here" (Griffiths).

She never considered trying to first publish in India because there was no publisher in India who would be interested in fiction by an Indian writer (Jussawalla) and it was first in England that her work became noticed. U.S. readers were slower to discover her, due, she believes to England's natural interest in India and the U.S.'s lack of comprehension regarding the foreignness of her subject.

But Desai only writes in English. This, she has repeatedly said,was a natural and unconscious choice for her: "I can state definitely that I did not choose English in a deliberate and conscious act and I'd say perhaps it was the language that chose me and I started writing stories in English at the age of seven, and have been doing so for thirty years now without stopping to think why"(Desai).

She is considered the writer who introduced the psychological novel in the tradition of Virginia Woolf to India. Included in this, is her pioneer status of writing of feminist issues. While many people today would not classify her work as feminist, she believes this is due to changing times: "The feminist movement in India is very new and a younger generation of readers in India tends to be rather impatient of my books and to think of them as books about completely helpless women, hopeless women. They find it somewhat unreal that the women don't fight back, but they don't seem to realize how very new this movement is" (Jussawalla).

Also, she says, her writing is realistic: "Women think I am doing a disservice to the feminist movement by writing about women who have no control over their lives. But I was trying, as every writer tries to do, even in fiction, to get at the truth, write the truth. It would have been really fanciful if I had made [for example, in Clear Light of Day] Bim and Tara modern-day feminists "(in Griffiths).

Desai considers Clear Light of Day, her most autobiographical book, because she was writing about her neighborhood in Delhi, although the characters are not based on her brothers and sisters. What she was exploring in this novel, she has said, was the importance of childhood and memories as the source of a life. She had wanted to start the book at the end and move backwards, into the characters' childhood and further, into the childhood of their parents etc., but in the end: "When I had gone as far back as their infancy the book just ground to a halt; it lost its momentum. It told me that this was done, that I couldn't carry it further. But I still have a sense of disappointment about that book, because the intention had been different" (Jussawalla). The character of Raja is identified with her in the sense that he is so immersed in all different types of literature and culture, and is so concerned with protecting the multicultural heritage of India. His worries about the Muslim neighbor family is not just about them particularly, but rather worry about the loss of all that the Muslim culture and literature contributes to India.

While Desai has taught for years at Mount Holyoke and MIT, and spends most of the year outside of India, she does not consider herself part of the Indian Diaspora. Although she does not fit in the Indian box anymore (Griffiths) as she said, she considers herself lucky for having not left India until late in her life, because she feels that she has been drifting away from it ever since: "I can't really write of it with the same intensity and familiarity that I once had." Yet she cannot feel at home in any other place or society (Griffiths).

Arundhati Roy

Arundhati Roy is known as an award winning author and also as a social activist and inspiration to all those who seek to support the poor and oppressed. Roy came in the limelight in 1997 when her book *The God of Small Things* fetched the coveted Booker Prize. This down-to-earth girl-next-door whisked off a whirlwind of controversy through her pen and her association with various social movements and activities. And this year again she is back in the public eye having been awarded the prestigious Sahitya Akademi Award (2005) for her collection of Essays *The algebra of infinite justice.*

The tale is based on twin children battling with the caste structures in India. Roy, herself, is the product of an inter-caste marriage. Her father is from a Hindu family of Bengal while her mother is a Christian. From the time she was very young, she knew in her heart that she wanted to be a writer. She studied architecture and taught aerobics but once Roy began writing screenplays, her writing career took off. Roy's debut novel, *The God of Small Things,* was published in 1997. It became an international bestseller, and in October 1997 won the coveted Booker Prize. Roy has since involved herself in causes such as the anti-nuclear movement and the Narmada Bachao Andolan and has written several essays in support of the causes she so strongly believes in. Arundhati is a towering intellect with a poetic fluency with words delivered in a soft modulated voice. She is also a dog-lover and her past times are writing and running.

6

History of Literature in the Caribbean

Caribbean literature is the term generally accepted for the literature of the various territories of the Caribbean region. Literature in English specifically from the former British West Indies may be referred to as Anglo-Caribbean or, in historical contexts, West Indian literature, although in modern contexts the latter term is rare.

Most of these territories have become independent nations since the 1960s, though some retain colonial ties to the United Kingdom. They all share, apart from the English language, a number of political, cultural, and social ties which make it useful to consider their literary output in a single category. The more wide-ranging term "Caribbean literature" generally refers to the literature of all Caribbean territories regardless of language—whether written in English, Spanish, French, or Dutch, or one of numerous creoles.

Territories Included in the Category "West Indian"

The literature of Anguilla, Antigua and Barbuda, Aruba, the Bahamas, Barbados, Belize, the British Virgin Islands, the Cayman Islands, Dominica, Grenada, Guyana, Jamaica, Montserrat, St. Kitts and

Nevis, St. Lucia, St. Vincent and the Grenadines, Suriname, Trinidad and Tobago, and the Turks and Caicos would normally be considered to belong to the wider category of West Indian literature. Some literary scholars might also include Bermuda, though geographically Bermuda is not part of the Caribbean and cultural ties with the region are not very strong.

Development of the Idea of West Indian Literature

The term "West Indies" first began to achieve wide currency in the 1950s, when writers like Samuel Selvon, John Hearne, Edgar Mittelholzer, V.S. Naipaul, and George Lamming began to be published in the United Kingdom. A sense of a single literature developing across the islands was also encouraged in the 1940s by the BBC radio programme *Caribbean Voices,* which featured stories and poems written by West Indian authors, recorded in London under the direction of producer Henry Swanzy, and broadcast back to the islands. Magazines like *Kyk-Over-Al* in Guyana, *Bim* in Barbados, and *Focus* in Jamaica, which published work by writers from across the region, also encouraged links and helped build an audience.

Many—perhaps most—West Indian writers have found it necessary to leave their home territories and base themselves in the United Kingdom, the United States, or Canada in order to make a living from their work—in some cases spending the greater parts of their careers away from the territories of their birth. Critics in their adopted territories might argue that, for instance, V.S. Naipaul ought to be considered a British writer instead of a Trinidadian writer, or Jamaica Kincaid and Paule Marshall American writers, but most West Indian readers and critics still consider these writers "West Indian".

West Indian literature ranges over subjects and themes as wide as those of any other "national" literature, but in general many West Indian writers share a special concern with questions of identity, ethnicity, and language that rise out of the Caribbean historical experience.

Two West Indian writers have won the Nobel Prize for Literature: Derek Walcott (1992), born in St. Lucia, resident mostly in Trinidad during the 1960s and 70s, and partly in the United States since then; and V.S. Naipaul, born in Trinidad and resident in the United Kingdom since the 1950. (Saint-John Perse, who won the Nobel Prize in 1960, was born in the French territory of Guadeloupe.)

Other notable names in (anglophone) Caribbean literature have included Earl Lovelace, Austin Clarke, Claude McKay, Orlando Patterson, Andrew Salkey, Edward Kamau Brathwaite (who was born in Barbados and has lived in Ghana and Jamaica), Linton Kwesi Johnson, and Michelle Cliff, to name only a few. In more recent times, a number of new literary voices have emerged from the Caribbean as well as the Caribbean diaspora, including Kititian Caryl Phillips (who has lived in the UK since one month of age), Edwidge Danticat, a Haitian immigrant to the United States; Andrea Levy of the United Kingdom, Jamaicans Colin Channer and Marlon James, the author of *John Crow's Devil, The Book of Night Women,* the unpublished screenplay "Dead Men", and the short story "Under Cover of Darkness", and Antiguan Marie-Elena John.

Caribbean Poetry

Caribbean poetry is any form of poem, rhyme, or song that gets its derivatives from the Caribbean. This type of media became popular primarily in the early 1900s with the works of poets Linton Kwesi Johnson, Kamau Brathwaite, and Derek Walcott.

The origins of Caribbean poetry lie in countries such as Jamaica and Barbados. These countries have been known as international hot spots for great poetry due to their unique styles, abstract ideas, and the addition of musical instruments to their style. Bongos were added for their emphasis on lyrics, and for their added mood.

Famous poets from the Caribbean genre could include Kamau Brathwaite, International Winner of the Sixth Annual Griffin Poetry Prize in 2006, Linton Kwesi Johnson, who became only the second living poet to be published by Penguin Classic series, and Derek Walcott, winner of the 1992 Nobel Prize for Literature. These poets write primarily about politics, war, and spirituality among other topics.

Experimental Vision in Caribbean Writings

The Caribbean obsession with history and the past has not prevented authors from experimenting with new writing techniques. Many Postcolonial writers have aligned their goals with those of the Deconstructionist movement, which seeks to identify and then dismantle binary opposites. Derek Walcott, for example, accomplishes this in "Pantomime", by creating a dramatic safe space that allows characters to work out deep-seeded feelings without worrying about the political and thus damaging baggage that might accompany such feelings. Wilson Harris takes on this practice also, in his novel Palace of the Peacock. But he approaches it via quite a different technique from Walcott's blurred lines of drama. Rather, Harris combines words and concepts in unexpected, jarring ways. Through this technique of combination, Harris makes clear that he seeks not only to erode specific binarisms in his text, but to display the underlying, linking root that prevents two categories from ever really existing in opposition. The ramifications of this tactic stretch well beyond the abstract, ranging from human psychology to political legacies. As the authors of The Empire Writes Back state,

> The antagonistic energies of the past transform themselves, in the present, into a creative syncretism...it is...above all the works of Wilson Harris which underwrite this view.

To accomplish his goal, Harris utilizes the experimental technique of "intentional oxymorons." Throughout the novel, he draws connections between words that on the surface bear no similarity to each other, as in "They were plainly astonished at the immaculate bridal veil falling motionlessly from the river's tall brink". As Harris himself explains in the movie 'The Landscape of Dreams" this quote demonstrates how on the surface the waterfall appears constant and thus motionless, but in actuality it comprises rushing water in steady motion.

Combinations like that fill Harris's writing. At times they reach even beyond this paradoxical confusion, and prove bewildering or frustrating to the reader. And when Harris makes the intuitively problematic claim that "Anything was everything in the whirling swift moment and in the fantasy of their shattered boat and life,'", the door opens to a limitless wealth of possibility. But perhaps the frustration these possibilities produce is intentional — or even necessary. For with the revelation of Harris's larger goals, one could no longer pronounce this technique gratuitous. The author begins to make clear these goals in such pointed examples as

He stood like a melodramatic rock in mother earth, born from a close fantasy and web of slave and concubine and free, out of one complex womb, from a phantom of voluptuousness whose memory was bitter and rebellious as death and sweet as life, every discipline and endurance and pain he felt he knew. But this boast sprang from a thriftless love of romance and a genuine optimism and self- advertisement and self-ignorance.

This passage, rife with paradoxes such as "melodramatic rock", hints that all opposites, indeed all colors in the spectrum, will in the end be woven into one large web...signaling deeper, shared roots from which these superficial opposites spring. Thus Harris hopes to point out that only through ignorance of the roots will we pronounce two such things opposite. Harris calls to the reader to push beyond the first appearance that a word may present in order to see the conflicts and opportunities that it masks, as he explains (in "A Talk on the Subjective Imagination"):

> Appearances are given, are apparently objective. The mystery of the subjective imagination lies, I believe, in an intuitive...grasp of a play of values as the flux of authentic change through and beyond what is given to us and what we accept, without further thought, as objective appearances. It is not a question of rootlessness but of the miracle of roots, the miracle of a dialogue with eclipsed selves which appearances mayu deny us or into which they may lead us.

And therein lies the possibility that the initial frustration the reader may experience becomes necessary — as the mind of the reader must stretch and grow in order to accomodate this penetrating vision for which Harris strives.

The authors of The Empire Writes Back explain in part why Harris begins with language in this quest. They cite Harris's perception of language as both a crucial element in the subjugation of slaves and indentures, and as the means by which the destructive processes of history could be reversed:

> Harris sees language as the key to these transformations. Language must be altered, it power to lock in fixed beliefs and attitudes must be exposed, and words and concepts "freed" to associate in new ways. There are, he points out, two kinds of relationship to the past — one which derives from the past, and one which is a dialogue with the past.

Thus Harris attempts to take his readers on a journey to the past, in which his language and the readers' investigation of it establish new channels of interrogation with notions of the past that each once held as fixed.

Combination and Humanity

Wilson Harris does not leave the reader merely with this abstract notion of unearthing connections between seemingly opposing words or concepts. Rather, he seeks to demonstrate how vital this tactic is to human existence. For in Palace of the Peacock's tale of the men going down the river in search of the kin of the mysterious Mariella, a series of tragedies occur, ultimately bringing each member's death. Harris seems to point to their inability to reconcile binarisms in the world around them and between each other as the prime factor in their demise. Therefore daSilva kills Cameron in an argument over whether the ringed bird is a witch—a question of semantics. Though its members perhaps do not realize it, from the beginning Harris makes clear the unity of the crew:

> The whole crew was one spiritual family living and dying together in a common grave out of which they had sprung again from the same soul and womb as it were.

But they struggle with each other, and with their own past, while illusory debates and dream visions isolate them from each other. In the end each seems to strive to reach realizations like that of Schomburgh in this passage:

> It no longer mattered whether Carrol was his nephew or his son or both. He had heard clearer than ever before the distant music of the heart's wish and desire.

Here Schomburgh sheds the illusory distinctions of "nephew" or "son" in favor of the deeper heart's connection, one more akin to the notion of the "spirtual family" above. But since the majority of the crew cannot reach these conclusions in life, since they allow illusions to fragment their unity, they "die". True to his technique of binary breakdowns, and echoing the African tradition of death not bringing the end to a soul — dealt with extensively in Erna Brodber's Louisiana — Harris demonstrates that only in physical death can they find reconciliation:

> He saw Cameron in the stream and in the sky where their joint flesh had flown and darted above the fantasy of their carnal death.

Though he hints at it all along, not until the end of the novel does Harris make clear the superficiality of the illusions (illusions like the structure of binary opposites) which divided and doomed the crew:

He had stopped a little to wonder whether he was wrong in his knowledge and belief and the force that had divided them from each other — and mangled them beyond all earthly hope and recognition — was the wind of rumour and superstition, and the truth was they had all come home at last to the compassion of the nameless unflinching folk.

Harris therefore concludes that these illusions of "rumour and superstition", which may have provoked a crew member to pronounce two objects opposite or sparked enmity between two friends or relatives, must give way to the deeper roots of connectivity which they mask. The crew, "nameless" and thus undifferentiated in death, realizes the compassion which holds them together, which in essence ties every human being to every other. In sum, Harris has personified the concept of binary opposites in the characters of the crew, shown how they (like other binarisms) are divided by superficial distinctions, and then shattered these distinctions in favor of connecting, common roots of compassion.

Postcolonial Combination

Wilson Harris extends his metaphorical search for connection beyond the sphere of the individual in Palace of the Peacock. He appears to desire erosion even of the binary opposition between past and present. To do this he consistently evokes mythic origins of life and the continuing story that the Guyanese landscape tells:

> The precipitous cliffs were of volcanic myth and substance he dreamed far older than the river's bed and stream. He seemed to sense and experience its congealment and its ancient flow as if he waded with webbed and impossible half-spidery feet in the ceaseless boiling current of creation.

But Harris adds a Postcolonial twist to this notion, as he seeks not only to attack distinctions between past and present, but the supposed power relations that historical legacy has left us with in the present. The presence of the Arawak woman on the boat exemplifies this point, for the Arawak presence, all but eliminated in the modern West Indies, once flourished alongside many other ancestral tribes in this region. The Arawak woman's role as guide, as Vigilance's savior from drowning, signals Harris's belief in the diverse roots of human life in the Caribbean despite present states of nonexistence or disempowerment. Thus the subjugated and outcast tribe member becomes a leader and heroine.

In this vein, Harris also wishes to wash away the distinction between colonizer and colonized which history has bequeathed. Therefore the crew, which sets out to dominate the land of peasants (much like the Europeans did for hundreds of years), in the end loses their power as they dejectedly come to understand that "they were the pursuers and now they had become the pursued,". The author further notes how false the idea of ruling over men rings as it appears in Donne's mind:

> Abstraction grew around him — nothing else — the ruling abstraction of himself which he saw reflected nowhere. He was a ruler of men and a ruler of nothing.

In sum, Harris has now turned his preoccupation with unearthing connections that prove the existence of binarisms illusory. Here he opens his eyes to the largest (and most germane to Postcolonial literature) spectrum. He has sought to combat those divisions of white and black, colonizer and colonized, which threaten to divide humanity even in the present day. In essence, Harris attempts the most broad based Deconstruction of binary opposites of any Postcolonial writer. Language, human relationships, and even historical legacies (in social strata) all fall within his sights. His startling combinations and mingling of life, death, and other such opposites, into one shared reality force the reader to cast aside traditional assumptions about origins and status. And therefore the most experimental aspect of Palace of the Peacock comes not in his drawing odd or baffling connections but in the scope of his vision.

Post-Colonialism

Other European nations joined the race to conquer the New World by this time, the English and the French, especially. With the virtual extermination of the Arawakan peoples, rapacious eyes were turned to their more war-like cousins: the Cariban peoples. This alternative source of labour also died from disease and captivity.

Many, rather than being taken into captivity, threw themselves in a ritual of suicide by the thousands off cliffs. All in all, the world saw—or maybe it did not see, for these are facts that do not appear in many history books—the virtual extermination of an entire people, an entire culture. Virtual, because there are a few thousand of these people whose ancestors fled into the jungles of Guyana.

Theirs is a history largely ignored in the writing and even more largely ignored in the reading; for, even today, many so-called post-colonial scholars must suffer the indictment of being too imprisoned within national and racial boundaries to bother themselves too much with such trivia. Such is the bliss of the ignorant or myopic. Or else, they render histories the same; colonialism, after all, they say, is colonialism.

But nowhere was the pathology of colonialism more deadly. Not before, not since. Today, the West Indies are a witness to statistics of awful proportions: there is no record of an Amerindian person on any of the islands where once they had lived so well and in such numbers.

The point of recalling this holocaust, unequalled still in the twisted history of this planet, is not to stress the cruelty of Europeans. As most of us would be aware, mythologies or religions explain the beginnings of humanity and society as something created from something else: from something base or simple—whether it be clay or egg, chaos or night — cometh forth something noble or complex.

West Indian society as we know it began in quite a unique and contrary fashion: the gods who landed found something inestimably precious, and they created out of it nothing, a void, in human, cultural and mythological terms. It is as if they found a most precious, fragile and fecund egg, then proceeded to suck the life out of it. Having devoured the indigenous meat, they sought to refill the shell, to remake the West Indies after a fashion into a wealth-generating thing. White peasant and criminal labour was brought in, but by then tobacco had been deposed by the more demanding King Cane. Since sugar cane needed more hardy human machinery, Africans were culled from their continent.

After Europe, stricken by conscience after a few hundred years, and now newly awakened to the idea that slave labour was no longer profitable, emancipated slaves into economic slavery in the mid-nineteenth century, Indians and Chinese were brought in as indentured labour. Other new "immigrants" were

North Africans, Portuguese, Jews, Japanese, Syrians, and so on. By the nineteen thirties and forties, the stage was set for the only man-made culture on that scale in human history: many peoples, all unwilling to be where they were, all longing for other lands, all pulled towards different cultural imperatives and "purities". Each group antagonistic to the other. What they shared like an unvoiced pain was the consistent erasure of their humanity, the corrosion of the human person. The master himself was not exempt, for the cruelty that he visited upon others meant the diminishment of his own human stature.

The luxury of the creation of whole and relatively harmonious societies is a recent phenomenon—phenomenon, because survival itself was nothing short of a miracle. Heterogeneity, even up to the sixties, meant that one obtained different groups living alongside each other but separate from and in great suspicion of each other. There were a series of cultural garrisons, a series of racial solitudes‹a situation that exists even now in Malaysia, Singapore and other places that proclaim themselves multi-cultural.

After centuries during which the human person was but an economic commodity and was as expendable as a coin, self was fragmented and unformed. And when self has yet to be recreated, society cannot labour into being. It is little wonder, then, that Anthony Trollope wrote of the West Indies: "No people there, in the true sense of the word." And closer to home, it is little wonder that V.S. Naipaul could have spoken of the "storylessness" and Orlando Patterson, the "historylessness" of the West Indies. To Naipaul's exclamation that "Nothing was created in the West Indies", Derek Walcott has replied that if nothing was created in the West Indies, then there was everything to be made.

What education was received made sure that White values and European civilisation remained paramount. Contiguously, all that was Black or local was disparaged. Consequently, the actual landscape of the writer was at odds with the landscape that inhabited the creative imagination.

Self was at odds with self. The individual was psychically fragmented and culturally schizophrenic, reflecting the condition of the society as a whole. The landscape itself seems to mirror this sense of futility: the West Indies, a fractured archipelago, a broken backbone. The point here is that writers, when they looked around for a language, for metaphor, in which to speak their wholeness into creation, found nothing but that which was borrowed from or imposed by Europe.

When they sought landscape, they found only jungle, volcano, plantation, beaches and sea, a landscape barren of the caveats of "civilised" society. When they groped for tradition, they found fragments, half-buried, half-excavated. When they glanced back for history, they found only indignity. Any quest for mythology yielded gods disappeared, broken or reshaped for having been placed upon the rack of experience.

The only dignity, it seemed, was in Europe. Consequently, there was a great deal of imitative stuff written during the thirties and forties. They all wanted to be Keats or Shelley, Tennyson or Coleridge, Wordsworth or Arnold. They wrote blissfully of autumn, winter, snow, and daffodils—elements quite foreign to their actual landscape, but which belonged to the landscape of their imaginations. They wrote in a language that was contrived, wooden, alien to what they felt, to their hopes, and to their mission, a mission not imposed by some political, policing body, but by the necessity of history itself. And this task, above all else, was the re-assembly of the individual into a thing of dignity, wholeness and worth. The novelist, Wilson Harris, writes about the West Indies as a "cultural environment whose promise of fulfilment lies in a profound and difficult vision of the person—a profound and difficult vision of essential unity within the most bitter forms of latent and active historical diversity". And that diversity, that bitter antagonism was both inner and outer, both social and psychical.

With the fifties and sixties came a renaissance of sorts, an eruption of the imagination that recognised worth outside of the metropolitan centres. But because writers were padlocked within the castles of their skins, because they were imprisoned within racial garrisons, the tendency was to write for or on behalf of narrow racial groups, their eyes glazed over with different nostalgias for racial beginnings outside the Caribbean. Always, home was elsewhere. Writers of African descent wrote as spokesmen for those who shared their racial heritage. The longing was to return to Africa, a movement that was solidified by Marcus Garvey, and that yielded what was to be a world-wide movement called Black Power. Those of East Indian descent looked to India, for what Naipaul terms an "Aryan" purity in Mimic Men; and everyone continued to look to Europe generally and to England specifically. This movement was triggered in part by the mass departure of writers from the West Indies: Edgar Mittelholzer and Jean Rhys were followed by the likes of C.L.R. James, George Lamming, V.S.

Naipaul, Edward Kamau Brathwaite, Wilson Harris, Samuel Selvon, John Hearne, Martin Carter, Roger Maise, Michael Anthony and Austin Clark. Derek Walcott was among the few to remain at home, writing out of Trinidad and St. Lucia.

Generally, it took distance from the West Indies and proximity to the "centre" to allow the scales to fall from their eyes. Each writer engaged in the painfully lonely task of writing himself or herself and the society into being, each in solitude putting back together the shattered vase of self and society. It is significant to me that not one of these was state-sponsored, although the temptation must have been great to accept such sponsorship. The one considerable talent which yielded, it occurs to me, was that of the poet Arthur Seymour, who headed the state-sponsored Guyana History and Arts Council which oversaw language and literature in that country. It is also significant that, of all, he is a failed talent, producing little more than politically sanctioned stuff which seldom rose above self-conscious nationalism, ideological absolutism. Yet, Seymour was among the first West Indian poets to have excavated fragments of the Indigenous Amerindian past in his poetry. To his discredit, he traded invaluable insights for the trinket of political influence.

The mould into which the human body is cast may be superficial, skin-deep; but skin, so easily ruptured, is not an easy thing from which to break free—so imperative is race, so tempting the old compulsion to return to the original state. The self-conscious, skin-conscious idea of belonging reduced art and literary thought to an ideological order based on race; thought and art predicated upon and predetermined by skin colour. To some extent, literary thought in the West Indies was affiliated to racial politics, both serving to polarise further a society that was fractured into so many pieces in the first place. Political militancy and coincidental artistic militancy may have been a necessary step in the evolution of literature, the individual and society, but it was a stage that presented the gravest dangers to all aspects of life, artistic and otherwise. This compulsion to write for one's skin is as grotesque as it is disturbing. In "What the Twilight Says", Derek Walcott writes:

> The future of West Indian militancy lies in art. All revolutions begin amateurishly, with forged or stolen weapons, but the West Indian artist knew the need for revolt without knowing what weapons to use, and just as a comfortable self-hugging pathos hid in the most polemical of West Indian novels, so there was in the sullen ambition of the West Indian actor a fear that he lacked proper weapons, that his voice, colour and body were no match for the civilised concepts of theatre.... The West Indian mind, historically hung-over, exhausted, prefers to take its revenge in nostalgia, to narrow its eyelids in a schizophrenic daydream of an Eden that existed before its exile. Its fixation is for the breasts of a nourishing mother, and this is true not only of the generations of slaves' children, but of those brought here through indigence or necessity....

Literature subsisting merely on ideology is little more than propaganda, things to persuade others and ourselves that our cause is great and just, our pain and deprivation tragic. Such a whine is emitted still in post-colonial societies to elicit the sympathy of the captors/slavers/masters and mistresses, white men and women. And West Indian literature is littered with such stuff, sooner forgotten; and, indeed, forgotten for the transience of their appeal. Derek Walcott, referring to this time when political posturing was very popular, writes:

> Most of our literature loitered in the pathos of sociology, self-pitying and patronised. Our writers whined in the voices of twilight: "Look at this people! They may be degraded, but they are as good as you are. Look at what you have done to them." And their poems remained laments their, novels propaganda tracts, as if one general apology on behalf of the past would supplant imagination, would spare them the necessity of great art.

The artist, then, needed to have turned away from this cloying temptation to stagnate, to rest easy in the lap of an illusory wholeness and healing, a place that offered immediate, localised reward and recognition. West Indian artists needed to break free of consolidated postures of protest, of flag-waving and fist pumping. Great art, as Walcott and Wilson Harris would agree, necessitated V.S. Naipaul's return to Miguel Street before he may return again to the enigma of his arrival; Edward Kamau Brathwiate's return to the West Indies after his rights of passage, his spiritual journey to Africa; Jean Rhys's imaginative turning back across the wide Sargasso sea to Dominica, especially, and to the West Indies generally. West Indian artists turn back to find themselves coming forward. It meant Wilson Harris embarking on an arduous journey, his characters engaged in a muscular struggle against themselves and their old racial and racist compulsions and roles which history had dictated to be theirs, a journey over many lives and deaths. The aim was always the sublime pleasure of intimate intercourse with rather than to inflict rape upon the landscape. It meant also poets like Walcott and Martin Carter stringing together with words—with the genius and patience born of love—the disparate islands with all their disparate peoples. Each bead or pearl a thing of worth, but only part of the jewellery recreated. It meant a simultaneous stringing together into one fantastic and precious item those beads or fragments within their individual selves. The beads are different; the jewellery sparkles with the colours of a rainbow.

But in order that this be done, West Indian artists needed to have removed their pursed and longing lips from the breasts of cultural mothers who were theirs and not theirs. They needed to have descended from the laps of luxuries, as it were, and to crawl on their hands and their knees, searching the land, listening to its tremors which were as the rumble of their own thoughts; feeling its pulse which was but the beat of their own hearts; harkening to the rush of surf, the torrent of their own blood.

If the vase of individual self lay shattered upon the stage of the West Indies, and if the society lay likewise, broken like islands upon the floor of the world, then so did language. Pieces of English, French, Dutch, Spanish. Pieces of Hindi, Arabic, Chinese. All these great languages; but they were but shards; shards, sharp, everywhere. And when the poet—crawling, humble assembler of things—picks up each shard, blood is drawn. But this is a sacrifice of necessity: the artist in search of form and language to envelope and convey artistic substance—form and language born of other forms and other languages, but different from all that went before. Each putting together, each reintegration, is a triumph of creation, unique creation. For broken things, however painstakingly reassembled, bear the marks of breakage, of fracture and fragmentation. So that the joy of completion is always marked with sorrow; what is found anew is the child of the old, but free from too great a resemblance to the parent.

The calligraphy of bamboo leaves from the ancient languages, Hindi, Chinese, and Arabic, on the Antillean sky. From the Ramayana to Anabasis, from Guadeloupe to Trinidad, all that archaeology of fragments lying around, from the broken African kingdoms, from the crevices of Canton, from Syria and Lebanon, vibrating not under the earth but in our raucous, demotic streets.

Each writer sat with an individual vocabulary to capture the story of broken humanity, stories to capture the "storylessness" of a people. There was the fundamental metaphor, but no uniform use of language; for uniform use, like uniform tradition, is alien to the Caribbean. Now, it is alien to the whole world. Language—like the person, like the society—was composed of shards on the ground. Pieces that bore the promise of a fractured wholeness, something "torn and new", to use the words of Edward Kamau Brathwaite in The Arrivants. Like paradox, always paradox. For the place began with an end, was born in death. And twilight contains the contours of the morning. Language, then, which has served to revitalise tired old tongues, was theirs to create. And this they did, each writer and critic bringing forth some kind of theory which was not theory but vision, a vision of survival in the sun, in the cauldron of their discontent. Each writer fashioned metaphor with healers' hands in a vocabulary different from the other, though the image be the same. It is impossible to mistake the language of Wilson Harris for that of V. S. Naipaul or that of George Lamming, the poetry of

Edward Kamau Brathwiate with that of Martin Carter or Derek Walcott.

A remarkable confession indeed from someone who is a Methodist-Christian-Mulatto-hybrid. And one of the greatest poets of our time. This issue of tradition, of choice of tradition, has been and is of vital significance in West Indian literary thought. Cultural tradition is frequently yoked to ethnicity and subsists largely on homogeneous constraints, an idolatry of absolutes. They offer the temptation of wholeness, of a time, place and people without taint by contact. West Indians offered themselves up to cultural motherlands (or fatherlands) depending on the race to which they affiliated themselves: Chinese traditions for the Chinese-West Indian; to the Indo-West Indian, India; to the West Indian of African descent, Africa. And Europe offered a tempting model for all to live and write or paint or act by.

Yet, it was not simply a matter of "to the colour of your skin, choose". In Walcott's brilliant play, Dream on Monkey Mountain, for instance, Makak is tempted by the vision of a White woman to seize upon his kingly African heritage. His reward would be to taste of her white flesh. But Makak is an old West Indian wood-cutter, and he may don princely African robes and live out his dreams of revenge, but his power is both illusion and delusion. He is, after all, still being manipulated by the White woman, the symbol of European cultural tradition. It is not simply a case of becoming white, of bleaching the mind and the skin; rather, it was to become more African than the African while contorting the mind ignominiously to European rhythms. On the other hand, Makak is tempted by Moustique, his friend on Monkey Mountain, who offers yet another absolute model by which to live and kill: capitalism. But Moustique is Black. These are the kinds of demons, in the end, which the West Indian must wrestle and vanquish. These are temptations that each of us still face, even now; even now, most of us are defeated by those temptations.

The great challenge which West Indian artists have taken up is not which tradition to choose, which cultural imperative to obey, which traditional monolith before which to genuflect. Rather, the great challenge was not to choose at all. For to have chosen one tradition was to have betrayed all others. Conversely, if they reject each, they have all from which to choose. The truth is that no heterogeneous or hybrid civilisation—and, today, the whole world is heterogeneous, hybrid—can afford to accept a total or implacable model upon which to base art or life. Yet, outright rejection of all models, or any model for that matter would be the folly of the vacuous. In "The Phenomenal Legacy" Wilson Harris ties together the issues of the old compulsion to choose one model of tradition with the more demanding new direction that art makes:

> The literature of the West Indies and its corresponding literary thought have broken free of ossification in the face of a Medusa-like history. They have evolved beyond chattering despair, bawling vengeance and self-embracing narcissism. They have gone, also, beyond the paved road of conventional prose, derivative poetry and postures of remorse. Instead they have turned away from the temptations offered by singular models of culture and tradition, choosing all instead. What is left is obedience to a much more demanding aesthetic which seeks to capture and dramatise the recreation of self and a society which that self may call home.

7

Trends in South African Literature

South Africa has had a rich history of literary output. Until relatively recently, realism dominated the production of fiction in South Africa—perhaps authors felt an overriding concern to capture the country's turbulent history and the experiences of its people.

Fiction has been written in all of South Africa's 11 official languages—with a large body of work in Afrikaans, in particular. This overview focuses primarily on English fiction, while also touching on major developments in poetry.

Elleke Boehmer writes, "Nationalism, like patriarchy, favours singleness—one identity, one growth pattern, one birth and blood for all... [and] will promote specifically unitary or 'one-eyed' forms of consciousness." The first problem any student of South African literature is confronted with, is the diversity of the literary systems.

Olivier notes, "While it is not unusual to hear academics and politicians talk about a 'South African literature', the situation at ground level is characterised by diversity and even fragmentation". Mossman adds that "One of the enduring and saddest legacies of the apartheid system may be that no one - White, Black,

Coloured (meaning of mixed-race in South Africa), or Asian - can ever speak as a "South African." The problem, however, pre-dates Apartheid significantly, as South Africa is a country made up of communities that have always been linguistically and culturally diverse. These cultures have all retained autonomy to some extent, making a compilation such as the controversial *Southern African Literatures* by Michael Chapman, difficult. Chapman raises the question:

> [W]hose language, culture, or story can be said to have authority in South Africa when the end of apartheid has raised challenging questions as to what it is to be a South African, what it is to live in a new South Africa, whether South Africa is a nation, and, if so, what its mythos is, what requires to be forgotten and what remembered as we scour the past in order to understand the present and seek a path forward into an unknown future.

South Africa has 11 national languages, Afrikaans, English, Zulu, Xhosa, Sotho, Pedi, Tswana, Venda, SiSwati, Tsonga, and Ndebele. Any definitive literary history of South Africa should, it could be argued, discuss literature produced in all eleven languages. But the only literature ever to adopt characteristics that can be said to be 'national', is Afrikaans. Olivier argues, "Of all the literatures in South Africa, Afrikaans literature has been the only one to have become a national literature in the sense that it developed a clear image of itself as a separate entity, and that by way of institutional entrenchment through teaching, distribution, a review culture, journals, etc. it could ensure the continuation of that concept."

Part of the problem is that English literature has been seen within the greater context of English writing in the world, and has, because of English's global position as *lingua franca*, not been seen as autonomous or indigenous to South Africa - in Olivier's words, "English literature in South Africa continues to be a sort of extension of British or international English literature." The African languages, on the other hand, are spoken across the borders of Southern Africa, e.g. Tswana which is spoken in Botswana, and Tsonga in Zimbabwe, and Sotho in Lesotho. South Africa's borders were drawn up by the British Empire, and like all other colonies, these borders were drawn without regard for the people living within them.

Therefore in a history of South African literature, do we include all Tswana writers, or only the ones with South African citizenship? Chapman bypasses this problem by including 'Southern' African literatures. The second problem with the African languages is accessibility, because since the African languages are regional languages, none of them can claim the readership on a national scale comparable to Afrikaans and English. Sotho, for instance, while transgressing the national borders of the RSA, is on the other hand mainly spoken in the Free State, and bears very little relation to the language of Natal for example, Zulu. So the language cannot claim a national readership, while on the other hand being 'international' in the sense that it transgresses the national borders.

Olivier argues that "There is no obvious reason why it should be unhealthy or abnormal for different literatures to co-exist in one country, each possessing its own infrastructure and allowing theoreticians to develop impressive theories about polysystems". Yet political idealism proposing a unified 'South Africa' (a remnant of the colonial British approach) has seeped into literary discourse and demands a unified national literature, which does not exist and has to be fabricated. It is unrealistic to ever think of South Africa and South African literature as homogenous, now or in the near or distant future, since the only reason it is a country at all is the interference of European colonial powers. This is not a racial issue, but rather has to do with culture, heritage and tradition (and indeed the constitution celebrates diversity).

Rather, it seems more sensible to discuss South African literature as literature produced within the national borders by the different cultures and language groups inhabiting these borders. Otherwise the danger is emphasising one literary system at the expense of another, and more often than not, the beneficiary is English, with the African languages being ignored. The distinction 'black' and 'white' literature is further a remnant of colonialism that should be replaced by drawing distinctions between literary systems based on language affiliation rather than race.

Afrikaans

Afrikaans is a language akin to the Germanic languages and in particular Dutch. It has its origins in the 17th century, but was only officially recognized in 1875 when the *Genootskap vir Regte Afrikaners* was established. Afrikaans is spoken throughout South Africa, and is the mother tongue of both whites and coloureds (in the South African sense, meaning a specific independent culture rather than the disparaging European or American use of the term). The literary history is thus short, but surprisingly vibrant. The major literary histories are HP Van Coller's *Perspektief en Profiel,* JC Kannemeyer's *Geskiedenis van die Afrikaanse literatuur,* and Dekker's

Afrikaanse Literatuurgeskiedenis. Lewis Nkosi claims that "in South Africa there exists an unhealed—I will not say incurable—split between black and white writing." This split occurs because, Nkosi claims, black writers are "largely impervious for the most part to cultural movements which have exercised great influence in the development of white writing." The Afrikaans literary system, in contrast to the African languages, engages with European artistic movements such as symbolism, expressionism, modernism, post-modernism, Dadaism and the like, offering literature familiar to a European or American audience.

Poetry

Some of the early names include Leipoldt and Langenhoven, who wrote the national anthem (*Die Stem*). Early poetry often deal with the Anglo-Boer War, and it is only in the 1930s that poetry reaches a significant literary standard. N. P. van Wyk Louw is the vanguard of the new movement, called *Dertigers,* along with his brother WEG Louw, and Elizabeth Eybers, although they were all to write in future literary periods. Olivier notes Van Wyk Louw's predominance: "It was only in the Thirties that a fully developed theory about Afrikaans as a national literature was launched by the erudite poet, N P van Wyk Louw, in his two collections of essays *Lojale verset* (1939) and *Berigte te velde* (1939)". Van Wyk Louw introduced international literary theories and movements into the South African literary scene on a much larger scale than any of his predecessors, and his "theory provided the intellectual and philosophical space within which poets and novelists could exercise their craft without fear of transgression; in short, it became the paradigm for Afrikaans literature"

(Olivier). DJ Opperman started writing in the 1940s, and was to have a particularly prominent role with his anthology, *Groot Verseboek*. The next major paradigm shift came in the 1960s, with TT Cloete and Ingrid Jonker, who, after her death, attained cult status. Cloete et al. discuss this literary watershed in *Rondom Sestig*. TT Cloete is further noteworthy for his compilation, *Literêre Terme en Teorieë* (1992), which is one of the most encompassing works on literary theory available on the global market, although written in Afrikaans. Some modern poets of note include Joan Hambidge, Hennie Aucamp, Ernst van Heerden, Antjie Krog and Gert Vlok Nel. Breyten Breytenbach is regarded by many as one of the best, if not the best, Afrikaans poet. He spent a number of years in prison for his political beliefs during apartheid and later lived in France. Breytenbach's latest work, "Die windvanger" was published in 2007. The major poetry anthologies are DJ Opperman's *Groot Verseboek*, Foster and Viljoen's *Poskaarte*, Gerrit Komrij's controversial Die *Afrikaanse poësie in 1000 en enkele gedigte*, and André P. Brink's *Groot Verseboek*, a remake or reworking of Opperman's anthology.

Prose

Being a predominantly agricultural society, the *plaasroman* (farm novel) plays a prominent role in early as well as later novels. One of the archetypes is CM Van den Heever's *Laat Vrugte*, which lay the foundations for parodies in the 1960s and later such as Etienne Leroux's *Sewe dae by die Silbersteins*, André P. Brink's *Houd-den-bek* and Eben Venter's *Ek stamel ek sterwe*. Even some English novels, such as JM Coetzee's *Disgrace*, remind one of the plaasroman. As urbanization became more prominent during the time of the two World Wars, other forms emerged, notably the *dorpsroman* (town novel) such as Lettie Viljoen's *Karolina Ferreira,* Etienne van Heerden's *Die Swye van Mario Salviati,* or Alexander Strachan's *Die Werfbobbejaan.* Afrikaans writing tends to be critical of conservative culture, and during the Apartheid regime, critical of politics as well. André P. Brink and Etienne Leroux deserve special mention, Brink not only because he is accessible to English readers (he writes in English and Afrikaans, e.g. *Duiwelskloof* is available as *Devil's Valley*), but also because the vast oeuvre he produced (prose and drama) sets him apart as arguably the greatest South African writer.

Leroux produced less, but had a profound influence on the literary scene. His characters are often outsiders, and his satirical view on South African issues embodies alchemistic, Jungian and Cabbalistic theories and philosophies, with the novel reading like a palimpsest with different levels of meaning. This style had a profound influence on writers such as Ingrid Winterbach (Lettie Viljoen), Alexander Strachan, and Etienne van Heerden's magical realist novels. With the war in Angola, *grensliteratuur* (border literature) started playing an important role, such as Dine van Zyl's *Slagoffers,* Christiaan Bakkes's *Skuilplek* and Alexander Strachan's *'n Wêreld sonder grense.*

After political changes in 1994, an emphasis on the past has become an important feature as South Africans attempted to make sense of their past, of which Dan Sleigh's *Eilande* and André P. Brink's *Duiwelskloof* are examples. *Triomf* by Marlene van Niekerk deals with poor Afrikaners in a legendary suburb of Johannesburg, where the Apartheid regime demolished the old black township Sophiatown, in order to build houses for the white lower-class. *Triomf* has been translated into English by Leon de Kock. Another writer who often regresses to earlier times is André P. Brink, e.g. *Anderkant die Stilte* (in English available as *The Other Side of Silence*) which is set during the German occupation of Namibia. Andre Brink was the first Afrikaner writer to be banned by the government after he released the novel *A Dry White Season* about a white South African who discovers the truth about a black friend who dies in police custody. In recent years, gay and lesbian writing has also begun to feature, e.g. Johann de Lange, and Eben Venter's *Ek stamel ek sterwe.*

Political turmoil and the opening of South Africa's borders after the 1994 elections have resulted in many writers moving abroad, or writing about their time spent overseas, e.g. Jaco Fouché's *Ryk van die Rawe.* Other contemporary issues include crime (Jaco Fouché's *Die avonture van Pieter Francken,* Etienne van Heerden's *In stede van die liefde* and others) and other government issues such as corruption. In short, Afrikaans prose tends to be critical of the dominant ideologies and the government of the time, the society inhabiting this space and the people living within this society. From a European perspective, Afrikaans prose produces works of a high standard and is artistically and intellectually capable of engaging with the best European and American writers.

Drama

As with the prose and poetry, Afrikaans drama is often intellectually and stylistically modern and complex, as influenced by French, German, Russian and Dutch playwrights. *Siener in die Suburbs* by PG Du

Plessis, Reza de Wet's *Vrystaat Trilogie* and *Drie susters twee*, Breyten Breytenbach's *Boklied* and André P. Brink's *Bagasie* deserve mentioning. Breyten Breytenbach was jailed for his (alleged) involvement with guerrilla activities against the Apartheid regime, but was subsequently released. As with the other genres, engaged literature remains important, and plays such as Brink's *Die jogger* deal with brutal violence committed by the security forces during apartheid, whereas current high levels of violent crime are addressed in plays such as Mike van Graan's *Die generaal* and Deon Opperman's *Kaburu*.

South African English Literature

Prose

One of the first literary works of note is Olive Schreiner's *The story of an African farm*, which can be linked to Van den Heever's *Laat Vrugte* as a *plaasroman*. The novel was a revelation in Victorian literature: it is heralded by many as introducing feminism into the novel form. However, Mossman argues that "The most frequently taught work of South African literature in American classrooms is *Cry, the Beloved Country* (1986) by Alan Paton". A possible reason for this is that it was made into a film starring James Earl Jones, and it depicts a typical racist situation which fits well with American perceptions of South African society. Alan Paton also produced *Too late the phalarope*, another text criticizing Apartheid politics, in particular the Immorality Act which forbade interracial sexual relations. During the 1950s, Drum became a hotbed of political satire, fiction, and essays, giving a voice to urban black culture. Around the same time, future Nobel laureate Nadine Gordimer began publishing her first stories. Her most famous novel, *July's People,* was released in 1981, depicting the collapse of white-minority rule. Athol Fugard's Tsotsi was also made into a film, although Fugard is usually better known for his dramas. Several influential black poets became prominent in the 1970s such as Mongane Wally Serote, whose most famous work, *No Baby Must Weep,* gave insight into the every day lives of black South Africans under Apartheid. Another famous black novelist, Zakes Mda, transitioned from poetry and plays to becoming a novelist. His novel, *The Heart of Redness* won the 2001 Commonwealth Writers Prize and was made a part of the school curriculum across South Africa. Miriam Tlali was the first black woman to publish a novel in South Africa with *Muriel at Metropolitan* (1975) (also known as *Between Two Worlds*). John Maxwell (JM) Coetzee was also first published in the 1970s. He became internationally recognised in 1983 with his Booker Prize winning novel *Life & Times of Michael K.* His 1999 novel *Disgrace* won him his second Booker Prize as well as the 2000 Commonwealth Writers' Prize. He is also the recipient of the Nobel Prize for Literature in 2003. South African English writing has produced two Nobel Prize winners: Nadine Gordimer and JM Coetzee.

Naturally, racial friction is often depicted in South African literature of all languages. But there is a marked difference between how white writing depicts black characters and how some black authors depict whites: one emphasizes that people are not what the stereotype claims, the other argue that the stereotype is substantiated. For instance, Miriam Tlali writes, "The Republic of South Africa is a country divided mainly into two worlds. The one, a white world — rich, comfortable, for all practical purposes organised — a world in fear, armed to the teeth. The other, a black world; poor, pathetically neglected and disorganised —voiceless, oppressed, restless, confused and unarmed—a world in transition, irrevocably weaned from all tribal ties." This clearly provides a one-sided view of South African realities, of course ignoring Soviet involvement in the arms trade during the freedom struggle, the reality of poor whites (as depicted in Marlene van Niekerk's *Triomf*), and essentially the fact that South Africa in the years of Apartheid was a more complex environment than the one often depicted in reductionist texts (literary and journalistic). Her stereotypical and demonizing depiction of "Boers" (Afrikaners) highlights the same reductionist tendency: "they have an insatiable lust for persecuting non-whites, [their] perfect efficiency in this respect was motivated by the unmistakable burning desire you find in most of them, that is, to sit on the necks of the non-whites." This contrasts sharply with specifically Afrikaans works under Apartheid (e.g. Leroux, Brink, Krog, Van Heerden), who tend to address the absurdity of Apartheid and the humanity in the Other, rather than perpetuating stereotypes.

Other prominent texts listed by Mossman are *Mine Boy* by Peter Abrahams, Alex La Guma's *Walk in the Night*, Breyten Breytenbach's *True Confessions of an Albino Terrorist*, Nadine Gordimer's *Burger's Daughter*, Andre Brink's *Dry White Season*, Richard Rive's *Buckingham Palace, District Six*, Andre Brink's *Rumours of Rain*, Nadine Gordimer's *July's People*, Sipho Sepamla's *Ride on the Whirlwind*, and Mongane Serote's *To every birth its blood*. Miriam Tlali was the first black woman to produce a novel, *Murial at the Metropolitan* (*Between Two Worlds*). David Lambkin also deserves mentioning, *The Hanging Tree* reading like a Leroux novel with various Jungian and alchemistic substrates.

Drama

Athol Fugard's *Master Harald and the boys* is a drama about race relations, and *Boesman and Lena* depicts the hardships suffered by South Africa's poor. Athol Fugard's plays have been regularly premiered in fringe theatres in South Africa, London (The Royal Court Theatre) and New York. Another noteworthy drama is Zakes Mda's *We shall sing for the fatherland.*

Recent plays have addressed the high levels of violent crime, such as Lara Foot Newton's *Tshepang,* Athol Fugard's *Victory* and Mpumelelo Paul Grootboom's *Relativity.*

Poetry

Tony Ullyatt's *The Lonely Art: An Anthology* includes South African English poetry. English poetry in South Africa is often considered 'good' by whether or not it criticises Apartheid, or whether or not it depicts life 'as it is', rather than the Afrikaans emphasis on literary merit taken from Russian Formalism and introduced by Van Wyk Louw.

Colonial Adventure

The first fictional works to emerge from South Africa were produced by immigrants who often felt alienated from the South African landscape - at the same time as they were fascinated by its harsh beauty. These colonial writers were unsettled and intrigued by what they perceived as exotic elements of indigenous cultures. Their attitude to indigenous South Africans was, at best, ambivalent, if not hostile. This is especially true of the writers of adventure-type stories, in which colonial heroes are romanticised and black South Africans' role is reduced to that of enemy or servant.

One such writer was Rider Haggard, who wrote many mythical and adventure stories, beginning in the early 1880s. His most famous book is *King Solomon's Mines* (1886), a bestseller in its day (and filmed several times up to the 1980s). Like subsequent novels such as *Allan Quartermain* and *She* (both 1887), its central character is the hunter Allan Quartermain, Haggard's ideal of the colonial gentleman.

These novels follow his various adventures in the "darkest Africa" of the European imagination, fixated on mysterious white queens and hidden treasures in ancient cities (built by other than black people). The point of view is that of the heroic Englishman, and indigenous peoples are portrayed either as dangerous savages or faithful servants (Quartermain's Zulu retainer eventually gives his life for his master).

Although Haggard wrote many other adventures and fantasies, it is his highly coloured African works that are still read today.

South African Voices

Olive Schreiner's novel *The Story of an African Farm* (1883) is generally considered to be the founding text of South African literature. Schreiner was born on a mission station and worked as a governess on isolated Karoo farms, an experience that informed the novel. It tells the story of several characters representing aspects of South African society of its day. Lyndall, the young heroine, is the focus of Schreiner's feminist concerns. Bonaparte Blenkins is a portrait of the "imperial rogue" and thus allows Schreiner to express her nascent anti-colonial ideas (she later supported the Boers in their war of freedom against Britain).

There is also Tant Sannie, the Boer woman, the kindly German Uncle Otto, and Otto's son Waldo, who expresses the universal themes of the novel in his concern with spiritual meaning.

The novel draws on the post-romantic sensibility of *Wuthering Heights,* and depicts rural South African life with authenticity and brio. It has been criticised for its silence with regard to the black African presence in South Africa, but it is still a key text in the formation of a truly South African voice. Schreiner's other work includes a critique of Cecil John Rhodes's brutal form of colonialism, *Trooper Peter Halkett of Mashonaland* (1897), and the polemical *Women and Labour* (1911).

Douglas Blackburn had a certain amount in common with Schreiner, yet he was also a very different kettle of fish. He was a maverick British journalist who came to South Africa when the Transvaal was still a Boer republic, and stayed during the Anglo Boer War and beyond. In several newspapers, he denounced British colonial attitudes as well as satirising Boer corruption.

He wrote two novels set in this world, *Prinsloo of Prinsloosdorp* (1899) and *A Burgher Quixote* (1903), capturing with a great deal of sly humour the personality and situation of the Boer at the time.

His later novel *Leaven* (1908) is a moving denunciation of "blackbirding" and other iniquitous labour practices, and is one of the first South African novels to portray what life was really like for peasants forced into urban labour. *Love Muti* (1915) attacks British colonial attitudes.

Blackburn is not read much today, but his work is an important contribution to a developing South African literature - and style. Herman Charles Bosman, for one, seems to have learned from Blackburn's ironic humour.

Emergence of Black Writing

It was not until the 20th century that literature by black South Africans emerged. The first generation of mission-educated African writers sought to restore dignity to Africans by invoking and reconstructing a heroic African past.

The first novel by a black South African was *Mhudi* (completed in 1920 but only published in 1930), by Solomon (Sol) Thekiso Plaatje. This epic story follows the trajectory of the Tswana people during and after their military encounter with the Zulus under Shaka, the Zulu conqueror of the 19th century, and encompasses their earliest encounters with the white people moving into the interior.

Viewed as the founding father of black literature in South Africa, Plaatje was also the first secretary general of the then South African Native National Congress (now the African National Congress) at its foundation in 1912.

His *Native Life in South Africa* (1916) was a seminal text in the study of land dispossession in South Africa. He also wrote a diary of the siege of Mafeking during the Boer War, and translated Shakespeare into seTswana language.

South African literature, Thomas Mofolo's *Chaka* reinvents the legendary Zulu king (commonly referred to as Shaka). Mofolo portrays him as a heroic but tragic figure, a monarch to rival Shakespeare's Macbeth. He is concerned to find in African history characters to rival those of the European literary tradition, which is based on the epics of ancient times, with their gods and heroes. Mofolo, however, also invests Shaka with a complex personality, in which good and evil are at war - in contrast to white colonial historians who made him a simplistic monster of tribal savagery. Completed in 1910, the novel was published in 1925 and the first English translation came out in 1930.

Shock and Satire

Just as Olive Schreiner had drawn fire from the colonial elite for her liberal views, so did William Plomer, decades later, shock colonial society with his novel *Turbott Wolfe* (1926), written when he was only 19 years old. It tackled the highly sensitive issue of inter-racial love, though it is hardly a roistering sexual chronicle. It was, however, an indictment of white South African attitudes at the time, and a mere suggestion that there might be some human sympathy, let alone sexual attraction, between a white person and a black person, horrified many. There is also open discussion of the political and racial situation in South Africa. Along with his contemporaries and sometime collaborators Laurens van der Post and Roy Campbell, Plomer left South Africa soon after the publication of his novel. He settled finally in Britain, where he became known primarily as a poet.

Between the Wars

Perhaps the dominant figure of South African literature in the period between the two world wars was Sarah Gertrude Millin, whose reputation has faded considerably since her death. This is due to her politics: she was initially a devout supporter of Jan Smuts' government, but later became something of an apologist for apartheid. Her views on the "tragedy" of racial miscegenation were put forward in *God's Stepchildren* (1924). Seen in terms of racial hierarchies, with whites at the top and blacks at the bottom, Millin's views represented those held widely at the time. Her later novels continued to deal with the "predicament" of coloured (mixed-race) people in South Africa, or attempted to describe the world of indigenous peoples.

The Forties

The 1940s saw the beginnings of a flowering of literature by black South Africans, as a generation of mission-educated Africans came of age. Among them was HIE Dhlomo, whose work preached a "return to the source" - the wisdom of finding traditional ways of dealing with modern problems.

His work includes several plays and the long poem *The Valley of a Thousand Hills* (1941). Poets such as BW Vilakazi, who wrote in Zulu, gave new literary life to their indigenous languages.

Peter Abrahams, an important voice who began writing in the 1940s, was of mixed-race descent. His early novel, *Mine Boy* (1946), was published in the same year in which a large miners' strike was violently suppressed by Smuts' government.

Mine Boy depicts life in black areas of the time, and dramatises the problems of rural people in a depressed urban environment - a theme that was referred to as the "Jim comes to Jo'burg" phenomenon in South African literature. Later works by Abrahams (who left South Africa and settled in Britain before finally moving to Jamaica) include *The Path of Thunder* (1948), which deals with interracial love; *Return to Goli* (1953), about his journey back to report on life in Johannesburg; and his autobiography *Tell Freedom* (1954).

Another South African writer who emerged in the 1940s, Herman Charles Bosman, has become one of the country's best-loved authors, particularly for his short stories set in the Groot Marico farming district. These tales, first published in the late 1940s, are a sometimes-gentle-sometimes-savage portrait of Afrikaner storytelling skills and social attitudes.

Bosman uses the voice of narrators such as Oom Schalk Lourens who relate the stories as if from their own viewpoint, but in a way that allows the reader to see through their prejudices and blind spots. Among the most famous are *Unto Dust* and *In the Withaak's Shade.*

Bosman's first collection of stories was published in *Mafeking Road* in 1947. A colourful character, who was jailed for the mysterious murder of his stepbrother, Bosman also wrote poetry, novels, and much journalism, often satirical.

One of his best works, *Cold Stone Jug* (1949), is a semi-fictionalised account of his time in jail. All his books have been reissued in new 2001 editions to coincide with the 50th anniversary of his death.

Bosman had satirised social attitudes in South Africa, but it was the work of a former schoolteacher - published in the very year in which the Afrikaner Nationalists came to power and established apartheid - that brought the world's attention to the situation of black people in South Africa. And it was written by a white man.

Cry, The Beloved Country (1948) is possibly the most famous novel to have come out of South Africa. When it was first published, it was an international bestseller, launching its author, Alan Paton, to worldwide fame. The novel put South Africa on the map of international politics by making visible to Western audiences the effects of racial prejudice and the oppression of black people.

It is the story of a black priest who travels to Johannesburg in search of his son, who had fallen victim to the corrupting influence of the city. The novel explores themes of corruption and forgiveness, putting forward a liberal-humanist view of South Africa's racial politics - as well as Paton's deeply felt Christianity. The novel has a lovely poetic language, with extensive use of Biblical cadences, though Paton has also been criticised for a possibly condescending portrayal of black people.

He later got involved in South African politics through the Liberal Party, of which he was a leader; he opposed the apartheid state while refusing to countenance the use of violence against it. He also wrote biography, much journalism, poetry and two further novels.

The Drum Decade

The 1950s was the decade in which the African National Congress and its alliance partners launched the massive Defiance Campaign, a huge peaceful affront on white supremacy. It was the decade in which the Freedom Charter, the central document of the anti-racist movement, was written on the basis of contributions from all over the country. And it was the decade in which the apartheid state responded with massive treason trials for those who defied it.

The 1950s also saw a new generation of black writers talking about the conditions of their lives in their own voices - voices with a distinctive stamp and style. The popular Drum magazine in the 1950s was their forum, and encouraged their emergence. It depicted a vibrant urban black culture for the first time - a world of jazz, shebeens (illegal drinking dens), and flamboyant gangsters (tsotsis).

Reportage blurred into fiction: there were satirical stories ridiculing the discriminatory and repressive policies of the state, while others provided harrowing details of the effect of apartheid legislation on people's lives. These writers recorded urban deprivation, but also the resilience of people who survived "without visible means of subsistence".

Es'kia (formerly Ezekiel) Mphahlele later described the style of Drum writers as "racy, agitated, impressionistic, it quivered with a nervous energy, a caustic wit". These writers may have been politically cynical rather than directly invovled in politics (and their dominant sexism has been noted by many), but they did create a vibrant voice that speaks in the truly original tones of the urban black experience in South Africa, and for that alone are highly valued.

Their work ranged from the investigative journalism of Henry Nxumalo to the witty social commentary of Todd Matshikiza; others such as Nat Nakasa, Can Themba and Mphahlele moved toward embodying their visions of black South African life in poetry or fiction.

Later, Nakasa edited a literary journal, The Classic, that published work such as Themba's story The Suit (1963), now regarded as a classic of South African literature. It has been adapted for the stage and is still touring the world in Peter Brook's production. Themba was banned by the apartheid state and died in exile, an alcoholic, in 1968, but others such as Mphahlele pursued their literary careers.

Lewis Nkosi became a noted literary critic in Europe and the United States. Other notable writers connected in some way to Drum include William Bloke Modisane, Arthur Maimane, Dyke Sentso, James Matthews, Peter Clarke, Richard Rive, Jordan Ngubane, Alex La Guma and Casey Motsisi.

Modisane wrote the autobiography *Blame Me on History* (1963), Matthews has written much poetry and a novel, and Rive wrote *Buckingham Palace, District Six* (1986), about life in that coloured Cape Town area, and two novels about South African states of emergency, decades apart, *Emergency* (1964) and *Emergency Continued* (1989).

The Drum Decade, edited by Michael Chapman, and *A Good Looking Corpse,* by Mike Nicol, anthologise and comment on key works of this era.

E'skia Mphahlele's autobiographical *Down Second Avenue* (1959) is a landmark in the development of South African fiction. Set in a village and a township near Pretoria, the text records in evocative language the resilience of various female characters in Mphahlele's life, who defy poverty and urban squalor to bring him up. At the same time, they are presented with complexity and depth - his grandmother, for one, is a rather tyrannical figure.

Mphahlele went on to write critiques *The African Image* 1962, short stories *Man Must Live* 1946, *In Corner B* 1967, as well as further novels, including *The Wanderers* 1971, in some ways an extension of the autobiographical form of *Down Second Avenue.* It articulated his own experiences, first as an adult in South Africa and then his move into exile (he settled in Nigeria in 1957, returning to South Africa in 1977). He also wrote poetry and autobiography.

Taken as a whole, Mphahlele's oeuvre represents one of the most important views of the life experience and developing views of a politically aware South African; this is the work of a black man taking the urban scenario as his subject matter and moving beyond the sometimes contradictory messages of the mission-educated generation.

Gordimer: liberalism to radicalism

At the same time as the Drum generation was creating the first urban black voice, one of South Africa's most important white writers was beginning her long, distinguished career.

Nadine Gordimer published her first short stories in the early 1950s; in 1991 she was awarded the Nobel Prize for Literature. Between those two dates, her many novels and short stories articulated key issues for white South Africans sympathetic to the plight of disenfranchised blacks, as well as providing for the outside world a devastating picture of what it was like to live under apartheid.

In her fiction, Gordimer moves from the position of a white liberal with a perhaps mildly or unconsciously paternalistic attitude towards her black compatriots, into a much more radical position that attempts to give voice to the black liberation movement, while at the same time articulating the contradictions in which white liberals and radicals were often caught.

Her second novel, *A World of Strangers* (1958), shows the first fruitful but often frightening encounters between white and black people in the heady days of Sophiatown. By the time of *The Late Bourgeois World* (1966), Gordimer is dealing directly with the effects of the black liberation movement on white South Africans, showing the divided soul of the white liberal in a morally ambivalent situation. *The Conservationist* (1974) pits Afrikaner land hunger against the indigenous population in an often phantasmagoric narrative.

Burger's Daughter (1979) depicts the involvement of radical white activists in the liberation struggle. *July's People* (1981), perhaps Gordimer's most powerful novel, projects into the future the final collapse of white supremacy and what that might mean for white and black people on an intimate level.

Her other works (and her short stories are regarded as among her finest work) deal with issues such as love across the colour line and, more recently, the emergence of South Africa into a democracy after the release of Nelson Mandela in 1990 - a society still dealing with a myriad contradictions.

Figures of the Sixties

In the early 1960s, the State of Emergency used by the apartheid state to crack down on dissidents, the banning of political organisations such as the African National Congress and the Pan African Congress, and the jailing of leaders such as Nelson Mandela, sent many black writers into exile. Among them was Alex la Guma, a Marxist and ANC leader who saw the purpose of his work as the exposure of the dreadful conditions of South Africa's oppressed.

His novella *A Walk in the Night* (1962) shows the life of crime to which slum inhabitants are driven, and *And a Threefold Cord (1967)* contrasts the existence of a black worker in a white home with her employers' affluent life.

The later novel, *In the Fog of the Season's End* (1972), possibly his best, shows the developing consciousness of a man dedicated to the underground struggle for freedom. As a "listed person", little of La Guma's work was available in South Africa until 1990, when the liberation movements were unbanned.

At the same time, in the 1960s, the Afrikaans literary scene had a rush of new blood, as writers such as Jan Rabie, Etienne Leroux, Breyten Breytenbach and Andre Brink emerged. Publishing first in Afrikaans, these writers were increasingly politicised by the situation in South Africa and their contrasting experiences overseas.

Breytenbach, who began as one of the most linguistically radical new poets in Afrikaans, left South Africa in 1960, where he became a vocal critic of the apartheid state. Later, in the 1970s, he returned to South Africa and was arrested and jailed for work he was doing for the liberation movement.

From this experience came his extraordinary prison memoir, *True Confessions of an Albino Terrorist* (1996). It is as much interior monologue as it is a record of his prison years, mixing surreal visions and Zen attitudes.

Breytenbach's return visits to South Africa are recorded, mixing reportage and imaginative commentary, in *A Season in Paradise* (1976) and *Return to Paradise* (1993). His prison poetry was published in English in *Judas Eye* (1988). Breytenbach remains as caustic about politics and power under an ANC government as he was under a Nationalist one. His essays have been published in *The Memory of Birds in Times of Revolution* (1996).

Andre Brink stayed in South Africa to see his novels become the first Afrikaans works banned by the government. He began to write in English as well as Afrikaans, and his novels have become as important a part of South African English-language literature as they are in Afrikaans. Having published several novels in Afrikaans during the 1960s, it was his novel *Looking on Darkness* (1973) that was first banned.

His immensely powerful novel *A Dry White Season* (1982), focused on the death in detention of a black activist, and caused great irritation to the apartheid state, while conscientising many white South Africans. It was also banned, then unbanned. Later novels by this prolific novelist include *An Act of Terror* (1991), dealing with an Afrikaner dissident turned "terrorist", and *On the Contrary* (1993), a playful reworking of South Africa's colonial history.

During this period, Bessie Head emerged as a leading South African woman writer, with the role of women as a central concern. Of mixed blood, and with a traumatic family history, Head left South Africa to avoid its racial policies and lived in Botswana, where she felt more at ease.

Her novels show a marked sympathy with ordinary peasant women; her heroines are poor but strong-willed, women who have to face up to various forms of prejudice.

Her first novel was *When Rain Clouds Gather* (1968), followed by *Maru* (1971), *The Collector of Treasures* (1977), and *A Question of Power* (1973). *The Collector of Treasures* is her most autobiographical work, dealing with the traumas of her own illegitimate mixed-race birth, her mother's suicide and her own nervous breakdown.

Another writer to make his name in the 1960s was Wilbur Smith, South Africa's most popular literary export. He is a worldwide bestselling author who now stands in the ranks of the money-making elite as far as popular fiction is concerned. In many ways he is the heir to the tradition of Rider Haggard - some would say politically as well.

His long, fast-moving adventure stories deal in sex and violence, often set against a backdrop of political turmoil. It is here that Smith reveals attitudes that were not out of place in apartheid South Africa. As with Haggard, black characters are often either menacing or servile; there are few who are treated simply as human beings with full interior lives to match those of his sexy, strong white heroes.

His earliest novels are probably his best: *Where the Lion Feeds* (1964) and *The Sound of Thunder* (1966) are set in the era of the foundation of gold-mining in South Africa. Others go as far afield as the state of Israel, Ethiopia during the Italian invasion, piracy in the age of sail, or, more recently, investigate the pharaonic times of Ancient Egypt.

There is no doubt that Smith has a propulsive narrative gift; some readers, though, may be irked by his often sexist and racist assumptions, as well as repelled by the frequent blood-letting.

The 1960s also saw the emergence of a new generation of white South African poets, among them Douglas Livingstone, Sidney Clouts, Ruth Miller, Lionel Abrahams and Stephen Gray. Their work ranges from powerful apprehensions of natural life (Livingstone) to more interior, meditative considerations (Abrahams), and a sardonic socio-political sensibility (Gray).

Gray has also written novels, plays and much criticism. Abrahams has written two semi-autobiographical novels, *The Celibacy of Felix Greenspan* (1977) and *The White Life of Felix Greenspan* (2002).

The Soweto Poets

In the 1970s, South Africa experienced a literary revival of black voices that had been silenced by repression. The 1970s are widely regarded as a defining period for the development of political consciousness among black South Africans, with the rise of the Black Consciousness (BC) movement, of which the martyred Bantu Steve Biko was a leading figure, and the schoolchildrens' revolt of 1976.

BC advocated an affirmation of black cultural values and a racial solidarity in the face of state oppression. Literature became a vehicle to promote the political ideals of anti-apartheid popular movements. Many of these productions were designed to mobilise audiences against state policies, and the genres of drama and poetry were utilised for their immediacy of impact.

The most notable writers from this period are Mongane (Wally) Serote, Sipho Sepamla, Oswald

Joseph Mbuyiseni Mtshali, Christopher van Wyk, Mafika Gwala and Don Mattera. Couched in graphic language designed to arouse the emotions of listeners, their poems were often performed at political rallies.

While Mtshali's poems, first published in 1971 in *The Sound of a Cowhide Drum*, asked for generalised sympathy for the plight of poor black people, and Sepamla was at first considered a "contemplative" poet, the tone soon changed. By the time of *The Soweto I Love* (1977), Sepamla's poetic persona is fully identified with the oppressed.

Sepamla also wrote a novel of this turbulent time, *A Ride on the Whirlwind* (1981). Sepamla, apart from being a leading arts teacher, has written several other novels, and his *Selected Poems* were published in 1984.

Serote's early poems, in volumes such as *Yakhal'inkomo* (1972) and *Tsetlo* (1974) are short and sharp. They deal with the life and attitudes of a politically aware black person, looking at his society and its discontentment. In later volumes, Serote begins to develop an epic, incantatory voice, with the long poems of *Behold Mama, Flowers* (1978) and *Come and Hope with Me* (1994), winner of the Noma Award for Publishing in Africa.

Serote (who became an ANC leader) is also the author of the novel *To Every Birth Its Blood* (1981), a remarkable account of political activity in the 1970s. It graphically recreates state violence, initial black apathy and ultimate black involvement in "liberatory" violence. Serote's later novel, *Gods of our Time* (1999), reconstructs civil and military campaigns which led to the demise of apartheid.

These novels do not simply record the grim life of people in the ghetto but go on to celebrate the resilience of the human spirit in the face of adversity. Other interesting fiction to deal with the Soweto revolt and subsequent political activity include Miriam Tlali's *Amandla* (1980) and Mbulelo Mzamane's *The Children of Soweto* (1982). Don Mattera has written an account of life in Sophiatown, and its destruction, *Memory is the Weapon* (1987).

The Emergency Years

Increasing internal and external pressure on the apartheid state led, in the 1980s, to its most repressive measures yet. While sanctions were imposed from outside, a mass democratic movement, based on the ideals of the Freedom Charter, arose within the country.

The state responded with successive states of emergency that brought white troops to the townships; a state of civil war existed in all but name.

In the face of this, the driving need for politicised work was felt, as it had been in the 1970s. Poets such as the orator Mzwakhe Mbuli reached vast audiences, while novelists such as Menan du Plessis and Mandla Langa engaged with the business of resistance to apartheid. Yet, at the same time, some felt the need for a move away from rhetoric and toward the depiction of ordinary life.

In his 1986 essay, *The Rediscovery of the Ordinary* Njabulo Ndebele expressed this view, seeing politically determined work as inimical to a full depiction of rounded humanity in fiction.

His own fiction, in the award-winning collection, *Fools and Other Stories* (1983), demonstrated that it could be done with grace. Although written in the wake of township rebellion, the book is not polemical but evokes township life with subtlety. It probes the formative experiences of young men growing up in a township, vividly evoking the rhythms and speech of township life. The main story, *Fools* was later reworked into a movie with an all-South African cast.

JM Coetzee, one of South Africa's most lauded writers, began publishing in the 1970s, but achieved prominence in the "emergency years". Like Ndebele, he eschewed fiction of direct political statement, though his complex post-modern work deals in subtle ways with issues of power, authority and history.

One of the key works of recent South African writing, Coetzee's novel *Waiting for the Barbarians* (1980) tackles issues germane to South Africa by telling the story of an official at the outpost of an unidentified empire, one under stress from a barbarian threat that may or may not be imagined. His next novel, *Life and Times of Michael K* (1983), won the Booker Prize in Britain.

This story of a poor man of colour trying to survive in a civil-war situation, never taking sides, is very powerful, as is *Age of Iron* (1990), which takes the perspective of a white academic who is dying even as the townships explode with violence.

Coetzee's next novel, *Disgrace* (1999), won him a second Booker Prize and caused huge debate in South Africa over its depiction of a postapartheid reality in which the wounds of the past have not been healed - and new ones are being inflicted. Coetzee is also an illustrious literary academic *Doubling the Point* (1992), and has published a memoir of growing up in South Africa, *Boyhood* (1998).

His more recent works include *The Lives of Animals*, edited and introduced by Amy Gutmann (1999); *The Humanities in Africa - Die Geisteswissenschaften in Afrika* (2001); *Stranger Shores: Essays, 1986 to 1999* (2001); and two more novels, *Youth (2002)* and *Slow Man* (2005).

After Apartheid

Questions were asked of writers as apartheid came to an end with the release of Nelson Mandela in 1990 and over the transitional period leading up to the democratic election in 1994.

What, they were asked, will you now write about, now that apartheid, and racial tension, your primary topics as South African writers, have gone? Well, apartheid may have died, but its effects linger on, and as writers such as Coetzee have demonstrated, the issues of power that haunted the apartheid era are still in many ways with us.

Certainly, while there has been no sudden post-apartheid renaissance, there are many important writers dealing with South Africa today, and processing its past, which is still in many ways with us.

Among them, one of the most acclaimed is Zakes Mda, who worked for many years as a playwright and poet before publishing his first novels in 1995. He started with a bang - with two novels, *She Plays with the Darkness* and *Ways of Dying*. The latter, the story of a professional mourner, won the M-Net Book Prize.

His next novel, *The Heart of Redness* (2001), won the Commonwealth Prize; it contrasts the past of the 19th century, when the prophetess Nongqawuse brought ruin to the Xhosa people, with a present-day narrative.

Ivan Vladislavic is another author pushing into the post-apartheid future, with distinctly post-modern works that play with the conventions of fiction as much as they speak about contemporary realties in South Africa today. He has published two collections of stories, *Missing Persons* (1990) and *Propaganda by Monuments* (2000), and two novels, *The Folly* (1993) and *The Restless Supermarket* (2001).

Lesego Rampolokeng came to prominence in the 1980s, through the Congress of South African Writers. His is one of the most irreverent voices to hit the South African literary scene over the past decade. Using a vibrant mix of rap-styled poetry and township idiom, he displays no loyalty to any figures of authority. His poems are published in *Horns for Hondo* (1991) and *End Beginnings* (1993). A powerful live performer of his work, he has collaborated with musicians as well.

K Sello Duiker is a young novelist who has recently made a splash in South Africa, with two novels, *Thirteen Cents* (2000) and *The Quiet Violence of Dreams* (2001), coming out in quick succession. Both have won him awards and critical acclaim. Set in the urban landscape of Cape Town, the two novels see the world through the eyes of the underdog, a street kid in the first and an ostracised gay student in the second.

Mark Behr has been one of the most compelling and controversial additions to the South African literary canon. His first novel, *The Smell of Apples* (1997), was first published in Afrikaans. It tells of white South Africans who were brainwashed by the apartheid system, and went on to win several prizes.

Soon after that, Behr admitted that he had been a spy for the apartheid police while a student activist; a graphic illustration, if one were needed, of the divided loyalties felt by many whites in that period.Behr's second novel, *Embrace* (2000), deals with the formative experiences of a young homosexual.

There are many South African writers worth checking out. Many are still dealing with the legacy of apartheid and the struggle against it, as South Africa finds a new national - and hybrid - identity. One is Zoe Wicomb, whose new novel, *David's Story* (2001, winner of the M-Net Book Prize), interrogates the past and present of an anti-apartheid activist, as does Achmat Dangor's *Bitter Fruit* (2001).

Mike Nicol's first novel, *The Powers That Be* (1989), brought a magic-realist sensibility to South African literature, and his latest, *The Ibis Tapestry* (1998) is a post-modern take on the secrets of South Africa's apartheid abuses. Among Afrikaans writers now translated into English, notable works have come from Etienne van Heerden, particularly the marvellous *Ancestral Voices* (1989), and from Marlene Van Niekerk, with the hilarious and horrifying *Triomf* (1994).

Phaswane Mpe's *Welcome to Our Hillbrow* (2001) is a critically acclaimed view of the physical and moral decay in both the rural areas of Tiragalong and the urban ghetto of Hillbrow. Kgafela wa Magogodi is a poet who probes issues such as Aids in his collection *Thy Condom Come* (2000).

8

Literature of Singapore

The literature of Singapore comprises a collection of literary works by Singaporeans in any of the country's four main languages: English, Chinese, Malay and Tamil. While Singaporean literary works may be considered as also belonging to the literature of their specific languages, the literature of Singapore is viewed as a distinct body of literature portraying various aspects of Singapore society and forms a significant part of the culture of Singapore. A number of Singaporean writers such as Tan Swie Hian and Kuo Pao Kun have contributed work in more than one language. However, this cross-linguistic fertilisation is becoming increasingly rare and it is now increasingly thought that Singapore has four sub-literatures instead of one.

Literature in English

The immigrant cultures, and especially the Baba Chinese, were the earliest to use English for creative purposes in the Malaya peninsula. But poetic traditions were slow in taking root because immigrant populations were generally intent on more pragmatic needs. Sporadic attempts at writing poetry in English began in the late 1940s, but Singapore's most prominent poet, Edwin Thumboo, could still feel in 1970 that 'although we have had the language for 150 years we continue to be embarrassed by the fact that we have not produced any writers of the first rank' (Thumboo, 1970, p.2). While literature in Chinese worked on ethnic themes which kept alive associations with the parent country, and Malay literature pursued a nationalist policy, English offered itself as a liberating possibility. The earliest poetry was motivated by the nationalist ideal of a Malayan consciousness. Here is a brief example from Wang Gungwu, whose *Pulse* (1950) was the first volume of poetry in English from the region:

> Thoughts of Camford fading,
> Contentment creeping in;
> Allah had been kind;
> Orang puteh has been kind.
> Only yesterday his brother said,
> 'Can get lagi satu wife lah!'
> Ahmad was educated;
> The education was complete. —(Brewster, 1989, p.4)

Wang Gungwu and others of that generation could not reconcile the contradiction 'between our search for Malayan poetry and our decision to base that search on English forms' and gave up poetry. This experimental search for a localised poetic idiom was called Engmalchin, a portmanteau word standing for a linguistic mix of English with Malaya and Chinese. The only style it could sustain was self-conscious and limited: 'borrowed visions... in colonised hearts' as Thumboo later remarked. But it did lead to a kind of verbal ventriloquism, rich in sociological detail. Ee Tiang Hongs's 'Song of a Young Malayan', and the Singlish of Arthur Yap's '2 mothers in a hdb playground' are examples of the best that could be achieved in later extensions of this mode. The next generation of poets was oriented towards a symbolist and mythopoeic poetry, as in the case of Wong Phui Nam, of whom the Malaysian critic Lloyd Fernando wrote in 1969 that he had been able 'to get to grips with - rather than moan about - the detribalisation anxiety that has dogged the Malaysian writer for years'.

From the late 1950s onwards, the production of poetry in Malaysia and Singapore has been closely associated with institutions of higher learning, through journals, undergraduate friendships, and sponsorship. The University of Malaya was founded in 1949; in 1961 it split into two, the campus in Singapore becoming the University of Singapore, renamed National University of Singapore in 1981. The university provided young poets their first opportunity for publication, in journals (*The Cauldron* (1947-49), *The New Cauldron* (1949-60), *The Malayan Undergrad* 1951-7), *Write* (1957-8); and anthologies (*Litmus One* (1957), *30 Poems* (1958), followed by many others). The journals *Tenggara* (1967-) from Kuala Lumpur, and *Commentary* (1962-) and *Focus/* (1968-) from Singapore continue the tradition, supported later by the government with Singa.

Tertiary educational institutions have played a considerable role in the production and promotion of poetry in Singapore. Many individuals have contributed to shaping poetry in the region, chief among them Edwin Thumboo. The most visible part of what has been a many-sided contribution is the set of canon-forming anthologies he has edited (*The Flowering Tree* 1970, *Seven Poets* 1973, *The Second Tongue* 1976, *Anthology of ASEAN Literatures* 1985, and *Journeys*

1995). Singapore also has an industrious tradition of local criticism by writers/academics, supplemented by the steady interest of expatriates as well as academics from Australia and New Zealand. Thumboo's autobiographical essay (will give the student a first-hand account of how a poet has to strive very consciously to develop his own voice when using the legacy of an ex-colonial language. Comparisons between his views and those of Ee and Wong show how deeply poets have been preoccupied with the advantages and disadvantages attendant upon their poetic choices and decisions. Writers not represented here also have much of interest to offer in this connection, and the interested student will want to explore their work independently. The starting point for any such work should be Gene Tan's bibliography (1994), and the anthology of writings by Singaporean women compiled by Leong Liew Geok (1998).

Poetry

Singaporean literature in English started with the Straits-born Chinese community in the colonial era; it is unclear which was the first work of literature in English published in Singapore, but there is evidence of Singapore literature published as early as the 1830s. The first notable Singaporean work of poetry in English is possibly *F.M.S.R.*, a pastiche of T.S. Eliot by Francis P. Ng, published in London in 1935. This was followed by Wang Gungwu's *Pulse* in 1950.

With the independence of Singapore in 1965, a new wave of Singapore writing emerged, led by Edwin Thumboo, Arthur Yap, Robert Yeo, Goh Poh Seng, Lee Tzu Pheng and Chandran Nair. It is telling that many critical essays on Singapore literature name Thumboo's generation, rightly or wrongly, as the first generation of Singapore writers. Poetry is the predominant mode of expression; it has a small but respectable following since independence, and most published works of Singapore writing in English have been in poetry.

There were varying levels of activity in succeeding decades, with poets in the late 1980s and early 1990s including Simon Tay, Leong Liew Geok, Koh Buck Song, Heng Siok Tian and Ho Poh Fun. In the late 1990s, poetry in English in Singapore found a new momentum with a whole new generation of poets born around or after 1965 now actively writing and publishing, not only in Singapore but also internationally. Since the late-1990s, local small presses such as Firstfruits and Ethos Books have been actively promoting the works of this new wave of poets. Some of the more notable include Boey Kim Cheng, Yong Shu Hoong, Alvin Pang, Cyril Wong, Felix Cheong and Alfian bin Sa'at (also a playwright). The poetry of this younger generation is often politically aware, transnational and cosmopolitan, yet frequently presents their intensely focused, self-questioning and highly individualised perspectives of Singaporean life, society and culture. Some poets have been labeled Confessional for their personalised writing, often dealing with intimate issues such as sexuality.

Drama

Drama in English found expression in Goh Poh Seng, who was also a notable poet and novelist, in Robert Yeo, author of 6 plays, and in Kuo Pao Kun, who also wrote in Chinese, sometimes translating his works into English. The late Kuo was a vital force in the local theatre renaissance in the 1980s and 1990s. He was the artistic director of Substation for many years. Some of his plays, like *The Coffin is Too Big for the Hole* (1984) and *Lao Jiu* (1990), have been now considered classics. Stella Kon gained international fame with her now-famous play *Emily of Emerald Hill: a monologue*. About an ageing Peranakan matriarch, it has been produced in Scotland, Malaysia and Australia. The sole character has been played by men as well as women.

Fiction

Fiction writing in English did not start in earnest until after independence. Short stories flourished as a literary form, the novel arrived much later. Goh Poh Seng remains a pioneer in writing novels well before many of the later generation, with titles like *If We Dream Too Long* (1972) – widely recognised as the first true Singaporean novel – and *A Dance of Moths* (1995).

Beginning as a short story writer, Penang-born Catherine Lim has been Singapore's most widely read author, thanks partly to her first two books of short stories, *Little Ironies: Stories of Singapore* (1978) and *Or Else, The Lightning God and Other Stories* (1980). These two books were incorporated as texts for the GCE 'O' Levels. Lim's themes of Asian male chauvinistic gender-dominance mark her as a distant cousin to Asian-American writers such as Amy Tan. She has also been writing novels, such as *The Bondmaid* (1998) and *Following the Wrong God Home* (2001), and publishing them to an international audience since the late 1990s.

Han May is the pseudonym of Joan Hon who is better known for her non-fiction books. Her science-fiction romance *Star Sapphire* (1985) won a High Commendation Award from the Book Development Council of Singapore in 1986, the same year when she was also awarded a Commendation prize for her better-known book *Relatively Speaking* on her family and childhood memories.

Rex Shelley hails from an earlier colonial generation, although he began publishing only in the early 1990s. A Eurasian, his first novel *The Shrimp People* (1991) examines the regional Eurasian community and their experience in Singapore. The book won a National Book Prize. His three other novels, *People of the Pear Tree* (1993), *Island in the Centre* (1995) and *River of Roses* (1998) all examine similar themes of the Eurasian community in the Southeast Asia region. He has won the S.E.A. Write Award in 2007.

Su-Chen Christine Lim's works consider varied themes surrounding issues of gender, immigration and orthodoxy. In 1993, her novel, *Fistful of Colours,* was awarded the first Singapore Literature Prize. Her other novels take up the relationship between the Malays and Chinese immigrants in colonial Malaya, and the issue of land (*A Bit of Earth*).

Gopal Baratham, a neurosurgeon, started as a short story writer and later wrote politically-charged works like *A Candle or the Sun* (1991) and *Sayang* (1991), which courted some controversy when they were first published.

Augustine Goh Sin Tub who began his writing career writing in Malay, burst on the literary scene after his retirement with more than a dozen books of short stories, most of which were founded on his own personal history, thus making them part fiction and part non-fiction. Works like *One Singapore* and its two sequels *One Singapore 2* and *One Singapore 3* have found fans among the different strata of Singapore society and well acclaimed by all.

Around this time, younger writers emerged. Claire Tham and Ovidia Yu wrote short stories, while playwright Stella Kon put forth her lesser-known science-fiction novel, *Eston* (1995). Of the younger generation, Philip Jeyaretnam has shown promise but has not published a new novel since *Abraham's Promise* (1995). His first two books, *First Loves* (1987) and *Raffles Place Ragtime* (1988), were bestsellers in Singapore.

Kelvin Tan, a musician and playwright, has been sporadically in sight, publishing the works *All Broken Up and Dancing* (1992) and the *Nethe(r);* (2001). Colin Cheong can perhaps lay claim to being one of Singapore's most prolific contemporary authors, releasing three novels, one novella, two short story collections, and dozens of non-fictional works thus far. He won the Singapore Literature Prize in 1996 for his travel diary-like novel *Tangerine*. Daren Shiau's *Heartland* (1999) traces an eighteen-year-old's rites of passage from junior college through to enlistment and thereafter. The novel has been selected to be a set text at secondary school level.

Hwee Hwee Tan graduated with a First Class Honours from the University of East Anglia, and a Masters from Oxford University. She grew up in Singapore and in the Netherlands, and her cosmopolitan experience can be readily seen in her novels. Her snazzy, humorous prose can be read in *Foreign Bodies* (1997) and *Mammon Inc.* (2001), both published by Penguin Books. Simon Tay, currently the chairperson of Singapore Institute of International Affairs and a former nominated Member of Parliament, has a short story collection and a novel under his belt. These are *Stand Alone* (1991) and *City of Small Blessings* (2009).

Short Story

Singapore is a cosmopolitan Asian city, unique in that there are four major language groups promoted by the government. From the very beginning, English was chosen as the language of government, law and social discourse. Being the native language of none of the ethnic groups, its choice favoured none. The presence of the different ethnic communities with their strong cultural identities and heritage suggests that the influence they exert over the development of Singapore literature cannot be insignificant. Chinese literature dates more than 3,000 years while the classic Hindu tales of *Mahabarata* and *Ramayana* are well-known, passed from generation to generation and transplanted to the alien soil of Singapore, both by merchants who travelled to these regions in the 14th century as well as through the influx of migrant workers well into the 19th and 20 century. Further add to this rich mixture, Malay culture which has seen the integration of Portuguese and Dutch language and culture from its earliest colonial influences and the strong sway of Islam.

Yet, in the early history of Singapore literature, the threads of each literature developed very separately from each other. The Singapore short story written in Chinese in the sixties and early seventies had probably more in common with one written in Hong Kong in the same language. The Singapore short story written in English drew from Maupassant and Poe rather than reflected the rich cultural ethnicity of its populace. There was consequently no 'borrowing' between the ethnic languages to express the commonality of a Singapore identity. What is significant is that Singapore literature in each distinct language community individually faced the challenge of defining what that culture is in the context of an newly adopted homeland and coming to terms with change.

The short story written in English had its obscure beginnings in the then-University of Singapore. There, the first generations educated at tertiary level in the English medium began to experiment with the mode of expression of the short story. The first published record of the short story in English in Singapore was in 1959; *The Compact*, edited by Herman Hochstadt represented incipient efforts of local writers to produce a volume of stories in the English medium.

It was in 1978, in the introduction to the seminal *Singapore Short Stories*, Volumes I and II, the editor Robert Yeo observed that if the published output of short stories is compared to that of poetry in English in the same period, it will be seen that there are fewer writers of short fiction than there are poets. Nearly a dozen individual collections have been published but no book of short stories by a single author has appeared.

In the interim, there were only two other significant attempts to promote the short story form. These were *Stories from Africa and Asia*, edited by Chandran Nair and Theo Luzuka, and *The Sun In Her Eyes: Stories by Singapore Women*, edited by Geraldine Heng. These two collections were said to have registered the start of a "concerted effort in making the short story assimilate the Singapore life and locale."

Within the same year of publication of *Singapore Short Stories*, a modest volume of short stories made its mark on the local literary scene. *Little Ironies: Stories of Singapore* by Catherine Lim sold 3,000 copies on the local market within six months. This naturally rendered Yeo's earlier assertion untrue; this was the first collection of "short stories by a single author." Soon, other writers such as Goh Sin Tub, Lim Thean Soo and Gopal Baratham formed the wave of writers issuing collections of their works.

Today, the acceptance of Singapore short story in English as a unique genre is unquestioned. Little Ironies has since sold well over 45,000 copies and undergone ten reprints. It has been accepted by Cambridge Examinations Syndicate as the text for the General Certificate of Education, Ordinary Level Examinations. Lim has published seven collections of short stories to date. Her second book, *Or Else the Lightning God... & Other Stories* is also studied in schools and her other books have found their way into required reading lists.

Demand for collections of locally written short stories has also led to the re-issue of collections. Early anthologies by Gopal Baratham, Goh Sin Tub and Nicky Moey have been reprinted under new titles. Wong Swee Hoon's *The Landlord & Other Stories*, first published in 1984, was reissued in 1991 under the title *A Dying Breed* and included three new stories. Philip Jeyaretnam, then a relative newcomer to the literary scene, amazed literary circles when his debut collection, *First Loves*, clung to the top position of the "*Times* Best Sellers" List of Books for a record of more than forty weeks.

The significance of Jeyaretnam's achievement and that of his fellow writers marks the change of perception of local writing. Where once local literature had a less than popular following and there were prejudices regarding styles and standards of writing, the rising volume of sales of short story collections is the best indicator of an increasing acceptance of literary works locally written and published.

Perhaps the greatest achievement of Singapore literature of the first decade is the documenting of the growth of a national identity, a culture which could be marked as "Singaporean". It is interesting to note that as the literature developed, it strengthened the consciousness of what Singaporean means. To a great extent, Singapore literature has not been merely a reflector of this growing awareness. It has given the emergence of a national identity a certain impetus by disseminating these ideas.

1988 marked a landmark year for the short story in English with the publication of both *0, Singapore! Stories in Celebration* and *First Loves*. In the years that have followed "First Loves", there has been a noticeable increase in interest in all forms of local literature. The number of publication titles has escalated in every literary genre; whether it be the short story, novel, poetry anthologies and drama.

Two separate strains emerged from the single root that was planted in that first decade. What is common to both is the striving towards a greater sense of the universal rather than the local. Unlike the anthologies of the first decade which sought to locate the Singaporean within the context of his own community, the new anthologies seek to establish the Singaporean as part of a larger world community. As a result, one of the key concerns is the need to confront change.

The first strain is essentially an continuation of the mainstream which was established in the first decade of publishing. Woo Keng Thye and Lim Thean Soo both continued to produce anthologies well into the decade following the first. Nalla Tan, whose short stories appeared in *The Sun In Her Eyes* and *Singapore Short Stories*, Volume I produced a substantial collection of short stories entitled, *Hearts & Crosses* while in 1992, Singapore's most prolific short story writer, Catherine Lim brought out two collections published within the same year, *Deadline for Love & Other Stories* and *The Woman's Book of Superlatives*. Both women writers explore the fragile relationships between men and women, exploiting the familiar language and narrative structure of their earlier stories. However, the difference is significant, in that both writers raised the problems of women who were fast adapting to a modern environment and yet trapped within the social confines of their traditions and culture. The stories reflect the ongoing dilemma of the modern woman in Asian society where the society has changed dramatically but her own situation is not changing quickly enough.

Along with the established writers who continued to write, there have been a number of new writers. There have been some remarkable collections of note, amongst them, *Fascist Rock: Stories of Rebellion*, a debut collection for young Singaporean Claire Tham. The common theme that runs through its stories is the rigidity of society's demands and her protagonists fight against these established systems in various ways. True to O'Connor's dictum that the short story "attracts" the "outlaws'. of society, Tham's protagonists are essentially social misfits. Tham shows a dear understanding of the teenage mind. This may be because Tham wrote most of the stories in the anthology when she was seventeen years of age. She shows an admirable command of the written language, a quality which immediately brought her to the attention of the judges of the National Short Story Competition in 1984. Dr Kirpal Singh, then Senior Lecturer in the National University of Singapore, describes how he was struck by her vigour; a sense of life comes powerfully across... She is obviously well read and has a good command of the language... But the dialogues tend to sound false because of the formality of the expressions. It is as if she is afraid to record true conversations for fear of breaking grammatical rules. For example, there are no Singaporeanisms.

It is significant that Dr Singh takes issue with the "formality of the expression" and the lack of Singaporeanisms. Rather than a negative qualities, they reflect the writer's confident of a wider audience. Tham's ability to express herself well borders on the poetic. Her use of language is her strongest asset in the collection. Nevertheless, *Fascist Rock* was a promising first for this young Singaporean writer. This was followed by *Saving the Rainforest & Other Stories* in 1993 in which she continued to explore themes of the conflict between the individual and conventional society. In this second book, her characters continue to be quirky, rebellious although they seem slightly more adult than those of her first book.

Another young writer Terence Chua plumbs the depths of the imagination in his debut anthology, *Nightmare Factory* (1991). This collection of short stories is hard to categorise. There are elements of fantasy literature, science fiction and the modern fairy tale cleverly interwoven in the narratives. The presence of these elements which are universal in quality gives his stories a sense of timelessness and placelessness. Yet, there is an accompanying sense of familiarity about the experiences each of Chua's protagonists goes through. The book was quietly received, less than it deserved although Chua achieved the capability to locate the Singaporean experience in the universal.

What is also encouraging about new writers such as Tham and Chua is the fact that they have begun writing at a fairly early age. They are not afraid of experimentation, having had basic grounding as they are already famih'ar with craft and technique. Hence, the limits of creativity which marked the first decade have become extended and the vision of the new writers expands in scope and addresses larger issues than those that were seen in the first decade. Concern for deeper issues like morality, justice and equality finds greater expression in the stories of the second generation. One is also able to perceive a greater confidence and outspokenness about the younger writers which is affirmative of the growth of the Singapore short story.

9

Literature of New Zealand

The literature of New Zealand commenced with the oral literature (narratives, songs and chants) of the Maori and expanded into written literature with the arrival of the largely English-speaking colonists. Most New Zealand literary works appear in English, but Mâori publications grow apace.

Histroy of New Zealand Literature

New Zealanders have long been avid readers, but up until the mid-20th century most of the literature they consumed was imported from Britain. Historian and poet Keith Sinclair identified the 1950s as the time 'when the New Zealand intellect and imagination came alive'. This flowering of creative and critical talent was not sudden, but the climax of a process that had begun at least two decades before.

By the 1930s a new breed of New Zealand writers was emerging, assisted by the growth of universities and small publishing enterprises. The New Zealand centennial in 1940 provided a further boost to the local literary scene, and later that decade a state Literary Fund was established. By the 1950s there was a wider range of outlets for creative writing, including the influential magazine *Landfall*. New voices in poetry and drama were generating heated debate over identity and politics, while writers of novels, short stories, children's and popular fiction were also finding new audiences.

The 1930s saw the emergence in New Zealand of a new breed of writers, whose work usually embodied a reaction against established ideas and conventions. Often these writers were influenced by recent trends in literature overseas, notably modernism; and by social and political events such as the Depression.

A growing, if narrow, sense of nationalism was expressed, focussing on the dilemma of Pakeha who still looked to England as 'Home', but increasingly identified with New Zealand through ties of kinship and daily experience. Some major literary figures of the thirties, including short story writer Frank Sargeson, poets Allen Curnow, A.R.D. Fairburn, Denis Glover and R.A.K. Mason, and Glover's printer associate Bob Lowry, remained active in the 1940s and 50s.

University Influence

During the decade some significant changes occurred in the literary scene. More and more, those engaged in literary pursuits began to be associated with academia, rather than journalism as had previously been the case. Several magazines publishing new writing were founded by university staff and students; the most prominent of these was Phoenix, an Auckland University publication. The influential Christchurch periodical, Tomorrow, received strong university support.

Growth of Publishing

It became somewhat easier for New Zealand writers to be published. Several innovative small publishing enterprises, notably the Caxton Press in Christchurch, and the Unicorn Press in Auckland, provided alternatives to the mainstream local firms of Whitcombe and Tombs and A.H. & A.W. Reed. And the New Zealand Listener, which developed into an important forum for debate and creative writing, was established in 1939. The first Labour Government's support for literature and scholarship was shown in funding for a series of historical and critical publications to mark the country's centennial in 1940; this provided recognition as well as employment for a number of writers, historians and critics.

The War Years

In some ways war interrupted the work of New Zealand writers; in others it acted as a stimulant. For those who joined the armed forces, such as Eric McCormick, Bruce Mason and Dan Davin, experience of travel and danger gave creative impetus and a new perspective on their country of birth. New Zealand writing gained some international exposure through John Lehmann's Penguin New Writing from 1941.

New Zealand New Writing, a local adaptation of this publication produced between 1942 and 1945, was another vehicle for fresh talent. The belief that New Zealand culture was worthy of serious comment was behind a burst of critical writing, beginning in 1940 with the publication of Eric McCormick's ground-breaking survey Letters and Art in New Zealand. This was closely followed by a wide-ranging series of essays by Monte Holcroft, the first of which was entitled The Deepening Stream.

Post-war Developments

With peace came a sense of renewal and some crucial innovations that helped literature to flourish. New Zealand universities began to expand rapidly after the war, and once again, they proved havens for writers. The University of New Zealand also began publishing books in 1949. A controversial but significant move, championed by influential public servant Joe Heenan, was the establishment in 1946 of a government Literary Fund to provide writers with financial assistance.

New Outlets for Writing

Pre-war publishing enterprises, notably the Caxton Press, were revived, and new ones began, for instance the Paul's Book Arcade imprint of Blackwood Paul. Once Monte Holcroft took over the editorship of the Listener in 1949 even more creative writing was featured, and Maori writers were encouraged by the establishment of *Te Ao Hou* in the early fifties. But possibly the most momentous event was the founding by poet and editor Charles Brasch of Landfall. This quarterly journal, which first appeared in 1947, came to dominate literary life, though a number of other small magazines were soon set up in competition with it.

Poetry

The forties and fifties were favourable times for poets and poetry, and lively communities of poets sprang up in the main centres, particularly Wellington and Auckland. Debate about the nature of poetry led to some heated exchanges.

Allen Curnow's anthology, A book of New Zealand verse 1923–45, provoked a reaction from emerging poets such as James K. Baxter, Louis Johnson and Kendrick Smithyman, who objected to what they saw as Curnow's insistence on a nationalist agenda for poetry. They argued that New Zealand poets, now secure in their identity, should express themselves on universal themes in an international context. A related viewpoint was that New Zealand poetry should move on from expressing alienation and isolation and develop a more confident vision of nationhood, inclusive of Maori. Underlying the positions was a tension between modernist and romantic approaches to poetry.

The debate was advanced by a passionate speech at the 1951 Writers Conference in Christchurch by James K. Baxter, who claimed pre-eminence for the Wellington group of poets, which included himself, Alistair Campbell, W.H. Oliver, Louis Johnson and Hubert Witheford. Sparring continued throughout the fifties.

Publication opportunities for poets were plentiful: the Year Book of the Arts in New Zealand series began in 1945, continuing until 1951 when it was succeeded by New Zealand Poetry Yearbook. The 1956 Anthology of New Zealand Verse, compiled by Robert Chapman and Jonathan Bennett, published many of the younger poets whom Curnow had overlooked in his 1945 anthology, including some new women poets, for instance Mary Stanley. However others such as Ruth France (who used the pen name Paul Henderson), found it difficult to make their voices heard in a male-dominated literary milieu.

Drama

The depression and advent of 'talkies' in the late 1920s brought an end to the regular tours of New Zealand by British and American professional theatre companies, and thereafter a thriving local amateur dramatic movement emerged. Isabella Andrews was one of a number of playwrights who achieved success during the 1930s and 40s through the original play competitions of the New Zealand branch of the British Drama League. In the same period, the rise of left theatre groups provided opportunities for writers with radical political sympathies.

Although prominent figures such as Charles Brasch, James K. Baxter and Frank Sargeson wrote plays, the best-known playwright of the fifties was Bruce Mason. He addressed the question of cultural identity by exploring Maori themes and the disintegration of traditional values. In an era when professional theatre was tentative, Mason pioneered the solo performance and also contributed to the development of radio drama in New Zealand.

Novel and Short Story

Much fiction of the forties and fifties concentrated on the trials of an isolated individual in a hostile, puritanical society. This theme mirrored the actual struggle of many New Zealand fiction writers to make a living and achieve acceptance. Among those who produced significant novels were expatriates Dan Davin and James Courage, and younger writers including David Ballantyne, Ruth France and Janet Frame. Although Frank Sargeson's 'realist' narrative style with its blunt New Zealand idioms dominated, some fiction writers experimented with impressionism to convey the intensity of individual experience. Maurice Duggan transcended realist conventions in his short stories, drawing on a wide range of textual models, while Helen Shaw was one of several women short story writers who broke free of the prevailing focus on masculine concerns and pursuits.

Writing for Children

In the 1940s the School Journals produced by the School Publications Branch of the Department of Education changed in character to focus entirely on high-quality fiction. Many writers had their first stories published in the Journals, and some of the most prominent, including James K. Baxter, Maurice Duggan and Louis Johnson, were editors. However, the best-known children's stories of the 1950s, the Hutu and Kawa series by Avis Acres, achieved their popularity largely through enchanting illustrations.

Popular Fiction

Thrillers, romances and other popular writing presented an interesting counterpoint to the concerns of 'serious' fiction. Often these genres supported positive stereotypes about New Zealand and New Zealanders and deliberately avoided analysis of social and political issues, in a calculated attempt to appeal to both a local and international audience. This tradition, which had taken root in the thirties with the work of Nelle Scanlan, Rosemary Rees, Mary Scott and Ngaio Marsh, was carried on by romance novelist Essie Summers and crime novelist Elizabeth Messenger.

By the end of the 1950s, favourable conditions for New Zealand literature had been largely achieved. The time was ripe for emerging writers to challenge, subvert and transcend the concepts of nationhood which had been formulated in the previous decades.

Famous Writers

The confluence of Mâori and settler experiences led to the development of a rich literature. Writers from various cultural backgrounds, such as novelists Patricia Grace, Albert Wendt, Maurice Gee and children's author Margaret Mahy, are prominent in New Zealand.

Keri Hulme gained prominence when her novel, *The Bone People,* won the Booker Prize. Witi Ihimaera wrote the novel that became the critically acclaimed movie *Whale Rider,* directed by Nikki Caro. His works deal with Mâori life in the modern world, often incorporating fantastic elements.

New Zealand poetry began with Mâori songs (*waiata*) and the shouted lyrics of haka. *Ngâ Môteatea* is an important body of traditional song lyrics compiled by Sir Apirana Ngata. With the arrival of printing presses and the evangelisation of existing inhabitants, Mâori oral traditions gave way to English. New Zealand poetry after colonisation was modeled upon pre-existing English poetic forms and sentiments.Today, most New Zealand poetry published by the major publishers subscribes to a comprehensibly prosaic approach. New Zealand has a lively community of playwrights in theatre. One of the country's most significant and successful playwrights is Roger Hall. Support for playwrights and plays in New Zealand is provided by Playmarket, a national organisation which also publishes and sells plays and scripts. Playmarket also represents Mâori and Pacific Island playwrights.

10

Pakistani Literature: Evolution and Trends

Pakistan literature, that is, the literature of Pakistan, as a distinct literature that gradually came to be defined after Pakistan gained nationhood status in 1947, emerging out of the Indian English Literature tradition. The shared tradition of Urdu literature and English literature of India was inherited by the new state. Over a period of time a body of literature unique to Pakistan has emerged in nearly all major Pakistani languages, including Urdu, English, Punjabi, Balochi, Pushto and Sindhi.

History

The nature of Pakistani literature soon after independence aroused controversy among writers due to its being centered heavily on the negative events related to the India-Pakistan partition. Pakistani literature was expected to take a new direction along with the new state of Pakistan at this point, but did not immediately meet this expectation.

Saadat Hassan Manto (1912-1955), a prominent writer of short stories of the South Asia, produced great literature out of the events relating to the India-Pakistan independence. His literature is considered to be progressive in its tone and spirit. According to several critics it had not only evolved its own identity, but also had played a significant role in documenting the hardships and hopes of Pakistan in the latter part of the 20th century.

Today, Pakistani literature has taken a shape of its own by depicting the complex class system and common man. Contemporary authors such as. It also has evolved in merging Urdu literary forms and English literature leading to experimentation. Many writers of fiction borrow from English and vice versa. Pakistani literature's main platform is the Pakistan Academy of Letters, chaired by Iftikhar Arif.

Pakistani Poetry

Pakistan has a rich and diverse tradition of poetry. This tradition partakes of Urdu poetry, Pakistan's national language and the regional languages of Pakistan including Sindhi poetry, Pashto poetry, Punjabi poetry, Saraiki poetry, Baluchi Poetry, and Kashmiri poetry. Sufi poetry known as Sufiana Kalam has a strong tradition in Pakistan and the poetry of popular Sufi poets is often recited and sung.

Persian poetry, is still common in Pakistan because of the centuries of Persian influence on the region. Many sufi poets wrote their Kalam in Persian. Pakistan's national poet Allama Mohammad Iqbal also wrote many volumes of poetry in Persian.

Poetry is widely read across Pakistan. Gatherings for thr recitations of poetry known as Mushaira frequently take place. Verses of popular poets are also used as political slogans by political activists.

Pakistan is a country known for its love for its tradition and family oriented individuals. Because of this, poetry that speaks of love, passion and religion make up the lives of many Pakistanis.

Urdu, the official language in Pakistan together with English is the most widely used language in the whole country. Although there are other languages, most of the people in the urban area use Urdu.

A large collection of Islamic and Sharia literature are originally written in Urdu before other languages. Translations and interpretation of Qur'an are also written in Urdu.

The language therefore has a large following; it is also used as an official language in areas of India. In reality however, Urdu is in contract with Hindi.

In Poetry, Urdu sit he premier language for the South Asia and has rich traditional variety in poetic genres.

Subjective poetry called Ghazal is written in Urdu. Popular poets such as Mir, Ghalib, Dagh and Faiz all use Ghazal. On the narrative, descriptive and didactic purposes, Nazm in Urdu is used. Masnavi, a variation of Urdu is used for romantic and religious poetry. Marsia, on the other hand is used to commemorate the martyrdom of Hazard Imam Hussain, the grandson of Prophet Muhammad. Other variations of Urdu used in poetry include the following:

- Diwan
- Doha
- Geet
- Hamd
- Kalam

- Kulyat
- Musaddas
- Muhammas
- Naat
- Qasida
- Qat'a
- Rubai
- Sehra
- Soz

Urdu is one language that will give you them understanding that love, religion and tradition will give you a blessed future. You may only need to learn to love your predecessors and Urdu as your language.

Urdu is sometimes called the language of the army because of its past. The term Urdu came from the Turkic word army or tent. This word helped Indians relate to the soldiers because Urdu comes abridging several languages. It makes them understood in some extent without causing problem with other nationalities. Urdu remains spoken by various countries. Thus, the literatures written in Urdu are easily translatable to other language. It makes writing poetry in Urdu worthy of your time.

Pakistani Literature in English

English language fiction from Pakistan began to receive international recognition in the latter part of the 20th century, pioneered by figures such as Bapsi Sidhwa, the Parsi author of *The Crow Eaters, Cracking India* (1988) and other novels. In the diaspora, Sara Suleri published the literary memoir, *Meatless Days* (1989), Hanif Kureshi commenced a prolific career with the novel *The Buddha of Suburbia* (1990), which won the Whitbread Award, and Aamer Hussein wrote a series of acclaimed short story collections.

In the early years of the 21st century, a number of Pakistani novelists writing in English won or were shortlisted for international awards. Mohsin Hamid published his first novel *Moth Smoke* (2000), which won a Betty Trask Award and was a finalist for the PEN/Hemingway Award; he has since published his second novel, *The Reluctant Fundamentalist* (2007), which was shortlisted for the Man Booker Prize. Kamila Shamsie was shorlisted for the John Llewelyn Rhys award for her third novel, *Kartography* (2002); she has since published her fourth novel, *Broken Verses.*

Uzma Aslam Khan was shortlisted for the Commonwealth Writers Prize (Eurasia region) for her second novel, *Trespassing* (2003). British-Pakistani writer Nadeem Aslam won the Kuriyama Prize for his second book, *Maps for Lost Lovers* (2004). The first novel of Mohammed Hanif, *A Case of Exploding Mangoes* (2008) was shortlisted for the 2008 Guardian First Book Award. Emerging authors Kamila Shamsie and Daniyal Mueenuddin have garnered world wide attention.

In 1967 the expatriate Zulfikar Ghose published the riveting The Murder of Aziz Khan. This was the first cohesive, modern English novel written by a writer of Pakistani origin. The plot about a poor Punjab farmer destroyed by a group of industrialists, though fiction, was so close to the bone, that the chattering classes were abuzz, speculating "who-was-who". Ghose's remaining novels were set in South America, his wife's country and few reached Pakistan. However, his poetry appeared in the first two major anthologies of Pakistani English writing: First Voices (1965) which also included the young Taufiq Rafat; and Pieces Eight (1971) which introduced Adrian Husain, Nadir Hussein, Salman Tarik Kureshi and Kaleem Omar.

Over the next few years, the number of Pakistani English language writers grew rapidly. Adam Zameenzad published four novels and won a first novel award, as did Hanif Kureishi, while Nadeem Aslam won two. Tariq Ali embarked on a Communist trilogy, and an Islam quintet; Bapsi Sidhwa received a prize in Germany, an award in the USA, and published her fourth novel The American Brat (1993). Zulfikar Ghose, who had written around 10 accomplished novels, brought out the intricate and complex The Triple Mirror of the Self about migration and a man's quest for identity, across four continents.

Since 2001, Pakistani English literature has come into its own. Uzma Aslam Khan and Mohsin Hamid have made spectacular debuts too. Saad Ashraf, Sorayya Khan and Feryal Ali Gauhar have published accomplished new novels. However Pakistani women, who chose English as a creative vehicle, occupy a unique space. They must constantly challenge stereotypes imposed on them as women and as writers by the patriarchal narratives and cultures of both English and Pakistani literatures.

Saraiki Literature

Saraiki literature is the literature of the Saraiki language (sometimes written as Siraiki) which is mostly spoken in central Pakistan. Saraiki is the most widely spoken language in Pakistan and the first language of more than 120 million people in the

World. Among those 80 Million are in Pakistan (2008). It has a very rich culture and is the representative language of Sindh Valley Civilization.

The main Saraiki speaking areas are Multan, Bahawalpur, Dera Ghazi Khan, Dera Ismail Khan and most parts of Sargodha division. Saraiki is also spoken widely in Sindh and Baluchistan provinces of Pakistan. It has many sweet dialects and is considered as the language of love.

Saraiki is the language of love and literature. Rich cultural context and diversity of expression in the language have enabled Saraiki poets and prose writers to produce literature masterpieces. Saraiki poetry has different themes. Love for beloved and love for land can be identified as major ones. Sufi poets have used this language not only to speak to people but also to God. Saraiki people have a natural flair for poetry and literature. Most of the Saraiki literature is unrecorded for the reason that no formal patronage has been provided to poets and writers. Before the inception of Pakistan, Saraiki was written in Devnagri script and converting to Arabic/ Persian script resulted in the loss of a substantial part of literature.

During last two centuries, Saraiki motherland has produced a lot of legendary poets. Khawaja Ghulam Farid, Sachal Sar Mast and Shah Latif are some of famous Saraiki poets which are known world wide for their universal message of love.History Of Saraiki This is the first web site about Saraiki language and culture on World Wide Web to promote Saraiki language and culture all across the world. Saraiki is the most widely spoken language in Pakistan and the first language of more than 110 million people in the subcontinent. Saraiki is the 10th largest language out of more than

6000 languages in the world. It has a very rich culture and is the representative language of Sindh Valley Civilization. The main Saraiki speaking areas are Multan, Bahawalpur, Dera Ghazi Khan, Dera Ismail Khan and most parts of Sargodha division. Saraiki is also spoken widely in Sindh and Baluchistan provinces of Pakistan. It has many sweet dialects and is considered as the language of love.

Saraiki is the language of love and literature. Rich cultural context and diversity of expression in the language have enabled Saraiki poets and prose writers to produce literature masterpieces. Saraiki poetry has different themes. Love for beloved and love for land can be identified as major ones. Sufi poets have used this language not only to speak to people but also to God. Saraiki people have a natural flair for poetry and literature.

Most of the Saraiki literature is unrecorded for the reason that no formal patronage has been provided to poets and writers. Before the inception of Pakistan, Saraiki was written in Devnagri script and converting to Arabic/ Persian script resulted in the loss of a substantial part of literature.During last two centuries, Saraiki motherland has produced a lot of legendary poets. Khawaja Ghulam Farid, Sachal Sarmast and Shah Abdul Latif Bhittai are some of famous Saraiki poets which are known world wide for their universal message of love.

Poetry

Historically, the most celebrated poet in the Saraiki language is Khawaja Farid (1845–1901). His poems were written in a form of verse known as Kafi, a form rooted in a tradition of singing of poetry. Kafi should unite sound, imagery, feeling and subject matter. The following is an English translation of a few lines of one of Farid's poems:

> The beloved's intense glances call for blood
>
> The dark hair wildly flows The Kohl of the eyes is fiercely black
>
> And slays the lovers with no excuse
>
> My appearance in ruins, I sit and wait
>
> While the beloved has settled in Malheer I feel the sting of the cruel dart
>
> My heart the, abode of pain and grief A life of tears, I have led Farid

In Sindh, the most famous poet of Saraiki is Sachal Sarmast (1739–1829), the well known poet of seven languages. Recently, the famous sufi poet Hazrat Pir Mitha has also written a vast collection of religious poetry in Saraiki. Of the contemporary poets, most notables are 'Ashoo Lal ', ' Rifat Abbas' and 'Mumtaz Haider Daher'.

Saraiki Writings

Since the start of the consciousness raising efforts about common ethnic language in the 1960s, the number of Saraiki publications has increased. Most of the writings from the 1960s to the 1980s were political in nature and are â˜tarnished' with the ethnopolitical aims of the writers.Even though the number of publications has increased in the last and present decade, the Saraiki intellectuals themselves admit that there is not much readership, except perhaps for the works of some renowned contemporary poets, especially of the revolutionary poet Shakir Shujaabadi which sell like hot cakes'. Although writings in all the regional languages are suffering' from lack of readership due to similar reasons, in the case of Saraiki there are two added reasons. Firstly, most of the writers bring in colloquial phraseology (which varies from one variety to the other) in their writings and secondly, many writers, in their zeal to prove the antiquity of Saraiki language and to promote its Indo-Aryan feature, tend to use more Sanskrit words instead of the more common Arabic/Persian words in order to distinguish it from Punjabi and Urdu, thus blocking the understanding of the general readers.

11

History of Sri Lankan Literature

Sri Lankan literature is the literary tradition of Sri Lanka. The largest part of Sri Lankan literature was written in the Sinhala language, but there is a considerable amount of works in other languages used in Sri Lanka over the millennia (including Pâli, Tamil, and English). Up to the present, short stories are a very important part of Sri Lankan literature; the output of Sinhalese short story writers is greater than that of the Tamil and English writers combined and has elicited a greater measure of critical analysis.

Sinhalese Literature

Sinhalese literature dates back to well over 2000 years and is heir to the great Aryan literary tradition as embodied in the hymns of the Rig Veda, collection of Sanskrit verses composed by the ancient Indo Aryans around 1500 B.C.

Vyasa"s Mahabharata, Valmiki"s Ramayana, Kalhana"s Rajatarangini and Somadeva"s Kathasaritsagara are some of the masterpieces belonging to this great literary tradition, not to mention the Panchatantra composed by an anonymous Indian author in about the 3rd century A.C. which is the source of a good many European fairy tales as shown by the German Scholar Johannes Hertel in his "Das Pancatantra" (1914).

There is literary evidence to show that the Mahavansa, the great chronicle of Sinhalese royalty composed in Pali in the 5th century A.C. has drawn heavily from the ancient commentaries in the Sinhala languages known as the Sihalatthakatha.

The German Philologist Wilhelm Geiger has shown in his "Noch einmal Dipavamsa and Mahavansa" that the Mahavansa was based on an old Atthakatha (commentary) composed in old Sinhala prose. This work appears to have comprised of historical records of a religious nature and collections of legends.

These legends dealt with the early beginnings of the Sinhalese nation from a band of Aryan-speaking colonists from Bengal, deeds of the early kings, wars and other matters of historical importance.

The Mahavansa in itself is a literary masterpiece of the highest order. Composed in fine Pali verse, it narrates the adventures of Prince Vijaya, the founding father of the Sinhalese nation, the romantic union of Prince Gamani and Ummada-chittha, the wars waged by their son Pandukabhaya against his ten uncles, the campaigns of King Dutthagamani against the Dravidian invaders, the justice of the Tamil usurper Elara, the insatiable lust of the nymphomaniac Queen Anula and the self-sacrifice of King Sirisangabo, the paragon of Buddhist virtue, amongst other stories.

These wonderful narratives are based on actual fact, though they contain much literary embellishment. The Sinhalese possess a vast corpus of literature both in prose and in verse written in the Sinhalese language. The old literature has been preserved in palm manuscripts (pus-kola) penned with a stylus.

The oldest extant Sinhala prose work we have dates back to the ninth century. This is the Dhampiya-Atuva-Getapadaya, a glossary to the Dhammapada-tthakatha (a Buddhist story book in Pạli) compiled by King Kassapa V (913-923 A.C.) This is not to say that there existed no Sinhala prose work before this period. In fact the commentary to the Mahavansa, Vansatthappakasini, mentions a collection of a thousand stories known as the Sahassavatthu-ppakarana which is now lost to us. It is possible that some of its stories survive in the 14th century Saddharmalankaraya just as the tales of the lost Persian work Hezar efsaneh (thousand stories) survive in the Arabian nights (Alf layla wa layl).

There is reason to believe that the above work was based on some old Sinhala original. Another lost old Sinhala work, the Katha-vasthu is believed to be the source of the Rasavahini, a collection of popular tales in Pali compiled by Vedeha thera. Another early work, the Mahabodhi Getapadaya composed about the 12th century by an anonymous author is a glossary to aid students master the Mahabodhivansa, a history of the sacred Bodhi tree in Pali.

It is evident that many of the early Sinhala prose works were intended as accessories for comprehensive Pali works. Another such example, composed about the same period is the Jataka-Atuva-Getapadaya, a glossary to the Pali Jatakatthakatha which is a commentary of the Jataka tales narrated in connection with the supposed previous births of the Buddha.

However, it is the Polonnaruwa (10th - early 13th centuries) and the Dambadeniya (13th century) periods which mark the efflorescence of Sinhala prose literature. The 13th century is widely considered to be the golden age of Sinhala literature. The Amavatura (lit. flood of nectar) written about 13th century by the Buddhist lay disciple Gurulugomi is one such example. This work deals with the life of Prince Siddhartha Gautama, the founder of Buddhism. Besides, it also narrates a number of other tales connected with the Buddha or the Boddhisattva (as the Buddha is known in his supposed previous incarnations) such as the story of the beautiful Ditthamangalika and the outcaste, the story of King Ajatasatru the parricide and the story Angulimala the highwayman.

Gurulugomi is also credited with the authorship of the Dharmap-radipikava (the lamp of the good doctrine), a commentary to the earlier mentioned Mahabodhivansa. Gurulugomi"s works are characterised by the use of almost pure Sinhala (Elu) words and limiting Sanskrit and Pali loan words to the minimum.

In this respect, it differs considerably from the language of the getapadas (glossaries) which contained a good many Pali and Sanskrit loans. Other 13th century works of a religious character include the Buth-sarana (Refuge in the Buddha) an eulogy in praise of the founder of Buddhism by Vidyachakravarti and the Pujavaliya (Garland of offerings), a collection of Buddhist tales by Mayurapada Buddhaputra. However, none of these surpasses the Saddharma-Ratnavaliya (Garland of the jewels of the good doctrine) a collection of stories meant for the edification of the Buddhist laity by a monk named Dharmasena. This extensive work which has been largely based on the Dharmmapadatthakatha, a collection of Buddhist stories in Pali is renowned for the beauty of its style and the simplicity of its language. The stories of Sundara Samudda, Vasuladatta and of Tissa the fat are the more interesting tales narrated in the work.

The Indian tales " upon which the stories have been based " have been embellished and retold for the Sinhalese reader and therefore reflects contemporary social conditions to a significant extent. Martin Wickremasinghe (purana Sinhala stringe enduma) observes thus: "In the pages of the Saddharama Ratnavaliya are to be seen similes and descriptions which reflects the manners, customs, thoughts and ideas of its day. There is no other Sinhala work so helpful in the investigation of the conditions of the olden day Sinhalese." Other works of the period as well as those works of preceding and succeeding periods, also possess this characteristic. In fact, Prof M. B. Ariyapala (Society in medieval Ceylon 1956) has successfully reconstructed the society and life-style of the Sinhalese as it existed in the 13th century through a detailed study of the Saddharma-Ratnavaliya and other similar works. Another notable medieval prose work is the Saddharmalankaraya (ornament of the good law) composed by Jayabahu Dharmakirti in the 14th century.

The work, like the Saddharma-Ratnavaliya has a moral objective. Amongst other tales, it contains the story of King Dutugemunu (known as Dutthagamani in Pali works) and his exploits against the Dravidian invaders from the Chola country and the romance of his son Prince Sali with an untouchable (Chandala) maiden named Asokamala for whose sake he renounced the throne.

Other notable medieval prose works include the Thupavansaya, Elu-Attanagalu vansaya and the Dambadeni asna. These works may be categorised as historical literature as they mainly deal with the history of Buddhist edifices and relics. From the Kotte period (15th century) until the late 19th century we see a decline of Sinhala prose literature and a resurgence of Sinhala poetry such as war poems (hatan kavi) and message poems (sandeshas) modelled after Kalidasa"s Meghaduta. This is perhaps attributable to the fact that this period was a turbulent one due to wars against successive European colonial powers, namely the Portuguese (1505-1658), Dutch (1658-1796) and British (1796-1815) colonialists.

Such a situation would have naturally been conducive to the growth of poetry in the form of panegyrics and romances. As would have been noticed, the vast majority of the ancient and medieval Sinhalese literary works are of a religious (Buddhist) character.

This is due to the fact that Sinhala scholarship had traditionally been the domain of the clerical establishment, which accounts for the scarcity of good secular works in the language during the olden days.

However, beginning from the late 19th century we notice a surge in secular Sinhala literature. The Sinhala novel also had its beginnings during this period. These include Albert Silva"s Vimala (1892) and Adara Hasuna (1894). Another early novel which gained immense popularity was Simon Silva"s Meena (1905). Other early novelists include Piyadasa Sirisena, Sagara Palansuriya, Munidasa Kumaratunga, Hemapala

Munidasa, W.A. Silva and J.H. Perera. This period also saw the revision of old works on medicine and other subjects of scientific interest. Even such themes as the interpretation of dreams did not go unaddressed as is evident in Hisvelle pandit"s Svapna-malaya (1865). Reputed foreign works were also translated into Sinhala during this period, a notable example being Arabinishollasaya (1891) a translation of the Arabian nights. One of the greatest modern day Sinhala novelists was Martin Wickremasinghe, whose epoch making works Gam peraliya and Yuganthaya appealed to the hearts of a generation that was just beginning to shed the last vestiges of European socio-cultural domination in the island.

Other famous modern novels include Gunadasa Amarasekara"s Yali upannemi and Depa noladdo, Ediriweera Sarachchandra"s Mala-giya ettho and Valmath vi hasarak nudutimi, K. Jayatilleke"s Aprasanna Kathavak and Siri Guna-singhe"s Hevanella.

Sinhalese Poetry

Poetry is the pulse of a nation. It reflects its world view and cultural attainments, its literacy and its romanticism. In short, a nation given to poetry is a cultured nation. The Sinhalese have, of all the arts, excelled in poetry. Sinhala, the language of the Sinhalese, is a poetical language. It lends itself easily to metre and rhyme due to its grammatical flexibility and rich vocabulary comprising of a large number of synonyms. Sinhala itself is a mellifluous language with a high vowel content and is comparable to French and Urdu, widely regarded to be the two most romantic languages in the world. A specimen from a late 18th century poem, the "Kalingabodhi Jataka-Kava", a versified form of the story of Prince Sulukalingu contained in the "Kalingabodhi Jataka", composed by the poet Dunuvila will bear this out. Cited below is a quatrain from the poem describing the prince"s journey to the forest.

> Nil digu varal kusuman benda gothala
> Pul rathu upul mal savanata sadala
> El gevi kal kiyana liyagi asala
> Lol hera giye
> Kumarindu mana pinala

(The prince heard the heart-captivating songs of the pretty women in the fields of rice who had arranged their long flowing hair with flowers and tucked full blossomed red lotuses behind their ears, and went away, full of joy, but not captivated by them).

According to Prof. Sen-arat Paranavithana (Brahmi inscriptions in Sinhalese verse Journal of the Royal Asiatic Society of Ceylon. 1945), the earliest extant specimens of Sinhalese metrical compositions may be dated to the first century B.C.

At least four of the early Brahmi inscriptions of Sri Lanka have been identified as poetical compositions.

As may be gleaned from literary sources such as the "Pujavaliya" (13th century) the reign of King Aggabodhi I (568-601 A.C.) was a period of great literary activity. Twelve famous poets, namely Demi, Bebiri, Kithsiri, Anuruth, Dalagoth, Dalasala, Dalabiso, Puravadu, Sakdamala, Asakdamala, Suriyabahu and Kesub-Kotha-Epa flourished during the king"s reign.

The Sigiri graffiti scribbled on the mirror wall (Kedapath pavura) of the ancient rock fortress of Sigiriya built by King Kassapa I (477-485 A.C.), may be dated to the 7th - 8th centuries.

These verses which are predominantly on secular themes are largely addressed to the Sigiri frescoes, paintings of beautiful bejewelled, bare-breasted female figures on the western face of the rock. A good many of the verses are therefore of an amorous or romantic nature. Two specimens of the graffiti are given below (trans. by S. Paranavithana and W. G. Archer).

> We spoke but they did not answer
> Those ladies of the mountain
> They did not give us
> The twitch of an eyelid
> The girl with the golden skin
> Enticed the mind and eyes.
> Her lovely breasts caused me to recall
> Swans drunk with nectar.

One of the greatest literary monuments of the medieval period is the "Kavsilumina" (The crest gem of poetry), a 13th century "maha-kavya" (lengthy, ornate poem taking after the Sanskrit model) composed by King Parakrama Bahu II (1234 " 1269).

This masterpiece which contains 770 verses divided into 15 cantos is a versified form of the "Kusa Jataka" which related the story of the Bodhisattva (as the Buddha is known in his supposed previous births) born as the ugly Prince Kusa and his romance with the lovely Princess Pabhavati.

Much of the medieval Sinhalese poetry has been based on the Jataka tales. Such are the "Kavya-Sekharaya" (Diadem of poetry) written in 1450 by Sri Rahula which is based on the "Sattubhasta Jataka" and the Guttilaya of Vetteve thera (15th century) based on the "Guttila Jataka".

The Kotte period (15th " 16th centuries) marks the efflorescence of Sinhalese poetry. The largely secular "Sandesha" (message) poems gained immense popularity during this period. The Sandesha poems are based on Kalidasa"s Meghaduta (cloud messenger). The essence of the Sandesha poem is the despatch of a message through the agency of a living being, very often a bird.

The oldest Sandesha poem of which we have any evidence is the "Mayura Sandeshaya" (Peacock"s message) dating back to the 13th century, if not earlier. The work no longer exists, though examples from it are cited in the classical Sinhala grammar "Sidath-sangara" (13th century).

The "Thisara Sandeshaya" (Swan"s message) is dated to the 14th century, while the "Gira Sandeshaya" (Parrot"s message), "Hansa Sandeshaya" (Goose"s message), "Parevi Sandeshaya" (Dove"s message), "Kokila Sandeshaya" (Cuckoo"s message) and "Selalihini Sandeshaya" (Starling"s message) belong to the 15th century.

Other Sandesha poems include the *Sevul Sandeshaya* (Cock"s message), "*Hema Kurulu Sandeshaya*" (Oriole"s message) "*Ketakirili Sandeshaya*" (Hornbill"s message), "*Nilakobo Sandeshaya*" (Blue dove"s message) and "*Diyasevul Sandeshaya*" (Black swan"s message).

An unusual Sandesha poem is the "Nari-Sath-Sandeshaya" of "Shiladipati" composed in 1833, describing the pilgrimage of seven women from the village of Nathagane to Dambulla.

What enamours one most to the Sandesha poems are its rhyme and detailed description of the people and places to be seen in the course of our feathered friend"s journey.

One of the most descriptive Sandesha poems is the "Hansa Sandeshaya", which purports to be despatched from Kotte to the Sangha-raja Vanaratana at Keragala (a distance of roughly 48 kilometres) beseeching him to invoke the gods and bid them protect the king.

One of the earliest known hatan kavi is the "Kustantinu hatana" (the war of Constantine) describing the war the Portuguese Captain General Constantine de Sa (17th century) waged, and won, against a Sinhalese rebel named Antonio.

The "Maha hatana" (Great War) tells of the defeat of Constantine de Sa and his successors at the hands of the Kandyan King Rajasinghe II (17th century). Other notable war poems include the "Parangi hatana" (War with the Portuguese) describing the famous battle of Gannoruwa (1638) in which the Sinhalese forces routed the Portuguese army and the "Ingrisi hatana" (war with the English) describing the Kandyan King Sri Wickrama Rajasinghe"s victory over the British army in 1803. Sinhala love poetry also makes delightful reading. Some of the most popular verses are ascribed to Gascon Adigar and the Queen-consort of the Kandyan King Rajasinghe. Gascon who was of Portuguese or French descent had been brought up as a Kandyan from infancy, and being a man of martial prowess, became a favourite of the king.

Changing Trends

By 1950 there were a number of monthly poetry magazines being published in the country. Four of them, published from Colombo, were read nationwide. They were Dedunne (Rainbow), edited by P.B. Alwis Perera; Suwanda (Fragrance), edited by Kapila E.

Seneviratne; Meewadaya (Honeycomb), edited by John Rajadasa; and Amba Vanaya (Mangrove) edited by Sirisena Maitipe. P.B. Alwis Perera edited the largest-selling poetry magazine and was also the most formidable figure at kavi maduwas. Poetry magazines were also published from provincial towns. Kavi maduwas were held occasionally in the towns and sometimes lasted a whole day. Poetry collections of well-known authors sold in large numbers. Kavi kolayas, which carried important or sensational incidents narrated in verse form, were sold at bus stands, Sunday fairs and so on by men who recited them aloud to attract customers.

The poetry practised was metrical and the most popular metre was samudraghosha (every line has about 17 time units and ends with the same syllable and every stanza has four lines). Samudraghosha has been popular for at least 700 years. It was used in sandesa poems (the earliest model of which was Kalidasa's Meghadootam) which are supposed to have been inspired by the more recent Tamil Thudhu poems, in the Kotte period and before. (The Kotte period was the last period of Sri Lankan glory before the European invasions). The samudraghosha metre was used in most forms of popular poetry, such as pel kavi (poems sung at night while guarding fields), paru kavi (those sung while paddling boats) and goyam kavi (those sung while reaping paddy).

The important poets of the 1940s were Ananda Rajakaruna, S. Mahinda Thera and G.H. Perera. Ananda Rajakaruna was the seniormost of them. S. Mahinda Thera was a Buddhist monk, who wrote his name as 'Tibet Jathika S. Mahinda', which meant S. Mahinda of Tibetan nationality. 'S' stood for Sikkim.

Apparently he called himself a Tibetan national rather than a Sikkimese national because Tibet was better known in Sri Lanka. He was ordained a monk after his arrival in Sri Lanka. A remarkable aspect of his career as a Sinhala poet was that he became an ardent nationalist. He was also a sympathiser of the Lanka Sama Samaja Party (LSSP), which was founded in 1935 and which brought together the forward-looking and anti-imperialist sections of Sri Lankan society. G.H. Perera, a school teacher, was also a member of the LSSP, a nationalist and a social critic.

Among the younger poets of the late 1940s and early 1950s were P.B. Alwis Perera, Sagara Palansuriya, Wimalaratne Kumaragama and a host of others. The most sensitive poet was perhaps Wimalaratne Kumaragama. Most of the poets were left-leaning. When the right-wing United National Party Government held a poetry competition to celebrate Sri Lanka's Independence in 1948, none of the popular poets responded, saying that it was a fake Independence.

While poetry magazines and newspapers catered to popular poetry, another poetic tradition was kept alive through its main proponent, Munidasa Cumaratunga, who died in 1944 but whose fame remains to this day. This was a more learned stream of poetry. Munidasa Cumaratunga is the foremost Sinhala grammarian of modern times. He was a teacher and later the principal of a teachers' training college. A question by one of his pupils, which Cumaratunga could not answer, set him on a voyage of study which enabled him to develop concepts of Sinhala grammar in a scientific manner. He also learnt Sanskrit on his own and gained a thorough knowledge of it. He started a magazine by the name of Subasa to promote the correct use of Sinhala.

Cumaratunga was a versatile poet. He also edited and published several ancient Sinhala classics. He was a nationalist of a different order. He considered all Sri Lankans to be Helas, a term that could include all ethnic communities in the country. He and his associates founded an organisation called Hela Havula in order to promote their ideas. One of Cumaratunga's poems, "Piyasamara", written about his dead father, was considered by a distinguished contemporary, Martin Wickramasinghe, as a work fit for expansion into a mahakavya.

In a reinterpretation of Sri Lankan history by the Hela school, Vijaya, who is traditionally considered to be the founder of the Sri Lankan state, was no hero; he was only a usurper who temporarily seized a kingdom established long ago, one of the illustrious rulers of which was Ravana. It is interesting that Ravana is a hero of the Hela school in Sri Lanka as well as among Dravidian nationalists in India.

Another distinguished poet of the Hela school was Reipiyel Tennekoon, who in addition to his other voluminous works wrote a history of Sri Lanka in metrical verse. However, he preferred the traditional version of Sri Lankan history rather than the Hela version. Sunil Santha, a popular and talented singer of yesteryear, was a member of the Hela Havula; he sang a number of songs composed by the members of the organisation.

Another significant development in Sinhala poetry was the introduction of free verse. The most enthusiastic proponent of free verse in Sinhala was Siri Gunasinghe, a university don. Free verse was first introduced in Sinhala poetry by G.B. Senanayake in 1948. He inserted free verse between short stories in one of his collections. He did not call it poetry. He called it an intermediate composition between prose and poetry. However, Siri Gunasinghe introduced it with a vengeance in the mid-1950s. He considered metrical verse as worthless. He published two collections of verse called Mas le neti eta (Bones Without Flesh or Blood) and Abinikmana (Departure). Coming from a university academic, this criticism had a devastating effect on popular poetry. None of the earlier poets, including the erudite Munidasa Cumaratunga, had a university degree. Popular poets such as P.B. Alwis Perera tried to fight back but were unsuccessful.

The decline of Sinhala poetry perhaps began with the publication of Mas le neti eta in 1956. However, this also brought in a culture of fine introspective poetry. One of the dominant poets of this tradition was Mahagama Sekara. He was also a song writer. Some of his songs enjoyed mass appeal when they were sung by the noted singer Pandit Amaradeva. Other important poets who came later were Ratnasri Wijesinghe and Gunadasa Amarasekera. Ratnasri Wijesinghe is also a song writer and some of his songs have been popularised by Amaradeva. Gunadasa Amarasekera, a dental surgeon, won literary laurels early in life. When he was 20 years old, his story was among two Sri Lankan entries selected for an international short story competition conducted by the New York Herald Tribune. Other poets who deserve special mention are Sunil Ariyaratne, Parakrama Kodituwakku, Monika Ruwanpathirana and Eric Ilayapparachchi.

Even Martin Wickramasinghe, the doyen of Sinhala writers of this period, joined the chorus in condemning metrical poetry, poetry in samudraghosha metre in particular. His book of poetry, Theri Gee, is a Sinhala translation of some Theri Gatha (Psalms of the Sisters) ascribed to Buddhist nuns who were contemporaries of the Buddha. The originals were in Pali, in mellifluous metrical verse, but the Sinhala translations are in free verse.

However, Wickramasinghe later said that he did not like the free verse form. The new poets occasionally write metrical verse in addition to free verse, but they generally avoid the samudraghosha metre. Sirilal Kodikara is a poet of the early 1950s but whose form of poetry is akin to that of the new poets. In his early poems he adopted the samudraghosha metre, but when the trend went against the samudraghosha metre he adopted other metres.

Several Sinhala poets today seem unconcerned whether their poetry is actually "performed", but the effect is lost when poetry is not recited or acted out. Modern poetry is meant more to be read than recited. All these poets are talented, but they face a serious problem; Sinhala poetry has lost its mass appeal and the sales of books of poetry have dropped. A book of poetry today sells about 500 copies on an average. This is a sad situation in a country where such books sold thousands of copies a few decades ago. Perhaps Sinhala poetry needs to return to the metrical form, especially the samudraghosha metre, which today's poets appear to despise.

12

Literature of Bangladesh

The history of Bangladeshi and Bengali literature goes back hundreds of years. While it is impossible (and undesirable) to separate the literary trends of the two Bengals during the pre-independence period, post independent Bangladesh has given birth to it's own distinct set of literateurs and literature.

The earliest available specimen of Bengali literature is about a thousand years old. During the mediaeval period Bengali literature developed considerably with the patronage of Muslim rulers. Chandi Das, Daulat Kazi and Alaol are some of the famous poets of the period.

The era of modern Bengali Literature began in the late nineteenth century. Rahindranath Tagore, Kazi Nazrul Islam, Michael Madhusudan Datta. Sarat Chandra Chattopadhyai, Bankim Chandra Chattopadhyai, Mir Mosharraf Hossain and Kazi Ahdul Wadud are the pioneers of modern Bengali Literature.

Literature from Bangladesh is produced in many forms, from novels to poetry, and in several languages. It was during medieval times that Bangladesh's literature reached new heights as Muslim rulers became patrons of this art form. Well-known Bangladeshi poets of the era are Alaol, Chandi Das and Daulat Kazi. Toward the end of the 19th century Bengali literature entered a modern era, introducing literary geniuses such as Rahindranath Tagor, Kazi Ahdul Wadud, Kazi Nazrul Islam, Kankim Chandra Chattopadhyai and Mir Mosharraf Hossain.

Renowned Rabindranath Tagore's literary career encompassed more than 60 years of his life. During this time he produced an abundance of exquisite works including poems, songs, plays, novels, volumes of short stories. He also produced prose covering topics such as politics, society, literature and religion. Over and above this he engaged in many other activities such as painting, lecture tours through Europe, Asia and America, translating into English, educational reforms, religion and politics. Tagore is certainly a legend amongst the people of Bangladesh and throughout the world.

Shamsur Rahman is considered by many to be Bangladesh's greatest poet, having published some 60 collections of poetry. He has been acclaimed for bringing about a new dimension to Bengali poetry. Shamsur is in fact a journalist by profession and has won several awards for his contributions to Bangladesh's literature, including the Swadhinata Award, the Bangla Academy Award and the Ekushey Padak.

Kazi Nazrul Islam, also known as Rebel Poet (asbidrohi kobi), hit Bangladesh's literary scene with a bang when his poem entitled "bidrohi" was published. This poem touched the hearts of people and so affected the population deeply. Nazrul's literary works speak out against religious and social bigotry, oppression and other contributors to national discord. Nazrul is also popular for his song writing abilities, having produced some 3000 songs. His main works include Chayanat, Sanchita, Agnivina and Dolan Champa.

Bangladesh's literature and literary figures have not only had an immense influence within in the country, but have extended beyond borders, bringing to light many issues plaguing the nation as well as inspiring mankind.

History of Bangla Literature

Bangla literature has its roots in poetry. Bangla poetry has its roots in its people. Long before the print medium was invented, folk tales had been told from one generation to the next by singing verses created by ordinary people. Stories were constructed in the course of their lives from materials collected from their own experiences and from famous stories or themes composed by past generations of "Kobials" (or folk poets) and bauls (or street singers).

Kobials (folk poets) would often recite their compositions in front of appreciative audiences not only in their immediate neighborhood, but also often in far-away villages. The depth of logic, humor, wit, wisdom, emotive outpour and romanticism in their poetic pieces (created extemporaneously often in response to and as an anti-thesis of the points and arguments made by the rival poets sharing the same audience and performing stage) was informative and amazingly entertaining. Such was their melodious rendition that they would leave an indelible mark on the audience. The villagers would continue to recite these verses for a long time to come. The verses, which often included references to familiar characters from the great Indian epics Mahabharat and Ramayan would serve as beacons for thousands. The instructive power of some of these creations would later provide many with simple how-to guides to fulfillment in life and salvation after death.

Joydeb was one of the earliest and the most famous Bangla poets. His masterpiece Geetgobinda remains a fitting Baishnab poetry. Seeds of early Bangla literature were sown in the folkloric fertile ground. Madhusudan Datta who had a meteoric appearance in the Bangla literary firmament following Nabeen Chandra Sen, introduced blank verses and sonnets and presented to the world his masterpiece epic poetry Meghnad Badh Kabya. This is the true beginning of modern Bangla poetry. Shackles of the past thus destroyed by this rebel poet later helped Bangalees to reap a bumper harvest in the late nineteenth and early twentieth centuries. Bangla poetry reached its peak in the hands of Nobel laureate Rabindranath Tagore.

Even though he was most widely known as a poet, Tagore was simultaneously a novelist, playwright, lyricist, music composer, painter and philosopher. His book of lyrics called Gitanjali translated into English by himself earned him the Nobel Prize in 1913 despite reported objections from the English members of the Nobel award committee. If there was a bigger and better prize for Tagore - it was to be the hearts and souls of millions of Bangalees who lived during his lifetime or will ever walk on this earth since his passing away.

History of Bangla prose is relatively new. Bangla prose form was largely developed and introduced by the missionaries of Srirampur and by the Fort William College. Both had pragmatic and utilitarian ends in mind. New British officers of the East India Company were taught Bangla so that they could converse with the natives.

To this end Nathaniel B. Halhead published the Bangla grammar in 1778 - the title page clearly stated this obvious purpose. After Fort William College was established in 1800, the pundits were charged with the development of Bangla prose for the benefit of the English Administration. The missionaries of Srirampur, under the able guidance of William Carey (1761-1834; British orientalist and missionary born at Paulerspury, Northamptonshire, co-founder of the Particular Baptist Society, Professor of Sanskrit at the Fort William College), translated the Bible in Bangla in 1801 for spreading Christianity - noted as the pioneering work in Bangla prose.

The Bangla prose thus developed in the early 19th century was nothing more than a cocktail of Sanskrit, Arabic and Persian words and *"was pitiably amorphous in from"*. The first Bangla book of prose written by a Bangalee was the textbook Raja Pratapaditya Charita published in 1801. The author was Ramram Basu who later wrote another book Lipimala. In 1802, Batrisa Simhasana written by Mritunjaya Bidyalankar published. It was certainly an improvement on Ramram Basu. The same writer also published three other textbooks: Hitopadesh, Rajabali and Prabodh Chandrika.

It was not until 1815 when Raja Rammohan Roy published his first book of prose called Bedanta Grantha that a break with the tradition was established. The influence of Sanskrit, Arabic and

Persian words was minimized. In 15 years, from 1815 to 1830, Rammohan wrote thirty books in Bangla. According to Soumendranath Tagore, "the excellence that the Bangla prose [later] achieved in literary form under Bankim Chandra and Rabindranath owes its beginning to the Bangla prose developed by Rammohan". The above observation appears quite valid except in one detail. It does not accord any recognition to the pioneering work done by such writer as Iswar Chandra Bidyasagar, Bankim Chandra, Pyarichand Mitra and Tekchand Thakur. Indeed, Rabindranath Tagore regarded Bidyasagar (inspire of the fact that he was not a pure literary figure) as the father of Bangla prose.

Evidently, English style short stories, novels and plays are of relatively modern origin in the Bangla literature. Despite its late beginning, Bangla prose soon went through a complete course of evolution since then, rather quickly. According to Professor Sukumar Sen, the evolution of Bangla novelist tradition can be separated into four well-defined periods.

The Loric Period

Fable-centered literature of this period has been classified into two distinct streams. The first stream was purely romantic. These stories often deal with religious beliefs and rely on fatalistic endings. Examples include the Lausen's Adenture from Dharmamangal. Events were exciting and happenings romantic. Characters and story lines were inspired by the omnipresence of God. In the end they were rewarded or punished for their deeds in accordance with the Mahabharatic tradition.

The second stream, not unlike its predecessor, continued to be laden with religious preaching's and moral edicts. However, these were less exotic and less fanciful. Soon these started to deal with tales of ordinary people and their ordinary lives. The best examples of this period, according to Professor Sen, were the two stories in Kobikankan's poetry and in Bidyasundar by Bharatchandra. Stories in the Dharmamangal by the Seventeenth century poet Roopram Chakrabarty, who became as famous in his time as the best Bangla novelist Sarat Chandra Chatterjee would be almost three centuries later. In a century since 'Bidyasundar' was written by Bharatchandra quite a lot of stories were written - notable of which were Chandrakanta and Kaminikumar.

Most, however, resembled Bidyasundar and were reminiscent of the Loric style. These stories were written in verses and provided romantic setting for instructive materials for readers. A new era dawned with Pyarichand Mitra's trend-setting prose-based novel Alaler Gharer Dulal. Many criticized Mitra, however, for committing the same error, of not writing for entertainment value only. He too erred in making value judgments. It was claimed that he could not escape from the Loric past.

The Bankim Period

It is Bankim Chandra Chatterjee who finally dropped curtain on the Loric period by publishing his masterpiece Durgeshnandini. Bankim's novels can be classified into three groups: the first is full of English style romanticism; the second is modeled on Pyarichand Mitra (such as Bishbriksha, Krishnakanter

Will and finally those novels that were based on historical events (such as Mrinalini, Rajshingha and Sitaram.

The Tagore period

The Tagore period, which followed the Bankim period and co-existed with the Sarat Period, has to date been the most defining period in Bangla literature. Its essentially distinctive universal appeal, richness and variety of literary styles demand separate treatment and stratification. Tagore was not just a Bangla poet or writer. Tagore was a world phenomenon. Tagore's short stories are many and varied in their contents, tastes, presentation, universal appeal and inherent literary beauty. They differ from those of his contemporary writers; they differ from even his own novels and plays. In the latter, Tagore used quite a distinct artistic license. He went on to draw a much bigger picture. Here he observed and depicted people in their family and social settings. His penetrating insight into human minds and the many intricate ways they relate to other people around them in love and in conflict, in victory and in defeat, in happiness and in misery allowed him to map characters and stories precisely with a language that derived its adulthood from his pen.

The Sarat Period

Inspired by Bankim Chandra Chatterjee's writings, it was novelist Sarat Chandra Chatterjee who brought modern Bangla literature to the masses. His piercing analysis of human love, faith and frailties is unparallel. His intimate understanding of the social goings-on and the sympathetic albeit affirmative way he portrayed the unprivileged and the women in his stories testify his paramount love and affection for the deprived. His lovingly and masterfully crafted words, used by ordinary people of the street, and immaculate writing style made him easily one of the world's best-loved novelists. Like Bankim Chandra, he was a common man; he understood the common person's dilemmas with life and living conditions. His novels and short stories appealed to people of all walks of life. His mastery on this branch of the Bangla literature was so complete that it is not at all surprising to note that remaining under the full glare of Tagore's creative genius, Sarat Chandra was never to be influenced by it. On the contrary, Tagore has been so moved by his stories that even he could not resist from the occasional foray into the latter's familiar territory. Other writers of the Sarat tradition included famous novelists like Tarashankar Bandyopadhyay, Bibhutibhushan Bandyopadhyay (celebrated author of the Apu trilogy), Manik Bandyopadhyay, Balaichand Mukhopadhyay (pen-name was Banaful), Abadhoot and Bimal Mitra.

Countless novelists of the modern era since have tried many a different style and technique; many of them succeeded in varying degrees to reach the reading public at large. To date, however, no one novelist has received the same degree of love and affection as Sarat Chandra can so naturally and so mesmerizingly command.

Great Writers

Shamsur Rahman

Shamsur Rahman is indisputably the greatest living poet of Bangladesh, with more than sixty books of poetry to his credit. The renowned critic, Syed Manzoorul Islam, speaks of Rahman as having "produced a solid body of work which has permanently changed the geography and the climate of Bengali poetry. He has given it a new dimension and a meaning, he has created an ethos which belongs indisputably to him. He has given us a language, which we did not have. It is true he has built on the ground of the 30's poets, but he has developed the ground, explored into areas they thought too dark for exploration, has added new features to it, landscaped it and in the process left his footprints all over." The critic, Z. R. Siddiqui, describes Shamsur Rahman as one who is "deeply rooted in his own tradition." In his opinion, Shamsur Rahman "still soaks the language of our times, transcending the limits of geography. In his range of sympathy, his catholicity, his urgent and immediate relevance for us, Shamsur Rahman is second to none."

Shamsur Rahman did his Honours in English literature from Dhaka University. He had a long career as a journalist and was the Editor of a national daily, Dainik Bangla.

He has won numerous awards including Bangla Academy Award (1969), Ekushey Padak (1977), and Swadhinata Award (1991).

Rabindranath Tagore

Tagore's literary life extened over sixty years, and he reminds one of Victor Hugo in the copiousness and variety of his work: over one thousand poems; nearly two dozen plays and playlets; eight novels; eightor more volumes of short stories; more than two thousands songs, of which he wrote both the words and the music; and a mass of prose on literary, social, religious, political, and other topics. Add to these his english translations; his paintings; his travels and lecture-tours in Asia, America, and Europe; and his activities as educationist, as social and religious reformer, and as politician- and there you have, judged by quantity alone, the life-work of a Titan. Thia is not to say that his genius was no more than the capacity for taking infinite pains; but to note the element of steel and concrete that went to his making, and thus to dispose of the legend, that has grown in some quarters in recent years, of Tagore the pale-lily poet of ladies' table.

Not that the legend is entirely baseless. Tagore's almost continuous iteration, in his English translations, of the softer side of his poetry and his wistful-mystical message, is partly responsible for it. After having won world-fame with the mystical-devotional poetry of the English Gitanjali, he dug overmuch along that particular seam, producing a monotonously one-sided impression of his work. It is true that *The Gardener* and the subsequent volumes of translations gave some of his best lyrics, but they also gave many poems which were very thin and had nothing beyond a delicate fancy or a pretty sensibility to show for their author.

The Tagores were a cultured and wealthy family, and Rabindranath's father, Devendranath, was one of the leaders of the Brahma Samaj,. The poet's early life was spent in an atmosphere of religion and arts, principally literature, music and painting. In religion his inspiration was derived from the Vedas and the Upanishads, but with him as with many Hindus the Upanisadic monism was diversified by the Vaisnava dualism. In music Tagore's training was classical

Indian, though as a composer he rebelled against the tyranny of classical orthodoxy, and introduced many variations of form and phrase, notably from Bengali folk-music of the Baul and Bhatiyali type. he had some training in European music during his first visit to England, and some of his early songs were composed to the tunes of the Border Ballads and Moore's *Irish Melodies*. In later life he made some experiments on harmonaization in the European manner. As a writer the course of his life was early set. He was brought up on three languages- Sanskrit, Bengali and English- and the most formitive influences were those of the Sanskrit classics, the Vaisnava poets of Bengal, and the English romantics and post-romantics, most notably Shelley.

In 1901 he founded his school, the Santiniketan, at Bolpur as a protest against the existing bad system of education. The school was a great success and gave birth to Viswabharati. On revisiting England in 1911 he brought with him the English Gitanjali, and it's publication in 1912 and the award of the Nobel Prize for literature the following year made him world-famous. This was the first award of that prize to an Asiatic. The rest of Tagore's life was spent at Santiniketan, except for several travels and lecture-tours in which he carried his message of human unity to all the important countries of Asia, America and Europe.

As a novelist Tagore gave good pictures of upper middle-class life in Bengal in *Naukadubi, Chokher-Bali,* and later, in *Gora* and *Ghare Baire*. The last two, perhaps the best novels written by an Indian, are interesting studies of the impact of Western ideas on Indian life. His plays represent a large variety of types:

social comedies in prose, such as *Chirakumar Sabha*, *Goray Galad* and *Vaikunther Katha*; symbolical plays in prose, such as *Raja*, *Phalguni* and *Rakta Karabi*; and short romantic playlets such as *Malini*, *Chandalika*, and *Natir Puja*. *The Post Office* is generally regarded as a symbolical play, but is more aptly described as a fable. All these plays have songs, but Tagore wrote several plays, such as *Valmiki-Pratibha* and *Mayar Khela*, in which music predominates as in the European opera. Mention should also be made of the dramatic dialogues in verse, such as *Karna o Kunti* and *Viday-abhishap*.

In My Reminiscences (Jivan-smriti) Tagore has recorded the inner history of his early poetry. It is the history of his emergence from the unreal and self centered world of adolescence into the adult and super-personal world of man and nature. The emergence found expression in many early works: in the poem "Awakening of the Fountain" where the poet's soul was likened to a fountain imprisoned in a dark cave until one day the morning sun pierced the cave with its rays and set the fountain free. His gift of lyricism and song was fully in evidence in *Kari o Kamal* and *Manishi* and attained ripeness in *Chitra*.

The Ode to Urbasi which appeared in *Chitra* is the highest watermark of his aestheticism. Mysticism first appeared on a considerable scale in *Sonar tari*, and Tagore's philosophical and devotional-mystical poetry attained maturity in *Naivedya*, *Kheya* and *Gitanjali*. His stories in verse in *Katha o kahini*, *Palataka*, *Punascha* and other volumes and his epigrams in *Kanika* and in *Lekhan*. In addition he wrote many patriotic poems and songs and many poems having a social and political contents. His best reflective poems are to be found in

Balaka and some of his later books. He is happiest in the bondage of rhyme, but has also written some beautiful blank verse and free verse.

There never was a poet more of the earth, more earthy, than Tagore. The beauty and splendour of the earth he has proudly and lovingly sung in many a poem. But he also loves the earth, perhaps all the more, for her poverty and imperfection. 'Infinite wealth is not yours, my patient and dusky mother dust.... I have seen your tender face and i love your mournful dust, Mother earth.' In some poems he suggests that his love of the earth is older than his life.

Kazi Nazrul Islam

Kazi Nazrul Islam, popularly known *asbidrohi kobi* (Rebel poet) took the bengali literary world by storm by his poem, *bidrohi* or the Rebel. Probably no other single poem influenced the Bengali society and people so deeply, and this poem, alongwith many other patriotic poems and songs, inspired the freedom fighters during the struggle against the british, and also during the Bangladesh liberation war in 1971. Many regard him as the greatest poetic force in Bengali literature after world famous Rabindranath Tagore. Both Nazrul's poems and prose writing exuberate a certain force and energy, denouncing all social and religious bigotry and plurality, cultural differences and oppression as the principal reasons for national discord and disharmony. Many of his songs and poems were banned by the british administration in pre-partition India.

Nazrul also got equal prominence and popularity in writing songs, almost 3,000 of them, the largest by any Bengali poet and composing music. Many of his songs, particularly the love songs became instantly popular and are still revered. His songs are extremely romantic, lyric, appealing and rich in metaphors. All his works truthfully represent the life-style he led - the struggle of a poor childhood, his intense patriotism, and bohemian life as a poet.

Humayun Ahmed

Humayun Ahmed is a leading Bangladeshi writer, and the most prolific among his contemporaries. His phenomenal success is attributed to his ability to tell stories of contemporary Bengali men and women in simple and unostentatious language, portraying them with spellbinding intimacy. Although his characters belong to a broad spectrum of society, Humayun is at his best while depicting the Bengali middle class. His first novel, *Sankhanil Karagar*, published in 1972, caused a great stir among readers and the literary circles in Bangladesh. Since then, he has published more than a hundred novels. Many of his novels have been adapted successfully for television serials and plays. Ahmed did his Masters in Chemistry at Dhaka University and obtained his Ph.D. in Polymer Chemistry from North Dakota State University. He is a former Associate Professor of Dhaka University and an honorary fellow in writing at the University of Iowa. Lately Humayun Ahmed has turned his attention to film making. His film, *Aguner Parasaman*, won the National Film Award in eight categories. Another film *Sraban Megher Din* also enjoyed critical and popular success.

Selina Hussain

Selina Hossain is one of the most important women writers of Bangladesh. She has published twenty-one novels, seven collections of short stories, four collections of prose writings and four collections of stories for children. Her works are a moving account of the contemporary social and political crises and conflicts as well as the recurrent cycles of the life of the struggling masses. Quite a few of her novels have been translated into Indian regional languages and into French, Russian and English.

Commenting on the war of liberation in Bangladeshi novels, Kabir Chowdhury wrote that Selina Hossain's, Hangara, Nadi, Grenade (Shark, River and Grenade), "set in a remote riverine rural area of southern Bangladesh, dealing with illiterate common men and women, achieves a commendable integration of theme and style and brilliantly highlights the essence of all that is heroic, noble and glorious in our liberation war." Critic Syed Akram Hossain recalls Selina's Pokamakorera gharabasati and comments, "Her portrayal of life of a particular community living on the south-east coast of Bangladesh is informed by a deep awareness of life which transcends regionalism."

Hossain is the winner of Bangla Academy award, 1980 and Alaol Purashkar, 1981 among many others. In 1994-95 she won a Ford Foundation Fellowship for her novel, Gayatri Sandhya. Selina Hossain is currently serving in the position of Director of the Bangla Academy in Dhaka.

13

Postcolonialism in Commonwealth Literature

"Postcolonial Literature" is a hot commodity these days. On the one hand writers like Salman Rushdie and Arundhati Roy are best-selling authors; and on the other hand, no college English department worth its salt wants to be without a scholar who can knowledgeably discourse about postcolonial theory.

But there seems to be a great deal of uncertainty as to just what the term denotes. Many of the debates among postcolonial scholars center on which national literatures or authors can be justifiably included in the postcolonial canon. Much of the discussion among postcolonial scholars involves criticisms of the term "postcolonial" itself. In addition, it is seldom mentioned but quite striking that very few actual authors of the literature under discussion embrace and use the term to label their own writing.

It should be acknowledged that postcolonial theory functions as a subdivision within the even more misleadingly named field of "cultural studies": the whole body of generally leftist radical literary theory and criticism which includes Marxist, Gramscian, Foucauldian, and various feminist schools of thought, among others. What all of these schools of thought have in common is a determination to analyze unjust power relationships as manifested in cultural products like literature (and film, art, etc.). Practitioners generally consider themselves politically engaged and committed to some variety or other of liberation process.

It is also important to understand that not all postcolonial scholars are literary scholars. Postcolonial theory is applied to political science, to history, and to other related fields. People who call themselves postcolonial scholars generally see themselves as part of a large (if poorly defined and disorganized) movement to expose and struggle against the influence of large, rich nations (mostly European, plus the U.S.) on poorer nations (mostly in the southern hemisphere).

Taken literally, the term "postcolonial literature" would seem to label literature written by people living in countries formerly colonized by other nations. This is undoubtedly what the term originally meant, but there are many problems with this definition.

First, literal colonization is not the exclusive object of postcolonial study. Lenin's cla ssic analysis of imperialism led to Antonio Gramisci's concept of "hegemony" which distinguishes between literal political dominance and dominance through ideas and culture (what many critics of American influence call the "Coca-Colanization" of the world). Sixties thinkers developed the concept of neo-imperialism to label relationships like that between the U.S. and many Latin American countries which, while nominally independent, had economies dominated by American business interests, often backed up by American military forces. The term "banana republic" was originally a sarcastic label for such subjugated countries, ruled more by the influence of the United Fruit Corporation than by their own indigenous governments.

Second, among the works commonly studied under this label are novels like Claude McKay's *Banjo* and Chinua Achebe's *Things Fall Apart* which were written while the nations in question (Jamaica and Nigeria) were still colonies. Some scholars attempt to solve this problem by arguing that the term should denote works written after colonization, not only those created after independence; but that would be "postcolonization" literature. Few people understand the term in this sense outside a small circle of scholars working in the field.

Third, some critics argue that the term misleadingly implies that colonialism is over when in fact most of the nations involved are still culturally and economically subordinated to the rich industrial states through various forms of neo-colonialism even though they are technically independent.

Fourth, it can be argued that this way of defining a whole era is Eurocentric, that it singles out the colonial experience as the most important fact about the countries involved. Surely that experience has had many powerful influences; but this is not necessarily the framework within which writers from—say—India, who have a long history of precolonial literature, wish to be viewed.

For instance, R. K. Narayan—one of the most popular and widely read of modern Indian writers—displays a remarkable indifference to the historical experience of colonialism, a fact which results in his being almost entirely ignored by postcolonial scholars.

V. S. Naipaul is so fierce a critic of the postcolonial world despite his origins as a descendant of Indian indentured laborers in Trinidad that he is more often cited as an opponent than as an ally in the postcolonial struggle.

In fact, it is not uncommon for citizens of "postcolonial" countries to accuse Americans and Europeans of practicing a form of neocolonialism themselves in viewing their history through this particular lens. Postcolonial criticism could be compared to the tendency of Hollywood films set in such countries to focus on the problems of Americans and Europeans within those societies while marginalizing the views of their native peoples.

Fifth, many "postcolonial" authors do not share the general orientation of postcolonial scholars toward engaging in an ongoing critique of colonialism. Nigerian writers Chinua Achebe and Wole Soyinka, for instance, after writing powerful indictments of the British in their country, turned to exposing the deeds of native-born dictators and corrupt officials within their independent homeland. Although postcolonial scholars would explain this corruption as a by-product of colonialism, such authors commonly have little interest in pursuing this train of thought.

Although there has been sporadic agitation in some African quarters for reparations for the slavery era, most writers of fiction, drama, and poetry see little point in continually rehashing the past to solve today's problems. It is striking how little modern fiction from formerly colonized nations highlights the colonial past. Non-fiction writers often point out that Hindu-Muslim conflicts in South Asia are in part the heritage of attempts by the British administration in India to play the two groups of against each other (not to mention the special role assigned to the Sikhs in the British army); yet Indian fiction about these conflicts rarely points to such colonial causes. A good example is Kushwant Singh's *Train to Pakistan* (1956) which deals directly with the partition of India from an almost exclusively Indian perspective.

Indeed, "postcolonial" writers often move to England or North America (because they have been exiled, or because they find a more receptive audience there, or simply in search of a more comfortable mode of living) and even sometimes—like Soyinka—call upon the governments of these "neocolonialist" nations to come to the aid of freedom movements seeking to overthrow native tyrants.

Sixth, "postcolonialism" as a term lends itself to very broad use. Australians and Canadians sometimes claim to live in postcolonial societies, but many would refuse them the label because their literature is dominated by European immigrants, and is therefore a literature of privilege rather than of protest. According to the usual postcolonial paradigm only literature written by native peoples in Canada and Australia would truly qualify.

Similarly, the label is usually denied to U.S. literature, though America's identity was formed in contradistinction to that of England, because the U.S. is usually viewed as the very epitome of a modern neo-colonial nation, imposing its values, economic pressures, and political interests on a wide range of weaker countries.

The Irish are often put forward as an instance of a postcolonial European people, and indeed many African writers have been inspired by Irish ones for that reason. Yet some of the more nationalist ones (like Yeats) tended toward distressingly conservative—even reactionary—politics, and James Joyce had the utmost contempt for Irish nationalism. It is not clear how many Irish authors would have accepted the term if they had known of it.

Although postcolonial theory generally confines itself to the past half-century, it can be argued that everyone has been colonized at some time or other. Five thousand years ago Sumer started the process by uniting formerly independent city-states, and Narmer similarly subjugated formerly independent Upper and Lower Egypt. Rushdie likes to point out that England itself is a postcolonial nation, having been conquered by Romans and Normans, among others.

Not only is the term "postcolonial" exceedingly fuzzy, it can also be argued that it is also often ineffective. A good deal of postcolonial debate has to do with rival claims to victimhood, with each side claiming the sympathies of right-thinking people because of their past sufferings. The conflicts between Bosnians and Serbs, Palestinians and Jews, Turks and Greeks, Hindu and Muslim Indians, and Catholic and Protestant Irish illustrate the problems with using historical suffering as justification for a political program. It is quite true that Europeans and Americans often arrogantly dismiss their own roles in creating the political messes of postcolonial nations around the world; but it is unclear how accusations against them promote the welfare of those nations. In addition, when they are made to feel guilty, countries—like individuals—are as likely to behave badly as they are to behave generously.

It may make American and European scholars feel

better to disassociate themselves from the crimes of their ancestors, but people struggling for freedom in oppressed nations are more likely to draw inspiration from the quintessentially European Enlightenment concept of rights under natural law than they are to turn to postcolonial theory. Similarly, European capitalist market theory is far more attractive to most people struggling against poverty in these nations than are the varieties of socialism propounded by postcolonial theoreticians.

"Postcolonial" is also a troublesome term because it draws some very arbitrary lines. South African writers Athol Fugard and Nadine Gordimer are often excluded from postcolonial courses, although their works were powerful protests against apartheid and they have lived and worked far more in Africa than, say, Buchi Emicheta, who emigrated to England as a very young woman and has done all of her writing there—because they are white. A host of fine Indian writers is neglected simply because they do not write in English on the sensible grounds that India has a millennia-long tradition of writing which should not be arbitrarily linked to the British imperial episode.

Of those who write in English, Anita Desai is included, though she is half German. Ngugi wa Thiong'o is included even though he now writes primarily in Gikuyu. Bharati Mukherjee specifically rejects the label "Indian-American," though she is an immigrant from India, and Rushdie prefers to be thought of as a sort of multinational hybrid (though he has, on occasion, used the label "postcolonial" in his own writing). Hanif Kureishi is more English than Pakistani in his outlook, and many Caribbean-born writers living in England are now classed as "Black

British." What determines when you are too acculturated to be counted as postcolonial: where you were born? how long you've lived abroad? your subject matter? These and similar questions are the object of constant debate.

In fact, postcolonial theoretician Homi Bhabha developed the term "hybridity" to capture the sense that many writers have of belonging to *both* cultures. More and more writers, like Rushdie, reject the older paradigm of "exile" which was meaningful to earlier generations of emigrants in favor of accepting their blend of cultures as a positive synthesis. This celebration of cultural blending considerably blurs the boundaries laid down by postcolonial theory.

In practice, postcolonial literary studies are often sharply divided along linguistic lines in a way which simply reinforces Eurocentric attitudes. Latin American postcolonial studies are seldom explored by those laboring in English departments. Francophone African literature is generally neglected by Anglophone African scholars. Because of these failures to cut across linguistic boundaries, the roles of England and France are exaggerated over those of the colonized regions.

It can even be asked whether the entire premise of postcolonial studies is valid: that examining these literatures can give voice to formerly suppressed peoples. This is the question asked by Gayatri Spivak in her famous essay, "Can the Subaltern Speak?" Using Antonio Gramsci's arcane label for oppressed people, she points out that anyone who has achieved enough literacy and sophistication to produce a widely-read piece of fiction is almost certainly by that very fact disqualified from speaking for the people he or she is supposed to represent. The "Subaltern Group" of

Indian scholars has tried to claim the term to support their own analyses (a similar project exists among Latin American scholars), but the nagging question raised by Spivak remains.

It is notable that whenever writers from the postcolonial world like Soyinka, Derek Walcott, or Rushdie receive wide recognition they are denounced as unrepresentative and inferior to other, more obscure but more "legitimate" spokespeople.

This phenomenon is related to the question of "essentialism" which features so largely in contemporary political and literary theory. Usually the term is used negatively, to describe stereotypical ideas of the Irish as drunken, irresponsible louts. However, protest movements built on self-esteem resort to essentialism in a positive sense, as in the many varieties of "black pride" movements which have emerged at various times, with the earliest perhaps being the concept of "négritude" developed by Caribbean and African writers living in Paris in the 1930s and 40s. However, each new attempt to create a positive group identity tends to be seen by at least some members of the group as restrictive, as a new form of oppressive essentialism.

Faced with the dilemma of wanting to make positive claims for certain ethnic groups or nationalities while simultaneously acknowledging individualism, some critics have put forward the concept of "strategic essentialism" in which one can speak in rather simplified forms of group identity for the purposes of struggle while debating within the group the finer shades of difference.

There are two major problems with this strategy, however. First, there are always dissenters within each group who speak out against the new corporate identity, and they are especially likely to be taken seriously by the very audiences targeted by strategic essentialism. Second, white conservatives have caught on to this strategy: they routinely denounce affirmative action, for instance, by quoting Martin Luther King, as if his only goal was "color blindness" rather than real economic and social equality. They snipe, fairly effectively, at any group which puts forward corporate claims for any ethnic group by calling them racist. Strategic essentialism envisions a world in which internal debates among oppressed people can be sealed off from public debates with oppressors. Such a world does not exist.

Similarly, "strategic postcolonialism" is likely to be a self-defeating strategy, since most writers on the subject publicly and endlessly debate the problems associated with the term. In addition, the label is too fuzzy to serve as a useful tool for long in any exchange of polemics. It lacks the sharp edge necessary to make it serve as a useful weapon.

However, those of us unwilling to adopt the label "postcolonial" are hard put to find an appropriate term for what we study. The old "Commonwealth literature" is obviously too confining and outdated as well as being extremely Eurocentric. "Anglophone literature" excludes the many rich literatures of Africa, for instance, written in European languages other than English, and taken in the literal sense, it does not distinguish between mainstream British and American writing and the material under discussion. "New literature written in English" (or "englishes" as some say) puts too much emphasis on newness (McKay is hardly *new*) and again excludes the non-English-speaking world. "Third-world" makes no sense since the collapse of the Soviet Union and the Communist "second world." "Literature of developing nations" buys into an economic paradigm which most "postcolonial" scholars reject.

The more it is examined, the more the postcolonial sphere crumbles. Though Jamaican, Nigerian, and Indian writers have much to say to each other; it is not clear that they should be lumped together. We continue to use the term "postcolonial" as a *pis aller,* and to argue about it until something better comes along.

14

Women in Commonwealth Literature

Traditionally, the work of women writers has been undervalued due to patriarchal assumptions about the superior worth of male experience. One factor contributing to this prejudice is the fact that most of these women write about the enclosed domestic space, and women's perceptions of their experience within it. Consequently, it is assumed that their work will automatically rank below the works of male writers who deal with 'weightier' themes. Additionally, Commonwealth women writers in English are victims of a second prejudice, vis-à-vis their regional counterparts. Since proficiency in English is available only to writers of the intellectual, affluent, educated classes, a frequent judgement is made that the writers, and their works, belong to a high social strata, and are cut off from the reality of Indian life. The majority of these novels depict the psychological suffering of the frustrated housewife, this subject matter often being considered superficial compared to the depiction of the repressed and oppressed lives of women of the lower classes that we find in regional authors writings.

English education was introduced to teh South asian Commonwealth countries in the nineteenth century, serving as an ideological force behind social reform and control. There was an imperial mission of educating colonial subjects in the literature and thought of England, a mission that in the long run served to strengthen western cultural hegemony. Thomas Babington Macaulay's Education Minute of 1835 is regarded as a crucial document in this history. His arguments were based on an assumption of the innate superiority of English culture, a key sentence in his Minute being:

> [we] must at present do our best to form a class of interpreters between us and the millions whom we govern; a class of persons Indian in blood and colour, but English in taste, in opinions, in morals and in intellect.

The establishment of English colleges led to the creation of an English-educated, and predominantly elite, who eventually became critical of both their own religious orthodoxies, such as the caste system and child brides, and of British rule. The British-style education also had the effect of linking writers to literary traditions of the west, enabling South Asia writers writing in English to reach an audience in Europe as well as in India.

In the nineteenth century, both progressive and orthodox reformers supported female education in India, believing that social evils could be eliminated through education. However, the concept of education was limited to producing good homemakers and perpetuating orthodox ideology, as women were believed to support the traditional values of Indian society. Christian missionaries and British rulers, especially in Bengal where the British had made their first inroads in the mid-nineteenth century, started girls' schools, and in the 1880s, Indian women started to graduate from universities. The vast majority of girls, however, did not attend school, as education for women was mainly confined to the larger towns and cities.

Many critics see the use of the English language in India as one among many postcolonial mimic activities, resulting from the imposition of the English language as a part of British colonialist intervention in Indian education, language and literature. In India, some critics see the hegemony of English language and literature as a form of continuing cultural imperialism. Others argue that the widespread use, prestige, and expansion of English in India in recent decades are attributable to the post-war hegemony of the United States rather than to the British Empire, that is, its growing global currency as a medium of communication.

However, the English language can alienate a text from its culture of origin, a view put forward by the Indian author Shashi Deshpande. She bases her argument on the idea that the English language is in some ways harmful to Indian culture not because it is the language of the ex-colonizers, but because it has become the language of the privileged, elite classes in India. She admits that when she writes in English she is aware that her work will reach out to only a few English-speaking readers, most of whom will be thinking the way she does. The problem is that if an author writes in English with the purpose of changing social traditions, the language excludes the women whose involvement is most needed, English having no place in those women's daily lives. Another problem is the fact that writing in English also means using a language which most, or at least many, of one's characters do not speak. However, for many Indian authors English is no more than the medium through which they express themselves, and through which they can reach an international audience.

Indian Women Authors

Prior to the rise of the novel, many Indian women composed poetry and short stories in Hindi, Punjabi, Bengali, Urdu, Tamil, Malayalam and Kannada. Women were the chief upholders of a rich oral tradition of story-telling, through myths, legends, songs and fables. Once literacy began to filter through society, those stories were transformed into poetry and drama. The novel was not at first a common form, perhaps because the majority of women had less access to education than men. It was not until prose began to be used in the late nineteenth century by Bengali writers who had been exposed to European culture that the novel form took hold in India.

The volume of Indian literature written in English is smaller than that written in the various regional languages, and spans a smaller range of time, having only commenced with the spread of the English language and education. But in the last two decades there has been an astonishing flowering of Indian women writing in English, the literature of this period being published both in India and elsewhere. The authors are mostly western educated, middle-class women who express in their writing their discontent with the plight of upper-caste and class traditional Hindu women trapped in repressive institutions such as child-marriage, dowry, prohibitions on women's education, arranged marriages, suttee and enforced widowhood.

Poetry

Toru Dutt (1856-77) was the first Indian woman poet to write in English, and her work depicts archetypes of Indian womanhood, such as Sita and Savitri, showing women in suffering, self-sacrificing roles, reinforcing conventional myths in a patriotic manner. Her first book, published when she was twenty, was a book of verse translations from French, *A Sheaf Gleaned in French Fields: Verse Translations and Poems* (1876).

Kamala Das originated a vigorous and poignant feminine confessional poetry, in which a common theme is the exploration of the man-woman relationship. This style was subsequently taken up by other women poets such as Gauri Deshpande, Suniti Namjoshi, and Chitra Narendran.

The predicament of a single woman, spinster or separated, has also been a prominent theme in women's poetry. Tara Patel shows in *Single Woman* (1991) that in the harsh reality of the world, the quest for companionship without strings is a difficult one. Anna Sujata Matha in *Attic of Night* (1991) writes of the trauma of separation and the travails of a separated woman. Poetry for her seems to be an act of transcendence of agony, in the name of survival. But the image of woman she projects is strong and determined, and she argues for a sense of community, justice and companionship.

While in women's poetry we hear the voice of the New Woman's definition of herself and a quest for her own identity, we hear the conventional male voice and see a conventional, often negative portrayal of women, in men's poetry. An example is the six volumes of Nissim Ezekiel's poems, which depict women as mother, wife, whore, sex object or seductress.

Novels

Many Indian women novelists have explored female subjectivity in order to establish an identity that is not imposed by a patriarchal society. Thus, the theme of growing up from childhood to womanhood, that is, the Bildungsroman, is a recurrent strategy. Santha Rama Rau's *Remember the House* (1956), Ruth Prawar Jhabvala's first novel *To Whom She Will* (1955) and her later *Heat and Dust* (1975) which was awarded the Booker Prize, and Kamala Markandaya's *Two Virgins* (1973) are good examples. Sex is implied in these novels, but depicted more explicitly in *Socialite Evenings* (1989) by Shobha De, in which she describes the exotic sex lives of the high society in Mumbai.

As in poetry, the image of the New Woman and her struggle for an identity of her own also emerges in the Indian English novel. Such a struggle needs support structures outside the family to enable women to survive. Nayantara Sahgal uses this theme as the nucleus of *Rich Like Us* (1986). Other novels, such as Rama Mehta's *Inside the Haveli* (1977), look more towards issues of traditional Indian culture, particularly the debate on female education. Another example of the western educated female protagonist's quest for her cultural roots is Githa Hariharan's *The Thousand Faces of Night* (1992).

A number of Indian women novelists made their debut in the 1990s, producing novels which revealed the true state of Indian society and its treatment of women. These writers were born after Indian independence, and the English language does not have colonial associations for them. Their work is marked by an impressive feel for the language, and an authentic presentation of contemporary India, with all its regional variations. They generally write about the urban middle class, the stratum of society they know best.

Many of these authors, such as Chitra Banerjee Divakaruni in *The Mistress of Spices* (1997), use magic realism in their novels. Suniti Namjoshi stands out for her use of fantasy and surrealism, and Anuradha Marwah-Roy's *Idol Love* (1999) presents a chilling picture of an Indian dystopia in the twenty-first century. Other novels deal with various aspects of college life, such as Meena Alexander's *Nampally House* (1991), and Rani Dharker's *The Virgin Syndrome* (1997). Another theme to emerge is that of the lives of women during India's struggle for independence, as seen for example in Manju Kapur's *Difficult Daughters* (1998).

In the field of regional fiction, four women writers, Arundhati Roy, Anita Nair, Kamala Das, and Susan Viswanathan, have put the southern state of Kerala on the fictional map, while the culture of other regions has been represented by other women writers.

Anita Desai, in her psychological novels, presents the image of a suffering woman preoccupied with her inner world, her sulking frustration and the storm within: the existential predicament of a woman in a male dominated society. Through such characters, she makes a plea for a better way of life for women. Her novels have Indians as central characters, and she alternates between female-centered and male-centered narrative. Her later novels, written since she moved to the USA, reveal all the characteristics of diasporic fiction, that is, a concern with the fate of immigrants, and a growing distance from the reality of India, which is viewed from the outside.

As early as 1894 in Kamala, Krupabai Satthianadhan explored the cultural clash suffered by a Hindu woman who is given a western education in India, and the experience of being caught between two cultures has remained a prominent theme in writing by Indian woman. There are many Indian women writers based in the USA, Canada, Britain, and other parts of the world. Some are recent immigrants, while others, such as Jhumpa Lahiri, are second generation immigrants. These authors write about their situation in cross-cultural contexts - states of 'in-betweeness'. Expatriate representation has been questioned on several counts. Most expatriate writers have a weak grasp of actual conditions in contemporary India, and tend to recreate it through the lens of nostalgia, writing about 'imaginary homelands'. Distancing lends objectivity, but it can also lead to the ossification of cultural constructs, and even if memory is sharp and clear, the expatriate is not directly in contact with the reality of India.

The East/West confrontation, or the clash between tradition and modernity, is the impulse behind the works of acclaimed migrant writers, such as Meera Syal, Anita Rau Badami, Shauna Singh Baldwin, Uma Parameswaran, Chitra Banerjee Divakaruni, Anjana Appachana, and Kiran Desai.The theme of migration that leads to self-discovery, with a negation of the traditions of the country of origin, is a recurrent one among migrant authors, Bharti Kirchner's *Shiva Dancing* (1998), Ameena Meer's *Bombay Talkie* (1994), and Bharati Mukherjee's *Jasmine* (1989) being good examples.

Short Stories

Alongside poetry and novels, many collections of short stories, and anthologies of works by Indian women around the world have appeared, such as *Truth Tales* (1986), *Truth Tales 2: The Slate of Life* (1990), *Other Words: New Writing by Indian Women* (1992), *Right of Way* (1988), *Flaming Spirit* (1994), and *The Inner Courtyard* (1990).

Changing Image of Women in Fiction

The Hindu moral code known as The Laws of Manu denies woman an existence apart from that of her husband or his family, and since the publication of Bankim Chandra Chatterjee's Rajmohan's Wife in 1864 a significant number of authors have portrayed Indian women as long-suffering wives and mothers silenced by patriarchy. The ideal of the traditional, oppressed woman persisted in a culture permeated by religious images of virtuous goddesses devoted to their husbands, the Hindu goddesses Sita and Savitri serving as powerful cultural ideals for women. In mythical terms, the dominant feminine prototype is the chaste, patient, self-denying wife, Sita, supported by other figures such as Savitri, Draupadi and Gandhari. When looking at these narratives silence/speech can be a useful guide to interpreting women's responses to patriarchal hegemony. Silence is a symbol of oppression, a characteristic of the subaltern condition, while speech signifies self-expression and liberation.

The image of women in fiction has undergone a change during the last four decades. Women writers have moved away from traditional portrayals of enduring, self-sacrificing women toward conflicted female characters searching for identity, no longer characterized and defined simply in terms of their victim status. In contrast to earlier novels, female characters from the 1980s onwards assert themselves and defy marriage and motherhood.

Recent writers depict both the diversity of women and the diversity within each woman, rather than limiting the lives of women to one ideal. The novels emerging in the twenty-first century furnish examples of a whole range of attitudes towards the imposition of tradition, some offering an analysis of the family structure and the caste system as the key elements of patriarchal social organization. They also re-interpret mythology by using new symbols and subverting the canonic versions. In conclusion, the work of Indian women writers is significant in making society aware of women's demands, and in providing a medium for self-expression and, thus, re-writing the History of India.

The image of women in South Asian novels has undergone a change in the last three decades. Throughout this period, women writers have moved away from traditional enduring, self-sacrificing women toward conflicted female characters searching for identity. The interests of women writers have changed with South Asian society and its relationship with the West. This trend in writings by South Asian women clearly appears if onecompares the images of suffering women in Kamala Markandaya's Nectar in a Sieve and Meera Mahadevan's Shulamith to recent subversions and expansions of the traditional image in works by Chitra Fernando, Anita Desai, Kamala Das, Sara Suleri, and Anees Jung. In contrast to the main women characters in Markandaya's Nectar in a Sieve and Mahadevan's Shulamith, female characters in the 1980s assert themselves and defy marriage and family strictures. Chitra Fernando's collection of short stories Three Women, like Anita Desai's *In Custody,* portray women who want their individual worth realized and attempt to break through the suffering that traditional society offers them. The most recent books, of the last three years (1986-1988), explore an educated woman's search for identity and meaning — in autobiographical form, as in Kamala Das' My Story or in *Sara Suleri's Meatless Days,* or combining autobiographical and ethnographic form, as in Anees Jung's Unveiling India: A Woman's Journey.

Traditionally, marriage for women — except in certain matriarchal tribes in the south that remained unaffected by the Aryan invasion that began in 1500 B.C.E. — has entailed a most submissive feminine role. Although a woman ideally had power as a mother, as a wife she submitted to her husband and his family. Only recently have South Asian women in the dominant patriarchal tradition started to question aspects of this role, or decided against marriage altogether.

In Image of Woman in the Indo-Anglian Novel, Meena Shirwadkar claims that, following the changes in Indian society, novels have started to progress from depicting women characters solely as epitomes of suffering, womanly virtue to portraying more complex, real characters.

Tradition, transition and modernity are the stages

through which the woman in Indo-Anglian novel is passing. The image of traditional woman, the Sita Savitri type, was at once, easy and popular.... In India, with its strong bent for tradition, woman was expected mainly to live for others than for herself because "others" controlled and moulded the social structure. Even woman in life and literature herself voluntarily surrendered to the ideal of self-sacrifice.... Modern woman, in life, has been trying to throw off the burden of inhibitions she has carried for ages. Yet, a woman on way [sic] to liberation, trying to be free from inhibitions, is rarely seen in Indo-Anglian literature.

Shirwadkar's study, published in 1979, criticizes a literary tradition still overshadowed by the traditional, suffering ideal of womanhood. This ideal has persisted in culture permeated by religious images of virtuous goddesses devoted to their husbands. The Hindu goddesses Sita and Savitri still exist as powerful cultural ideals of women in South Asia. Both images tell women to devote themselves to their husbands to extremes of endurance, loyalty, and self-sacrifice. As Susan S. Wadley explains,

> [The god] Rama's wife Sita exemplifies the behaviour of the proper Hindu wife, devotedly following her husband into forest exile for twelve years, and eventually, after being kidnapped for a time by the evil Ravanawhom Rama finally destroys, proving her wifely virtue by placing herself on a lighted pyre.... Throughout North India, the women yearly worship Savitri, a goddess whose renown emanates from her extreme devotion to her husband, through which she saves him from the god of death. The story of Savitri isheld up as a prime example of the lengths to which a wife should go in aiding her husband. The good wife saves her husband from death, follows him anywhere, proves her virtue, remains under his control and gives him her power.

Meena Shirwadkar finds that the representation of women in Indo-Anglian literature fulfils this ideal of suffering devotion, which she calls the Pativrata tradition. She argues that "a graded change" has occurred, however, in Indo-Anglian fiction. "The early novels show [the] wife in her traditional role, mainly as a house-wife and child-bearer, and the writers are preoccupied with her suffering," she claims. Later novels, in contrast, show "the wives... to suffer more because of the incompatibility between her individuality and awareness of herself and the traditional views of her husband and her in-laws".

From women who endure namelessly fulfilling the ideal of the devoted wife-goddess, South Asian fiction by women has progressed to a conflicted yet liberating naming of one's one experience and that of other women. Although Easterners and Westerners can debate South Asia's traditional valuation of suffering, both must value the latest developments in South Asian women's writing. These women authors incorporate their experience in both worlds in an attempt to make new, empowering image for women. As Anees Jung points out: "Where the two experiences meet lies a revelation, and a story." Recent writers' stories realize both the diversity of women and the diversity within each woman. Rather than limiting the lives of women to one ideal, they push the ideal towards the full expression of each woman's potential.

Kamala Das: Reinterpreting Religious Tradition

Like Sara Suleri's autobiographical work, that of Kamala Das exemplifies recent texts in which South Asian women authors make the self-interested qualities so condemned in earlier fiction become liberating, positive, and creative forces. As they show themselves exploring their sense of identity — for writing autobiographically becomes in part public performance — they powerfully redefine their own lives. In *Meatless Days,* Sara Suleri interweaves the story of her life with that of her family and Pakistan's political history. Suleri's intellectual feminist attempts to define things and experience contrast to her mysterious mother's refusal to name food and her grandmother's supreme confidence in her own values and superstitions.

In *My Story,* Kamala Das, a poet famous for her honesty, tells of intensely personal experiences including her growth into womanhood, her unsuccessful quest for love in and outside marriage, and her living in matriarchal rural South India after inheriting her ancestral home. While at home, the rich families try to kill her with magic because they fear that her writing will reveal their immorality in. [In what sense does Das create a paradigm for the way repressive societies fear women's speaking, writing, and other self-defining forms of personal expression?] Like European women authors, Das seizes control of the society's own cultural codes, particularly those formed by dominant religious ideologies. She uses, for example, the terrifying religious image of Kali, the goddess of war and desctruction, in her defiant reaction:

> I hung a picture of Kali on the wall of my balcony and adorned it daily with long strings of red flowers, resembling the intestines of a disembowelled human being. Anyone walking along the edge of my paddyfield a furlong away, could see th Goddess and the macabre splash or red. This gave the villagers a fright.

Das often thus uses traditional religious imagery to sustain and dignify herself. She claims to search for an incarnation of the god Krishna in her love affairs and worships the god when the real men turn out to have flaws. Once, calmly facing death before a potentially fatal heart operation, she pictures herself as the goddess Durga and she titles one of her chapters "I Was Carlo's Sita," in which she tells about one of her affairs. Das reaches into her own religious tradition to find support for her defiant individuality

Meera Mehadevan's Shulamith

Meera Mehadevan's Shulamith exemplifies a recent novel in the sakti tradition that has the effect of showing the effect of the dominant Hundu culture upon the Jewish women of India. The novel's main character, Shulamith, experiences a "sense of dual fidelity" between her devotion to her husband and to her way of life. She chooses her way of life and remains in India when her husband leaves for Israel, but she withers away because she missies him and eventually dies as he returns. Second, Shulamith's initially ebullient sister-in-law, Mezuzah, allowed to date and remain single, soon suffers the consequences of violating traditional Indian-Jewish mores. Influenced by Western values of romance and freedom, the young woman falls in love with a non-Jewish youth and becomes pregnant. She then experiences shame, an agonizing abortion, and a horrible marriage because her mother will not let her either marry a non-Jewish man or bring shame on the family by having a child out of wedlock.

Shirwadkar explains the process that forces the Westernized young women to embrace family and tradition: "The ideas, tastes, manners adopted from the West appear to these girls attractive till some crisis or experience in their lives holds them back to the inherent culture" [Meena Shirdwadkar, Image of Woman in the Indo-Anglian Novel (New Delhi: Sterling, 1979), 49]. Mezuzah, or Maizie as she is called by most, becomes an image of the suffering woman: her values and personality change as she transforms first into a subdued, abused, barren wife living in poverty then into a hard-working, self-sacrificing nurse.

Shulamith appears particularly ambivalent because although Mahadevan portrays the young women Maizie and Naomi as victims of a patriarchal tradition, she makes Shulamith, who enforces social traditionalism and religious orthodoxy, a character to be highly respected. Mahadevan seems to sympathize with both sides of the conflict, but the positive image of the suffering woman remains constant. Mahadevan essentially has admiration for strong women who suffer and for younger women who learn to endure. In not being able to resolve the conflict she portrays, she returns to the traditional Sita-Savitri image.

Female Characters in Anita Desai's *In Custody*

Like Fernando's Three Women, Anita Desai's *In Custody* criticizes traditional society, but her novel focuses on a pathetic, trapped male character whose wife despises his inability to succeed financially. A terrified, insignificant person, Deven moves from mediocrity as a college lecturer to impending professional and financial ruin as he incurs increasing monetary debts, which he finally decides to endure rather than committing suicide. His wife gives him little support – in fact, the women in the book seem rather nasty, especially the enraged young wife of Deven's hero, the poet Nur. As the story progresses, however, Desai makes clear that just as the male characters are trapped in a world that offers no possibility for success, the female characters have even more right to feel frustrated with a sexist society that reduces them to clinging to these men who cannot provide them with what they want.

Unlike the evil Kunthi from Kamala Markandaya's Nectar in a Sieve, Desai's characters seem justified when they act out of self-preservation. Furthermore, unlike Markandaya's Rukmani and Ira who appear justified for their rebellion yet suffer punishment anyway, Fernando and Desai's women successfully defy traditional mores. The Urdu poet's young wife in Desai's In Custody, who rages at her limitations and writes in her own defense, stands out as the most outrageous of these woman. In fact, she radically redefines her experience by insisting on telling her story. This character's self-justification has continued in recent years as women writers tell their own stories and that of other women. When women make the lives of real women the center of their books, they go beyond creating sympathetic female characters to making claims for an alternative reality, an alternative truth. The illicit, self-interested qualities so condemned in earlier fiction become liberating, positive, and creative forces.

Desai shocks us near the end of her novel when she presents Nur's young wife's point of view in a letter to Deven, in which the woman claims that Nur married her because of her "gifts and abilities," not because of sexual entrapment as had been assumed throughout the novel. She challenges him to read her enclosed Urdu poems:

> Let me see if you are strong enough to face them and admit to their merit. Or if they fill you with fear and insecurity because they threaten you with danger — danger that your superiority to women may become questionable.... Are you not guilty of assuming that because you are a male, you have a right to brains, talent, reputation, and achievement, while I, because because I was born a female, am condemned to find what satisfaction I can in being maligned, mocked, ignored and neglected? Is it not you who has made me play the role of the loose woman in gaudy garments by refusing to take my work seriously and giving me just that much regard that you would extend to even a failure in the arts as long as the artist was male?

Deven's timidity prevents her defiant letter from gaining her acceptance in the world of Urdu poetry. Frightened of having to "enter that world on a mission of mercy or rescue," he tears up her poems. But her angry statements make the reader reevaluate what they previously had only seen through the eyes of a male character. By making women's frustration understandable, Desai subverts her book's primarily unsympathetic portrayals of women which turn out to have been Deven's — not the author's — perceptions.

But in fact, Desai does more than simply subvert a male society's attitude towards women, since she portrays a flawed Sita-like image in her main male character, not her female ones, who are too disillusioned and angry to want to fulfill self-sacrificing ideals. First of all, Deven suffers bitterly throughout In Custody because he has too weak a character and personality to refuse the burdens others place upon him. Second, whereas Nur's wife gains respect as a character by asserting her rights and abilities, Deven never manages such fiery rebellion. In contrast, he becomes noble at the end of the book by taking upon himself tremendous responsibilities: "He had accepted the gift of Nur's poetry and that meant he was custodian of Nur's very soul and spirit. It was a great distinction. He could not deny or abandon that under any pressure." Only as Deven decides to accept and endure whatever disasters befall him does he reach a kind of graceful inner strength: "Soon the sun would be up and blazing. The day would begin, with its calamities. They would flash out of the sky and cut him down like swords. He would run to meet them".

Chitra Fernando's Three Women

Chitra Fernando's stories portray most sympathetically women who reject traditional family life. In contrast, the least sympathetic female characters, those who hurt the sympathetic characters, cover up their selfishness by acting out their traditional roles. The first story, for example, "Missilin," portrays a plain, loyal, hard-working servant-woman, Missilin, who feels quite content with her lot. Rather than bemoaning that she will probably never marry, "She didn't care a jot. She wanted nothing to do with men."In reaction to hearing that a man, Gomis, expressed interest in her, she says haughtily, "'Ask him to poke his face in the chilibags". She slowly warms to him expecially after he gives her some scented soap. But when Gomis finally marries another woman, rather than being devastated, she throws away his gift and pushes all thought of him from her mind.

Yet Missilin's fiery resentment against men for the wrongs they commit against women disappears in the face of other social injustices, like class difference, which she never notices. Missilin and the rest of the community agree in thinking her employer Mrs. Ranasingha a "pious woman." Fernando makes transparent Mrs. Ranasingha's hypocrisy, however. She takes advantage of Missilin's obedience, by, for example, not letting Missilin visit her family when promised. It never recurs to Missilin to resent her employer. Indeed, Mrs. Ranasingha constantly reminds Missilin how much gratitude she owes for her employment, just as she constantly reminds herself and others of her piety by completingvarious "meritorious deeds" like almsgiving. The irony in the story, contrasting who really has worth and whom society considers worthwhile, reaches its peak at the end, after Missilin dies of tuberculosis. In order to feel virtuous, Mrs. Ranasingha pays for an almsgiving in her memory.

> The whole neighborhood commended heraction in the warmest terms. Mrs Ranasingha even felt mildly alarmed.... Of course, she wanted Nirvana. But she felt that to enjoy the worldly fruits of her meritorious deeds for her next two or three lives, at least, was only her due..... After briefly expressing the hope that Missilin would be born in better and better circumstances in this long cycle of births and deaths, he [the chief monk] passed on to the goodness of Mrs Ranasingha in having an almsgiving for a dead servant. And this, Mrs Ranasingha felt, was exactly how it should be.

Fernando here pokes fun at the small-minded selfishness of traditional society's values, but she takes Missilin seriously, evoking sympathy for an honest, self-sufficient woman unaware of how her employers exploit her In her other two stories, "Action and

Reaction" and "Of Bread and Power," Fernando presents women characters who are sympathetic because of their underdog status. In "Action and Reaction," Kusuma, brought to the narrator's aunt's house as a servant, grows from a pathetic child to a beautiful young woman. Her employer, Loku Naenda, whose personality echoes that of Mrs. Ranasingha in "Missilin," refuses to let her marry the man she loves, and society supports her in this decision. In this story, however, the exploited turns into the exploiter, because as she ages Kusuma takes over Loku Naenda's household, draining her of her money in order to pay for expensive meritorious deeds. As Kusuma turns into a replica of her employer, she becomes an equally unsympathetic character.

In "Of Bread and Power," the heroine Seela finally escapes the exploitation of her parents by remaining celibate, supporting herself financially, and living with her brother and another young man. She is the only female figure who breaks through tradition to build a happy life forherself. She seems a noble character when she asserts her worth and dreams against the wishes of her family. Interestingly, Fernando does not base this positive image completely on a breaking of tradition, because Seela only gains the confidence and money to leave her family from her grandmother. At the end of thestory, she argues with her brother's friend Somie, who wants to build society "based on justice, freedom and friendship." Seela responds: "'No... I - I want to be like my grandmother. She had no illusions. I want to be a good designer and understand myself and other people". Fernando in this story both shows a woman who breaks through tradition and suffering, but with the aid of her grandmother. Fernando does not reject the values of traditional society, but rather the greed and abuse they hide.

Anees Jung's *Unveiling India: A Woman's Journey*

Anees Jung, who first published *Unveiling India: A Woman's Journey* in 1986, also exemplifies another writer in search of new images of women. But in telling the stories of other women, her book becomes even more of a political, social statement, a sort of literary consciousness-raising. She explains the change that has taken place in Indian society so that now women will tell their own stories: "Not long ago a woman who spoke about herself was considered a loose woman. To voice a pain, to divulge asecret, was considered sacrilege, a breach of family trust. Today,voices are raised without fear, and are heard outside the walls of homes that once kept a woman protected, also isolated. Someof the women who speak here have stepped out. Others who have not, are beginning to be aware, eager to find expression. But let them speak for themselves".

Jung quotes the desperate, angry and hopeful stories of women from all over India. Her chapter "Women Find a Name" explores the wonderful consequences of Indian women renaming self and experience: "There are more women working today than there were a generation ago, more girls going to school and more women seen protesting in the streets, squares and homes. Their looks have not changed, their manner has. Individually they have gained a name, collectively an identity. Their new power was not imposed upon them but already existed, enclosed within walls. Now that power has stirred out into the open. Their new strength stems from personalities defining their own terms, lending grace to living". Jung's moving conclusion ends triumphantly, despite the sorrow and restrictions in so many of the women's lives she has presented. She affirms the constructive power of women.

She affirms herself at the same time, since she feels connected to the women of India, one of them. Jung herself, who grew up completely secluded in purdah, has remained unmarried and become a successful writer. She says about herself: "My reality no longer has one face. I have stepped out of an enclosed reality into one that is larger, more diverse, and mobile.... I continue to live out an experience for which I have yet to find a name". She presents her book, which begins with her own story and slowly blends into the story of other women as a "journey": "In the macrocosm of a vast land I find the microcosm of my own experience repeated and reaffirmed.... Coiled within the lives of these women I find myself transformed. The effort here is to probe the mystery of this experience and look beyond to another that is beginning to spell change and is centered in change.... It is the story of women who understand what survival is — a story with grace". The most important contribution that Anees Jung's vision of survival and grace makes to developing literary tradition lies in the way it moves beyond the Sita-Savitri ideal of woman as wife.

Kamala Markandaya's Nectar in a Sieve

Kamala Markandaya's Nectar in a Sieve portrays its positive woman characters as ideal sufferers and nurturers. "[T]he cause of her suffering springs mainly from poverty and natural calamity. The women are from the rural sections of society. They are the daughters of the soil and have inherited age-old traditions which they do not question. Their courage lies in meek or at times cheerful way [sic] of facing poverty or calamity"

Rukmani, the main character, and her daughter Ira display suffering hroughout the novel. Rukmani works hard and is devoted to her gentle husband. She endures blow after blow from life: poverty, famine, the divorce of her barren daughter, the deaths of her sons, her daughter's prostitution, and finally her husband's death. When she finds te emotional cener of her life, her relationship with her husband, threatened by the discovery that he fathered another woman's sons, she neither strikes out at him nor crumbles:

> Disbelief first; disillusionment; anger, reproach, pain. To find out, after so many years, in such a cruel way.... He had known her not once but twice; he had gone back to give her a second son. And between, how many times, I thought, bleak of spirit, while her husband in his impotence and I in my innocence did nothing.
>
> ...At last I made an effort and roused myself...
>
> "It is as you say a long time ago," I said wearily. "That she is evil and powerful I know myself. Let it rest."

She accepts the blow and moves on in life. In addition, when her son Raja is murdered, even her thoughts do not express rebellion. She moves from numbness to grief, thinking, "For this I have given you birth, my son, that you should lie at the end at my feet with ashes in your face and coldness in your limbs and yourself departed without trace[.]" Then she begins to wash the corpse and prepare it for burial. When two officials from the tannery, where Raja was killed, come three days later to try to bully her into saying they have no responsibility, she tells them what they want to hear, thinking, "What compensation is there for death? I felt confused, I did not know what they were getting at."When the officials turn to leave, she realizes that one of the men feels "shame and misery" and tries to make him feel better: "'You should not care,' I said very softly to him alone. "It does not matter.'" Her goodness and inner strength prevent her from becoming hard and bitter.

Rukmani survives. No pain or injustice can cause her to rebel or seek revenge. In fact, Markandaya subverts Rukmani's only violent reaction: when she finally physically attacksa shadowy figure in her home, thinking it a woman who has previously robbed her family of precious rice during a famine, the woman turns out to be her daughter Ira. Yet although Rukmani's general submissiveness may appear a weakness to Western readers, from another point of view she has incredible strength. These two views, which represent conflicting Western and Eastern values, explicitly appear in Nectar in a Sieve Rukmani confronts the Western doctor, Kenny, who urges, "'you must cry out if you want help. It is no use whatsoever to suffer in silence. Who will succour the drowning man if he does not clamour for his life?'" In response, Rukmani thinks, "Want is our companion from birth to death, familiar as the seasons or the earth, varying only in degree. What profit to bewail that which has always been and cannot change?" But Kenny, the Westerner, believes that, "there is no grandeur in want — or endurance." In contrast, Rukmani, the Indian woman, sees suffering as good for the spirit and endurance as a necessity, because she cannot change her situation. Looking at Rukmani only from the Western point of view leads one to misunderstand her character and the values that sustain her. The Western viewpoint equally misjudges the ideal of the devoted wife. Meena Shirwadkar, who hopes that women will emerge as uninhibited, multifaceted individuals in literature, perhaps regards the Sita-Savitri image from too Western a standpoint. She sees the role as a purely weak one forced upon women, when in fact Hindu culture conceives of self-sacrifice as a form of power.

Ira's sacrifice for others makes her prostitution therefore compatibile with the virtuous ideal. As a result of her motivations, she remains a sympathetic character although she violates traditional mores. That Markandaya means for our sympathy to hinge on her self-sacrifice becomes even more obvious when one compares her and another prositute in the story, the evil Kunthi. Initially, this beautiful, fiery woman has a bad reputation for sleeping with other men besides her husband. She appears an unlikable person who rejects Rukmami. But as the plot progresses into famine, she becomes a hateful, destructive figure. Not only does Rukmani find out that her husband Nathan fathered Kunthi's two sons, but Kunthi uses this knowledge of Nathan's secret, and of a secret of Rukmani's, to coerce them separately into giving her the family's hidden rice.

Kunthi's independence — she refuses to ask her married sons for food, and her husband has abandoned her — causes her to hurt others. She steals food from Rukmani's family so that she can regain some of her beauty for prostitution. Her illicit sexuality, unlike Ira's, always comes from self-motivated desire — first lust then greed; she represents a negative ideal of woman, using cruelty, trickery and other people to satisfy her needs and desires. She even appears as a carrion-eater who benefits from the collapse of others, in her most hateful scene with the saintly Rukmani.

After agonizing over whether to give Kunthi the rice Rukmani looks up and sees her: "there was Kunthi waiting by my side with the patience of one who knows what power she wields, patient, like a vulture." Feeding off the weaknesses of others, Kunthi contradicts the ideal image ofwoman as a nurturant, generative force.

Rukmani and Ira appear in Nectar in a Sieve as opposites of Kunthi. Their goodness originates in their acceptance of suffering, whereas Kunthi's evil originates in her refusal to sacrifice herself for others. As ideal images, Markandaya's heroines correlate with Shirwadkar's conception of how early Indo-Anglian novels portray women as Sita-like characters. By fulfilling cultural values, however, Rukmani and Ira find in their way of lifenot only suffering but also a sureness and inner peace. Shirwadkar claims that women in later novels lose even the satisfaction of this fulfillment, because they find themselves trapped between the traditional and modern requirements for women. Earlier images of calm, enduring women change to new ones, of frustrated women caught between the Sita-Savitri figure and the modern, Westernized woman.

Bibliography

Alamgir Hashmi. *Pakistani Literature: The Contemporary English Writers.* New York: World University Service, 1978; Islamabad: Gulmohar Press, 1987.

Allis, Jeanette B. West Indian Literature: An Index to Criticism, 1930-1975. New York: G.K. Hall, 1981.

Beebe, Maurice (Fall 1972). "Ulysses and the Age of Modernism". James Joyce Quarterly (University of Tulsa) 10 (1): p. 176

Benson, Eugene, and L.W. Connolly, ed. Encyclopedia of Post-Colonial Literatures in English. 2 vols. London: Routledge, 1994.

Berrian, Brenda F. Bibliography of Women Writers from the Caribbean, 1831-1986. Washington, D.C.: Three Continents Press, 1989.

Bloom, Harold, ed. *Caribbean Women Writers.* Philadelphia: Chelsea, 1997.

Brady, Anne & Cleeve, Brian (1985). *Biographical Dictionary of Irish Writers.* Lilliput.

Chatterjee, Gita. *Bengal's Swadeshi Samg+t.* Published in Banerjee, Jayasri (ed.), *The Music of Bengal.* Baroda: Indian Musicological Society, 1987.

Dance, Daryl Cumber. *New World Adams: Conversations with Contemporary West Indian Writers.* Yorkshire: Peepal Tree, 1992.

Fenwick, M.S. Writers of the Caribbean and Central America: A Bibliography. 2 vols. New York: Garland, 1992.

Jeffares, A. Norman (1997). *A Pocket History of Irish Literature.* O'Brien Press.

Jordan, Alma, and Barbara Comissiong. *The English-Speaking Caribbean: A Bibliography of Bibliographies.* Boston: G.K. Hall, 1984.

Markham, E.A., ed. *Hinterland: Caribbean Poetry from the West Indies and Britain.* Newcastle upon Tyne: Bloodaxe, 1989.

Morris, Mervyn, ed. *The Faber Book of Contemporary Caribbean Short Stories.* London: Faber and Faber, 1990.

Muneeza Shamsie. *A Dragonfly in the Sun: An Anthology of Pakistani Writing in English.* Karachi: Oxford University Press, 1997.

Rahman, Tariq. 1991. *A History of Pakistani Literature in English.* Lahore: Vanguard Publishers (Pvt) Ltd.

Welsh, Robert (ed.) & Stewart, Bruce (ed.) (1996). *The Oxford Companion to Irish Literature.* Clarendon Press.

Wright, Julia M. (2008). *Irish Literature, 1750-1900: An Anthology.* Blackwell Press.

Index